Critical Muslim 30

West Africa

Critical Muslim is published quarterly by C. Hurst & Co. (Publishers) Ltd. on behalf of and in conjunction with Critical Muslim Ltd. and the Muslim Institute, London.

All editorial correspondence to Muslim Institute, CAN Mezzanine, 49–51 East Road, London N1 6AH, United Kingdom. E-mail: editorial@criticalmuslim.com

ISBN: 978-1-78738-150-6 ISSN: 2048-8475

To subscribe or place an order by credit/debit card or cheque (pounds sterling only) please contact Kathleen May at the Hurst address above or e-mail kathleen@hurstpub.co.uk

Tel: 020 7255 2201

A one-year subscription, inclusive of postage (four issues), costs £50 (UK), £65 (Europe) and £75 (rest of the world), this includes full access to the *Critical Muslim* series and archive online. Digital only subscription is £3.30 per month.

A Cataloguing-in-Publication data record for this book is available from the British Library

Jordi Serra del Pino's essay 'Futures in Five Scenes', published in *CM29: Futures*, contained factual errors inadvertently introduced during the editing process for which we apologise. An amended version of Serra del Pino's essay can be found online.

Critical Muslim

Subscribe to Critical Muslim

Now in its eighth year in print, *Critical Muslim* is also available online. Users can access the site for just £3.30 per month – or for those with a print subscription it is included as part of the package. In return, you'll get access to everything in the series (including our entire archive), and a clean, accessible reading experience for desktop computers and handheld devices — entirely free of advertising.

Full subscription

The print edition of *Critical Muslim* is published quarterly in January, April, July and October. As a subscriber to the print edition, you'll receive new issues directly to your door, as well as full access to our digital archive.

United Kingdom £50/year
Europe £65/year
Rest of the World £75/year

Digital Only

Immediate online access to *Critical Muslim*

Browse the full *Critical Muslim* archive

Cancel any time

£3.30 per month

www.criticalmuslim.io

CM30

April–June 2019

CONTENTS

WEST AFRICA

ARTS AND LETTERS

REVIEWS

ET CETERA

WEST AFRICA

}

INTRODUCTION
THE LION'S STORY

Yovanka Paquete Perdigao and Henry Brefo

How should we present West Africa? Its vastness and immense diversity, rich cultural heritage and historical depth. How is West Africa perceived? How best do we enable an appreciation of the region and its people that avoids the pitfalls of cliché and superficiality? How could we collate a series of engaging stories, expositions and insights that were not just the usual ready-made and well-packaged versions of West Africa that already saturate news headlines? When should Africa's history begin? Should we start from the usual vector - colonialism? But surely there is more to the continent than just that! Should we source a pure native Africa of war and poverty? Or pursue a decidedly contemporary tone, fraught with corrupt elites and downtrodden citizens on one side, and young tech-savvy activists holding governments accountable, on the other? And, of course, we could not possibly ignore the diaspora as an adulteration of an organic image of this part of the world. No matter how negligent or well-meaning the effort to tread familiar landscapes was, the subtle sleight of colonial indoctrination gained through a predominantly white curriculum was evidently at play.

Let us begin with the words of the African writer Chinua Achebe. As he points out, 'until lions have their own historians, the history of the hunt will always glorify the hunter'.

This is not to say that Africa was delivered in the cradle of colonialism, with racism as its midwife. Rather, a way of recognising that Africa has a history and presence beyond its ill-fated encounter with the West. Peter Griffiths attempts to read the continent beyond the colonial prism and although he continues to be concerned with the notion of an African space, his exploration of African cities projects West Africa's unique identity in the face of a harsh free market urbanisation. Nigeria's Eko Atlantic, a high-rise real estate luxury development, cuts residents off from the local populace providing them a little taste of New York in Lagos. In Ghana and Ivory Coast similar urban utopias separate the modern nouveau riche from the masses, like a tale of two cities. A new Africa is slowly emerging on the horizon. Dementing the tracks laid by the Colonial powers, China is extending Africa's networks and connectivity by retrofitting and expanding colonial infrastructures to facilitate intra-regional trade and better coordination between neighbours. Colonial infrastructure had largely been aimed at connecting externally rather than internally: roads were built to mainly facilitate the extraction of raw materials and natural resources from the interior to the colonial metropolis. Instead, what we are witnessing now is the connecting of local people to markets, buyers to sellers and rural residents to urban centres. As often becomes the case when global capitalism enters the game, the line between assistance and exploitation becomes exponentially thin.

China walks this thin line in West Africa. While the perception may make it appear that things are being done differently, the concern still remains as we ask: at what price? Though this remains a muted point in Griffiths' critical but optimistic overview of West African urbanisation, the importation of Chinese ideas of urban futures in Africa gives pause for thought. It brings to the fore the rapacious competition in the projection of global futures in African cities against local interpretations of African urban development. It begs the question must the project of Africa be forever part of a totalising utopian history that surrenders cultural specificity to a globalised aesthetics. As Ziauddin Sardar, in a previous issue of *Critical Muslim*, cautions, the extrapolation of romanticised and universalised 'images', 'metaphors' and 'accustomed narratives' onto local structures, 'can become an instrument not just of colonisation of the future but also of enslaving our imagination'.

It is a little known fact that 'African urbanisation as we are told goes further back than Europe'. Indeed, before England was formed, following the battle of Hastings in 1066, West Africa had experienced a flourishing of great empires that thrived in Ghana and Mali, as beautifully captured in Jean Ndow's account of the griot tradition in the Senegambia region. The recitation of the Sundiata epic in its oral essence presents an Africa with an elephantine memory. It is an expression of culture that defies the singularity of authorship to enrol the community at large through oral performance. Memory is de-commodified and socialised as fundamental to the collective identity of the Mande people. The space of performance, according to Ndow, can be a radical site for restoring indigenous knowledge production, which currently is under threat from the primacy of literary cultures. However, through modern techniques and digital technology, Africa can preserve and project its traditions into the future as part of the dynamic process of self-restoration. In a way, she calls for the decolonising of knowledge production, beyond the Ivory tower, by incorporating cultural practice in the telling of the continent's illustrious history. What does decolonisation really entail, one may ask. Is it just a harking back to pastoral images of communal Africa or grand modernist utopian constructions of universal futures?

In recent times, the deafening clamour of decolonisation from African universities has reverberated through Ivory towers in the West, shaking its hegemonic foundations to their core. On 9 April 2015 students at the University of Cape Town called for the pulling down of the statue of Cecil Rhodes. This galvanised a movement under the uncompromising affirmation #Rhodes Must Fall. Causing a ripple effect across campuses in major African capitals and former colonial centres, Ghana, a veteran of decolonisation, joined the ranks. At the University of Ghana, they even demolished the statue of Gandhi. In a blogpost, a Ghanaian student argued that 'Gandhi was an unrepentant racist whose low and contemptuous view of blacks is well documented, both by himself and by historians'. School of Oriental and African Studies (SOAS), University of London, a beehive of left-wing politics with a murky colonial past, also saw its student population demanding a decolonised curriculum. The likes of Oxford and Cambridge even tagged along. For universities in the West it was a question of mindsets, which could be repaired through the inclusion of African authors on their reading list.

Unlike their western counterparts, West African students confronted the symbolic evocation of power, expressed through the capture of public spaces to selectively commemorate histories of racial conquest and triumph as national memory. The issue of mindset had been long resolved in the first bout of decolonisation that saw to Africa's political independence in the 60s and 80s. Accordingly, the students had brought down the mnemonic violence of colonial rule and apartheid, embodied in the dead grindstones of white hegemony. The world watched with stirring indignation when the statute of Rhodes crashed to the ground. Protagonists in this act were charged with vandalism and destruction of national treasure by the global public. Liberal opinion argued for a plurality of historic effigies as a compromise. Others snubbed them as tetchy millennials obsessed with political correctness.

Political correctness, initially designed to discourage racial discrimination, has become an effective weapon to undermine the legitimate concerns of minorities and intersectional communities as pedlars of victimhood. Ironically, the West experienced euphoria when the wall separating East and West Berlin came tumbling down brick by brick, marking the triumph of capitalism - without a single shot fired in Europe. But what about the rest of the world? The euphoria transformed into geopolitical enmity and competition for space exploration amongst Western superpowers with devastating effect on African lives. Caught in the middle, African states came to know the end of the Cold War as a searing succession of civil wars, coup d'état and armed movements mostly funded by Western capital. For the Congo, Sierra Leone, Mozambique and others, this wasn't simply a cooling of friendly relations between historic rivals, but a long summer of carnage.

Once again, when the statue of Saddam Hussein came crashing down there was jubilation around the world alongside the population of Baghdad. Those who participated in the statue's toppling were deemed national heroes. Little did we know that Iraq would become a killing field for war-mongers. The scenes of the Rwandan genocide flicker in my memory with all the red flashes of dismembered limbs and disembowelled corpses sprawled along the dirt road of Kigali. Since then Kigali under the stewardship of Paul Kagame has risen like the phoenix from the ashes of ruins and wreckages, clothed in a new image. An impeccably clean city with grand skyscrapers and tarred roads. Yet the west revels in deriding Kagame as a dictator, simply because he dares to imagine a new world, a better future, without their approval. The ambiguity of Western attitudes and response towards Africa partly stems from the conceited belief that Africa and its people are racially inferior. Therefore, African lives, hopes and dreams should await western tutelage and sanction.

In 1953, when Ghana expressed a desire for independence, the British administration grumbled that the country was not ready for self-rule.

Surely, it would benefit immensely under British guardianship, the argument resounded, up to a time where the mother colony deemed it appropriate for her dark pickaninnies to leave the nest. Ironically, Britain could not find the same maternal yearning for her colonial offspring aboard the HMS Windrush in 1948. Adorned with all the paraphernalia of Englishness, the black and brown sons and daughters of the Empire upon arrival were met with racial hatred and violence by the legitimate spawns of rule Britannia. Am I not a man and a brother, the iconic image of the supplicant slave, kneeling with his manacled hands outstretched, asks the 'other', his master, judge, jury and executioner. The same conflicting sentiment runs through the ongoing Brexit debate. The chants of let's make Britain great again and take back our borders, conjures the horrors of racism, the terror of living in the shadows of your dark skin. Lord Kitchener, the Jamaican calypsonian and of the Windrush generation, said it best, 'if you're white you're right, if you're brown stick around, if you're black go back'. For Chuku Umunna, politician and former member of the British Labour Party, this hasn't been that easy. Back in 2015, though tipped for leadership in the party he quickly withdrew his bid citing that 'mixed cultural and class background' were 'a chain round my neck'.

In *Playing in the Dark* (1992), Toni Morrison argues that the rejection of people of colour in the mainstream centres the 'unracialized, illusory white world' as the norm, by displacing and choking the representation of an Africanist presence. In this tepid and hot climate of racial tensions, Kalaf Epalanga, a celebrated Lusophone writer and musician, reminds us that the liberation of Africa remains incomplete without the fostering of strong bonds of solidarity across the African diaspora in centring a constituted image of a global Africa. Through Afrobeat - a cross pollination of musical interaction across the black Atlantic and African continent - Africa rides the waves of self-determination to rewrite its own history, without entreating Western sensibilities and sensitivies. Crossing linguistic, national and cultural borders, it uses the medium of music and dance to showcase the plurality of African cultural idioms constituted within an emancipatory ethic that enunciates the irrepressible presence of a unified 'global Africa'. Each generation according to Frantz Fanon is entrusted with the sacred responsibility of either inventing a new future or accepting the status quo. Thus Epalanga tell us, Afrobeat signifies a cry for resistance:

'Resisting to be labelled a victim, passive and at the mercy of Western charity, resisting being labelled an immigrant when many of these musicians were born in Europe and carry two or more nationalities.'

But in resisting Western hegemony we must go beyond the realm of music and dance to liberate the self, shackled in the signs and codes of representation that entrench debauched notions of cultural difference and reinforces racial stereotype. In a cartoon drawn by Mark Knight, that was published in the Australian newspaper *Herald Sun*, Serena Williams is depicted as a raving hysterical toddler, with large lips, hideous eyes, flat wide nose, and spitting out a dummy in an ape-like pose. Every inch of her appearance is amplified to harmonise with white disdain for difference - the black body. To add insult to injury, the visceral portrayal of Serena is contrasted with Osaka, a Japanese-Haitian, featured as a slender white woman with delicate features and blonde hair. The newspaper employed all the familiar racist tropes of black people in America, since Jim Crow. Yet the Australian Press Council, a watchdog responsible for promoting good media practice and upholding standards in Australia, ruled that the cartoon did not breach media guidelines but simply used exaggeration to illustrate the events that occurred at the US Open final. Supporters of Mark Knight spat back at his critics on social media with the claim that labelling his cartoon to be racist shows that the world has gone too PC. It seems that in the realm of satire, anything goes provided that the assault is aimed at a black body, at best a black woman. In contrast, Zahrah Nesbitt-Ahmed, in this issue, brings a dialectical thrust to the politics of identity, moving beyond the black and white binary, to interrogate that unnerving space between the self and the 'other'. Through a candid self-introspection of living with divergent religious and cultural identities with discontinuous narratives, she tells of the incredulity of South Asian Uber drivers and Mauritian and Nigerian work colleagues upon learning from her name, that she might be a Muslim. The question 'Are you A Muslim?' whenever asked, conceals the complex interplay of race and culture in demarcating parochial fixed boundaries of identification grounded on the appeal of imagined communities.

In other words, the construction of homogeneous ethnic, religious and racial identities within synchronic narratives have the power to exclude. In a bold exercise of self-affirmation she staunchly declares 'So, what am I? I am a Muslim woman, a Hausa woman, a Nigerian woman, a West African woman, an African woman, a Caribbean woman, with a Christian British-Caribbean mother and a Muslim Nigerian father'. There is no hierarchy in her multiple identities. As Henry Brefo argues, this partly stems from the notion of an organic history of Islam, reflecting Islamic encounters that produced conspicuous forms of local conversions. He contrasts this with the case of the Asante Kramo in Ashanti, Ghana, revealing that Islamic identities did not follow the same trajectories but were produced out of specific historic relations that entailed unique sets of interaction between Muslims and local populations. Asante Nkramo, Brefo suggests are a 'hybrid' socio-cultural group whose sense of identity owes much to, but is not limited to, the colonial reconfiguration of Ashanti political, social and economic space. Consequently, identities are negotiated as an outwardly elaborate performance that turns on a disavowal of historic affinities to emphasise cultural difference. Evidently, Africa possesses a complex history that has shaped intricate forms of self-formation outside of the black and white dichotomy. And as such decolonisation must also deconstruct linear interpretations of an African past beyond neat and ordered narratives that suppress historical deviation from the colonial presence. It should aim at restoring the public archives, bringing to full circle the fragmented and divergent histories of the continent as Ndow's essay argues.

This argument underlines Hang Zhou's contention with the negative portrayal of relations between the People Republic of China and West African states. Going beyond the dominant narratives of greedy shrewd Chinese imperialists versus servile juvenile Africans, he highlights the cultural exchanges between the two countries. Particularly, he notes the growing interest in African literature in China. This is a positive development, with the potential of countering Eurocentric notions of Africa as a dark continent, of no historical consequence or importance to the World. The emergence of African consciousness amongst the Chinese is a good indicator of cross-cultural interactions on both sides. Whilst we remain suspicious of the Chinese state's growing interest in Africa, it will also serve us well to try and understand how the ordinary Chinese citizen perceives and engages with Africa.

Recall Achebe's warning. Who will recount the lion's perspective? With this goal in sight, the philosophical underpinning of the decolonisation movement conceptualised under the term Consciencism was provided.

But it was Ngugi Wa Thiong'o who popularised and invigorated the movement in his seminal work, the thought-provoking essay Decolonising the Mind. Ngugi provided coming generations of Africans a road map to a comprehensive decolonisation, aimed at restoring the African personality on the world stage. He helped a broader audience understand that colonialism was not simply about the exploitation of land, labour and natural resources but also an assault on the African imagination, by implanting its memory on the African consciousness. Credit must be given where it is due, decolonisation as a political movement did not commence in Africa but India. In 1947, India painfully wrested itself from the hubris of British tyrannical rule. Africa took notice and since then has sustained the spirit of the movement, moulding its own version, whether it be manifestations of Pan-Africanism, described in Nouria Bah's essay, or the assertions of religious identity uncovered by Brefo. Today, the slogan decolonising the mind has found African leaders envisioning an Africa beyond aid, in practice beyond the bondage of IMF and foreign NGOs. Clearly, decolonisation is not just a black African story but holds resonance for all people of colour.

In challenging the colonial domination of Africa's historical imagination, the millennial generation, the pulse of Africa's future, are leaving indelible marks on the consciousness of public memory. They are navigating the monolithic manifestations of the past, whilst resisting its enduring omnipresence in an audacious manner to give life to new imaginings of space and time. The physical act of pulling down vestiges of colonialism in public spaces serves as a figurative performance of spatial emancipation.

In a millennial spirit, Joy Oluwagbemileke Jegede, Africa's youngest lawyer, goes beyond the common stereotypes associated with Africa's youth. In her 'Last Word', Joy illuminates that Africa, as the continent with the youngest population, has such an abundance of talent to offer the world. From the realm of economics, sports, politics and business, young Africans are paving a new path forward through their creativity.

The hunter has for too long been celebrated for his exploits of the hunt. The time has come for the Lion to tell his side of the story.

ARCHITECTURE, CULTURE, IDENTITY

Shanka Mesa Siverio

What would come to mind if West African Architecture was the title of this piece? A strange mix of images may surface. These are likely to range from traditional adobe construction, to geometric detailed carvings, to modern mega constructions of contemporary West African cities. The truth is that West African architecture is a little difficult to pin down. It would be reductive to suggest that it is anything by an architect of West African heritage because the story of individuals is often more complex than ethnic identity. Equally to suggest that it is simply anything constructed within West African boundaries ignores the complex political and cultural history of these regions and the reality of the architectural scene in this part of the world. The images we might have in our heads might come from direct experience, but more likely second-hand perceptions and impressions subconsciously developed. What we refer to as architecture is increasingly differentiated from other mere 'buildings' because of its ability to be processed and appreciated through a lens. This is true of architecture in general, but in the case of West African architecture, these images have a greater potential to be distorted in our imaginations than many other better understood categorisations.

In most cases, rarely do we think much further than the images in our mind's eye, though architecture is really, less easy to define. Architecture can be sculpture, technology and art, but it is more interestingly and accurately described as a political and cultural activity that results in the creation of our man-made environments. Since architecture rarely sways from established ideals into the realms of critique, it can also be thought of as the material expression of the dominant values and aspirations of a society. Even when it appears to be the work of one or two individuals, the creation of architecture – a highly political act – is the culmination of hundreds of economic, regulatory and cultural decisions. Fundamentally, none of us lives outside of architecture and even within our own homes, we are subject to its subtle but pervasive influence when we least expect it.

Therefore, to read architecture thoroughly will give you a good idea of exactly where we are as a society. We are as influenced by what we read on a daily basis in architecture as by what we read in words – if not more so since most of the time we are not actively engaged in the process. Ultimately, any perceptible sway over society at large will be as a result of the summation of many individual acts of architecture. Some of these acts will certainly have more impact than others. Size matters; but in today's digital, global era, influence can be felt in different ways and digital media can ensure that impact is decoupled from physical presence.

In this digital context, architecture includes not only the images and explanations of concept, style and problem solving but also the architects themselves. In response, architecture has produced the 'Starchitect'; an architect 'whose celebrity and critical acclaim have transformed them into idols of the architecture world and may even have given them some degree of fame amongst the general public'. Consequently, clients are now able to pre-determine the global social status (and therefore 'success') of their projects well before they are built. 'Starchitecture' has been described as 'the embodiment of our age, the constructed celebration of celebrity.' Whether you agree with this definition or not, it is clear that this notion of celebrity is important. Celebrity status holds influence in our world and it is undeniable that Starchitects, like Norman Foster and the late Zaha Hadid, have a special role to play in popular consciousness, whether this populace is interested in architecture or not.

It is therefore worth noting that, for the first time in history, 2018 we saw the first architect of (West) African, more specifically Ghanaian, descent, Sir David Adjaye, to be named in the *Times* 100 'most influential' people list, increasing his celebrity status. He has been described as a 'Starchitect' by many. As though to illustrate the point the *Evening Standard* featured an eight-page spread on him, with over half of the pages dedicated to portraits of Sir Adjaye clad in black and grey Giorgio Armani and Boss turtle necks. Though by no means an overnight success, or the only well-known architect of African descent, this is somewhat of a big deal within architectural circles, which are notorious for their lack of diversity amongst its practitioners and particularly amongst those who can be described as 'influential'.

The lack of diversity along lines of ethnicity - not to mention gender and socio-economic status – is relatively well acknowledged in the UK and for the last few years has been a feature of several studies. A recent 2018 survey demonstrated that only 6 per cent of practising architects are from Black, Asian and Minority Ethnic (BAME) backgrounds (a significant under representation of the population in general) and that 80 per cent of those surveyed (from all backgrounds) in the industry identified that racism existed within the profession. As one of the 6 per cent, this is no surprise to me, but the longer I stay in the profession, the more I am convinced this issue is more of a global problem reflecting old world orders. As bad as the problem is in the UK, it does not appear to be any better elsewhere. As one rising star of Nigerien architecture, Mariam Kamara, observes, there is 'a subconscious feeling that the West holds the monopoly on knowledge and know-how'. There is also plenty of evidence to suggest a deep-rooted trend of awarding sought-after commissions to European or American practices, over the home-grown talent across Africa and Asia. Aside from the odd survey and discussion on the side-lines, the profession as a whole has done little to challenge these trends.

As a famous ethnic-minority architect, Sir Adjaye undoubtedly faces some pressure to discuss these issues. Just as Zaha Hadid had openly spoken out about sexism in the industry, dubbing British Architecture a 'boys club', many have been expecting Sir Adjaye, to speak out about the other elephant in the room. Though race and culture are central to many of his largest commissions, such as the Smithsonian African American Museum in Washington, those expecting controversial or combative language from Sir Adjaye have been left waiting. He is after all the son of a diplomat. Sir Adjaye has instead, tended to take a more pragmatic approach to such issues. In a recent talk at the RIBA, he excluded himself from 'the world of privilege' and claimed that fame was needed to 'level the playing field for people of colour' in the creative fields. Like others before him have intimated, he ascribes the challenges of belonging within architecture as cultural, rather than racial conflict.

Culture is frequently more complicated than race or ethnicity. Anyone who has straddled two or more cultures will be aware of the subtle contradictions that can coexist and how difficult this is to explain. I can proudly and succinctly say I am ethnically Tamil, but I would need to draw you a diagram to express my cultural influences. It is also evident that culture can change over time. Sir Adjaye is of Ghanaian parentage, was born in Tanzania, travelled between several continents in his early years and later studied in the UK, eventually training in London at the RCA. Following early success, he taught at the Architectural Association (one of the world's most prestigious architecture schools) and practiced in London and New York as an internationally famous architect. Just below the surface, this cultural map speaks of a complex personal identity that has much in common with many white western architects – from whom, tellingly, we expect very little participation on the architectural discourse on race.

Like most other famous architects, Sir Adjaye was educated and practises within the traditions of the Western architectural education system. This educational system is ultimately what produces architects, critics and often clients as well. It is therefore responsible for a great deal of the production and interpretation of what we classify as architecture and thus plays an important role in the creation of our surroundings. The architectural establishment does not necessarily stem from one school of architecture, but the limited nature of this educational sphere of influence is best demonstrated by the aforementioned, Architectural Association (the AA). From its small home in Bedford Square, the AA is one of those establishments particularly notable for its recurrence in the CVs of prolific Starchitects known throughout the globe. The blue plaque which reads 'Most Famous Architects 1847–2016' at the AA's entrance, understates its impact on the twentieth and twenty-first centuries' global architectural legacy. In Africa, architectural researcher, Bruno De Meulder has argued that the AA led the research which ultimately shaped the post WWII building boom throughout Africa. Its influence today is no less profound.

We are all susceptible to groupthink and architects are no exception. In fact, I would argue that they are more susceptible than most since membership to the group is limited to the few willing to overcome the exceptionally high entry barrier, after which dissenting voices are harder to raise. Architecture school is where this group identity begins and where architects are taught the subtle codes of their profession. From an acceptable way to dress (anything from Cos according to the *Guardian*); to how to travel (bikes and scooters in, cars out); to the architectural heroes we are taught to idealise and which architecture publication you should be subscribing to, there is a very clear distinction between what is 'in' and what is 'out' of the acceptable mainstream circles of architecture. More seriously, these codes are those of both culture and knowledge. Throughout architecture school and later in practice, there are branches of knowledge that are revered and there are those that are simply refused access by the mainstream.

Most architects will testify that there are few, if any, non-Western thinkers who make it onto the agenda. The significant exception in the bias towards western modernism in design subjects is the respect for Japanese traditional design displayed, partly due to its twentieth century influence on many modernists. This dismissal of non-Western thought in building is exacerbated by the general bias away from traditional and vernacular forms of knowledge, best demonstrated by practice. In the UK, the 'community consultation' is a booming industry since most large regeneration schemes are required to undertake a process of consultation. However, it is frequently acknowledged as a tick box by many in architecture and planning and often separated from the design process itself. It is too frequently a marketing exercise, particularly where architects are not representative of the communities they are designing for. Understanding this, I usually dress my best whenever attending these events, knowing that I will undoubtedly feature in the photos as evidence of 'diverse outreach'.

Parallels can be drawn between this dismissal of traditional knowledge today and what has been observed of attitudes towards traditional methods in Africa in the mid twentieth century. In his thesis on modern African architecture based on a series of case studies, Antoni Folkers (co-founder of ArchiAfrika) argues that architects who 'were almost exclusively European, or of European origin' in twentieth century Africa, 'disregarded informal African architecture as irrelevant to the development of the African continent'. That architecture during the colonial era was 'dominated by European modern architecture' is not that surprising. This early formalisation of 'Architecture' under the European system was typical of many colonial era education systems. What is unique in the approach to African architecture is unquestioned assumption that prior to this introduction via the west, architecture in these countries simply did not exist in a true sense. Nonsensical as this is, the western-endorsed, formally accepted architecture that has made it into the history books is the legacy that we are left with.

The extent of change in architecture since the colonial era is evidently not enough, for many emerging African architects. Young architects such as Nigerian James George have also publicly spoken out about the trend towards awarding Nigerian projects to Western practices. Like others, he has argued for a more uniquely African approach to African urban problems, noting the significance of local approaches to the search for sustainable solutions. Why this trend has persisted for so long within architecture, when change has been more rapid in other areas such as art, music and literature is a question worth pursuing by anyone interested in equity in the way architecture is practiced and created.

Skills shortages could quite legitimately be one answer and indeed this is often the common reason given. There is a technical component to architecture which makes it unlike other artforms and leaves it more prone to shortages, in all countries at certain times. In Africa, Christian Benimana, managing director of Kigali based MASS Design Group, has noted the very limited number of architecture schools offering training, which often leads Africans to study architecture abroad. The statistics are revealing: in a high-profile, continental symposium of African architecture organised in 2017, all of the African participants were educated abroad. However, he also astutely notes that there are educational models beyond the western model of architecture school, which may be worth pursuing. African architecture schools were first established in the continent by their European counterparts in the mid-twentieth century, resulting in a system based entirely on the Western approach to architecture. Benimana is part of a group fuelling a profound shift in this system in a way that responds to the unique constraints and opportunities to be found in Africa. By establishing alternative forms of architectural education true to their context, MASS Design group are challenging the dominant assumptions which underpin the tendency to look abroad for architectural skills.

Another, more uncomfortable reason for this slow change in architectural attitudes is the entrenched cultural and knowledge-based 'caché' that western professionals possess, in general. This, it could be argued, is an inevitability of legal and professional systems based on western traditions as a direct result of colonial histories. But, added to this, is the prevalent myth of technological progress which has been a dominant narrative throughout the modern age. In architecture this myth drives the idea that there is a correct answer – a utopian future - that is fuelled by western technological advancement. Even in the era of early independence from European rule, this entrenched view often manifested itself as a rejection of African technologies and construction methods in favour of European ones, by both architects and clients. Advocates of African techniques such as the Egyptian architect Hassan Fathy were required to 'rediscover' methods such as African masonry techniques via France in order to apply them in projects in Senegal and Burkina Faso. Whilst, the advantage of hybrid solutions in innovative design cannot be denied, the practice of 'rediscovery' highlights the need to make traditional knowledge more palatable via the established western processes. Today, this type of sanctioning continues, with an implicit assumption that architecture is only worthwhile when recognised by the western architectural press and establishment. A preference towards western methods and technologies is still evident and further fuelled by the capitalist market economy.

The further continuation of this trend could now be dismissed as another inevitability; now, of globalisation and existing world orders. Could we reconcile ourselves that a little less variety and interest might be the price we have to pay for a globalised society? Unfortunately, this homogenising effect has problematic consequences which cannot be so easily brushed aside by today's leaders. Sustainable development has been the catchphrase of our planning system for the last ten years, but the truth is there is little sustainable about many of the projects that get given planning approval in the UK. The current dominant western model of the city simply cannot have universal relevance. Only slightly more nuanced is the argument in favour of 'genus loci', or simply put, what makes a place unique. Urbanists from Jane Jacobs to Jan Gehl have demonstrated the importance of unique development at the city level for thriving communities and economies. In support, we need only look to the most vibrant cities today, which at their core are diverse cities. We all instinctively know this. As Ziauddin Sardar has perfectly summarised, 'Monocultures dominate, isolate, alienate, decimate and finally bore themselves to death with uniformity.' This is as true for the individual as it is for the city or country.

West African cities are continuing to develop their identities using architecture, amongst other tools, after the process of decolonisation. This identity is important not just for national pride and belonging, but also for global image and competitiveness. The political narrative is easy to read in the selection of Sir Adjaye as architect of the Ghanaian Cathedral; soon to be one of Accra's most impressive iconic buildings. As the most famous architect of African descent he is uniquely placed to deliver an internationally recognised architectural icon which symbolises the progress of Ghana since independence and its arrival as a globally competitive city. Success and recognition are almost guaranteed by virtue of Sir Adjaye's pre-existing status, which fortunately, has already been sanctioned and approved by the western architectural powers. Ironically, it is likely to be this pre-approved status which gives him freedom to develop something that is, in his own words, 'unique to Accra and the Ghanaian nation'. The extent to which the project is more recognisably Ghanaian will be telling of both the national narrative and the true extent of the hard won 'freedom'.

Perhaps more important than its role in nation-building, both literally and in terms of identity, is architecture's role in shaping our personal identities and sense of where we fit in the world. Architecture has legitimately been conceived as an extension of the self, where the psychological concept of 'self' includes the physical items we identify with. Moreover, the aesthetic and symbolic nature of architecture ensures that this identity is communicated at a collective level. That African images and symbols have been missing from the forefront of collective consciousness for so long has undeniably had an impact on the identity of Africans from within the continent and on the various diasporas throughout the globe. Effectively, in architecture the narrative has been clear: it is the role of the African, along with many other non-dominant nationals, to aspire to the images of beauty and taste developed in the West. How this narrative limits the creation of a personal identity might be compared with the concepts of physical beauty that have been applied to the body in a way that is highly damaging to individual identity and self-worth.

Even more directly, our behaviour and habits are altered by the design of our physical environments. A variety of tools are available to the designer who wishes to make his or her stamp on the way we live. Mis-use of these tools can be as simple and misguided as designing out opportunities for residents to hang their washing outside in order to 'tidy up' an estate or neglecting to consider how safe vulnerable users might feel in a space. These are the kind of examples that create disconnection between space and the user at a very basic psychological level. Where clashes occur, the user is left disorientated and 'out of place'. Whilst this kind of poor design can occur anywhere, it is evident that where designers identify and interact least with their users, clashes are more likely to occur. This has been compounded at the scale of the continent in Africa where the architectural story has been dominated by international development from afar.

This profound impact on the psyche of individuals is perhaps the strongest argument for diversity and empathy, if not greater representation, within architecture. It's not simply a case of East v West or anti-colonial sentiment, but an argument pertinent to all non-dominant cultures and anyone who has ever felt at odds with their daily surroundings. However, it is clear that this is the least likely reason that we might begin to see change in architecture. Since rarely are the user's needs at the forefront of architectural projects, no matter what the rhetoric. It also takes a great political and architectural freedom to challenge the status quo. Up until recently, such freedom has had to be won in the West. It is reassuring then, to note that we also see the reverse process in action; architects who have developed an international reputation and therefore opportunities to create from within West Africa by virtue of the sensitive, user-focused approach to uniquely African problems.

One of the more significant events, demonstrating a shift in global perspectives towards West African architecture, has been in London. In 2017, the Serpentine Pavillion was designed by Burkinabe architect, Francis Kéré; the first African architect ever commissioned for this task. The pavilion is given to a different architect every year and though a modest commission, is a highly prestigious one. In 2017, for the first time we saw a move away from the usual display of Western and Japanese forms that have tended to dominate. The aesthetic that Kéré chose to work with was typical of his true-to-roots style. However, it was not a simplistic translation of a personal style into the grounds of Kensington Gardens that made the work so interesting. The effect was a challenge to dominant aesthetic sensibilities, ideas of beauty and even the inherent prejudices towards all 'native', but particularly West African and Islamic design culture. Where once this aesthetic would have been dismissed as pretty but irrelevant, or worse considered unworthy of the commission, it has been elevated to its correct position of both art and architecture by way of realisation in the context of the Serpentine Pavilion. This would have been unthinkable not long ago. The pavilion, though temporary, will have a ripple effect that continues to multiply with every new project that recognises the value of a knowledge-culture system that is both global and West African.

The realisation of the pavilion is as important for all non-dominant cultures as it is to West African nations. The contribution of 'sub cultures' to urbanism and architecture is relatively well discussed in academia. Research has tended to focus on spatial attitudes towards minority groups within the urban environment; from the role of skate-boarders, to young mothers, to the homeless, many have sought to give attention to the silent minorities within architecture. Sadly, the gap between theory and practice is striking. This is in part due to a failure of individuals and policy to apply theory. At an individual level, it is evident that architectural theory when read in a book is easily persuasive, but when told as a story by the elderly lady who wants to hang her washing outside, much less so. Policy and regulatory frameworks are often even slower to catch up, requiring a significant political shift before change can happen. The problem that is common to the elderly lady and the early nation builders of West Africa can be summed up as the false belief that some people are the beneficiaries of a superior culture, rather than the co-creators in its development. This is entrenched in both policy and personal attitudes.

There is recognition of this from within West Africa and in Europe and the West. History has spread the West African diaspora all over the globe and as a result there are hybrid narratives that return to the West African Nations and continue to exert international influence. Kéré received a scholarship to study in Berlin and practices in both Berlin and Burkina Faso. Similarly, Kunle Adeyemi, works between the Netherlands and Nigeria. Adeyemi is one of the newer names to reach western architectural press. His work often goes far beyond the simple creation of an aesthetic that is true to its roots based on local observations. Like Kéré's school in his home town, Gando, Adeyemi's floating school in Makoko tackles problems of poverty and place in a way that is authentic to the existing culture and geography. Building methods have been chosen that reflect the available resources and traditions of the people and the visual language of the architecture, though innovative and by no means traditional, can be traced to local traditions. Solutions are not only sustainable but also beautiful in the full sense of the word. This is not so unusual in many locations throughout West Africa perhaps but it is interesting to see this acknowledged and appreciated within the mainstream architecture press.

There are of course many other West African architects who have, for years, gained recognition within West African circles and have forged international links. Nigerian, Demas Nwoko; Ghanaian, Joe Osae-Addo; and Senegalese Pierre Goudiaby Atepa are amongst the prolific practitioners who have bridged the apparent gap between the colonial past and the present. Yet, the illusion of an unfulfilled architectural history exists and these remain names that are overshadowed by their European counterparts. This void continues to impact on the challenges faced by African architects from within Africa. In her work for her practice based in Niger, atelier masōmī, Mariam Kamara, who also happens to be Sir Adjaye's protégé under the Rolex mentoring scheme, describes the local preferences for European methods and involvement, regardless of true expertise. It is a view that many who have worked with NGO's within Africa will be able to support. Her words are particularly revealing because they stem from recent first hand experiences of working within her home-city of Niamey in Niger, following her education in the US. The question is a practical one that recognises the complex nature of any potential answers, when she asks: 'How then, as African architects, can we convince people on the ground that we mean business, that we are just as competent, and that we can provide real solutions to local problems?'

The answers will likely come from many different sources since the question itself arises as a result of assumptions that have been left festering for years. Olajumoke Adenowo is an architect answering these questions in a different way. At fifty, Adenowo, has succeeded beyond her years in Nigeria since starting her own practice at the age of twenty-five. Her brand of architecture has a more distinctly commercial feel than many of the others discussed and it is perhaps for this reason that she has gained commissions for large scale Nigerian projects such as the National Theatre and Abeokuta City masterplan, which could have also gone to commercial foreign firms. Significantly, Adenowo has developed an international presence from entirely within her nation. She studied architecture in Nigeria and developed skills at Nigerian practice Femi Majekodunmi Associates before starting her own firm in Lagos. She is also one of the few high-profile female voices adding to the debate, directly discussing the role of women in developing Nigerian society. Like some of her peers, she might not be a household name in the west yet, but has significant presence in West Africa and within international academic and business circles.

If the architectural press is any measure, there appears to be a tipping point in the way that African architecture is perceived on the distant skyline. Terms such as 'Afrofuturism' and 'African Renaissance' feature and encourage a new-found enthusiasm within their general audiences. Attention is given to the innovations which stem from indigenous architecture and styles. Emerging African architects are discussed with interest. The narrative is one of rediscovery and general consensus that the path of African architectural development, once stunted by colonialism, is experiencing a revival. Caught up in the enthusiasm, you could easily overlook that this handful of articles is dealing with a whole continent.

However, if, as the science fiction writer, William Gibson, claims, 'the future is already here – it's just unevenly distributed', the examples here do indeed suggest a significantly more diverse future than past for architecture. In an industry where practitioners really begin to build their careers and flourish in their forties and fifties, Sir Adjaye, Kéré, Adeyemi and Adenowo, in architectural terms, are still teenagers and just getting started. Many of the other architects mentioned as 'emerging' talent in architectural circles are also in this age bracket or younger and still gearing up to the peak of their careers. When compared to the timeline of independence for many of their home nations, these are the early examples of the first generation of architects who grew up after the end of colonial rule and are reaching the architectural-coming-of-age.

They have, by virtue of the exceedingly slow changes in architecture, benefitted from a greater openness within the industry towards differing paradigms, even if it has just been seen on the side-lines. The arrival of African architecture in mainstream western discourse has openly challenged what has come before and created a small but perceptible climate of change in the industry. The comparisons with West African literature are apparent, though architecture is lagging about forty years behind. However, it is possible that we might now see quite accelerated change thanks to communications-technology. The architectural press is no longer limited to the monthly supplement from the RIBA and the internet has offered vast opportunities for the proliferation of 'alternative' ideas. The accessibility of information is enhanced by innovative digital programmes which have sought to increase knowledge of African architecture, such as ArchiDatum and ArchiAfrika and further propagated by the shared economy and collective commons. We are no longer limited to one story which depicts African architecture as something to be dismissed as a minor character in the fairy tale we had mistaken for reality.

Architecture in general is still seen as the domain of the white man, and although I have focused on West Africa I could have offered an analysis of many parts of the globe that would have been similar. This need not have been the case if we include wider definitions of architecture, but perceptions have a way of influencing our material reality and we have all suffered the consequences. Our cities and buildings are far from the ideal offering of sanctuary and expression to the multitude of cultures and identities that exist. It is, therefore, of great relevance who our architects are. We need more minorities becoming visible in architecture, if only to ensure that they are also heard along with many others who represent a different way of thinking about and identifying with space.

WE WERE ONCE FRIENDS

Henry Brefo

Asante Nkramo, Asante Nkramo. When I first heard the words, they rapidly sizzled and disintegrated in the ether like unintelligible jargon. It was only after a few rings in my ear that it developed into a concept, and then later came to indicate a term, an appellation of a social group. Currently in my adulthood the phrase, whenever expressed, evokes a designated socio-cultural group whose habits, mannerism and bearing straddles across two distinctive cultures.

On a research trip to Ghana, whilst boarding a *trotro* one of the passengers painstakingly argued with his fellow interlocutor that the *Ashanti Nkramo* was different in temperament and bearing than the so called original Nkramofo (Muslim), often assumed to be from the northern part of the country. Apparently, the *Asante Nkramo* are not as devout as their northern brothers; they pick and choose which aspects of Islam marry well with their Ashanti traditions. He strongly protested that some even drink alcohol, pour libation to the ancestors and do not observe Jummah, except for during Ramadan. Here also there was an exception, that their commitment to Ramadan lies in the hereafter and of course the jubilant atmosphere of communal exchanges of kindness and generosity. His opponent seated in front of me, dismissed the argument as complete humbug. In his view, all Muslims were the same, and even the Ashanti becomes corrupt under the influence of religion. He stressed that the African is ruined by either the white man's or brown man's religion, which has rendered him a 'bustard to reason' by entrusting his care and wellbeing to a divine (non) existence instead of his labour and intellect.

To emphasise his point, he pointed to the pile of filth and scattered heaps of soiled bottles and polythene bags nestling along the pavements. He wryly observed that Ghana is one of the most peaceful and religious countries in the world. Yet godliness is clearly not next to cleanliness. A passenger next to my left chuckled, struggling to hold off his laughter. He continued, that the quick-tempered Muslim is nurtured on rage, through the rallying cry of the Qu'ran and hadiths, to pursue Jihad, even for very trivial matters. But they say Islam is a religion of peace. Clearly, he was no expert on either Islam, the Qur'an or Christianity but his speech was redolent of the Marxist logic 'religion is the opiate of the masses'. With the slight exception of his apparent lack of formal education, I would have taken him for a socialist. On second thought, he was probably a living praxis and embodiment of Marxism. At certain points in the conversation, it was difficult to tell which tradition of thought influenced his incisive exposition, be it phrenology, anthropology or flat out eugenics. One can't possibly say.

As the conversation waged on, almost teetering on the brink of an unholy war, the passengers interjected in annoyance, shouting both men down as ignorant and tribalist, non-believers. One elderly gentleman reprimanded the two contenders in a raspy drawl indicative of his seniority, 'religion is not independent of *kulture*, the two influence and shape each other in complex ways'. I later found out that the seventy-something gentlemen coiffed in a traditional Akan cloth that majestically hung from his right shoulder to the left casting an imperial mien, used to be a religious education teacher in a secondary school before his retirement. Emblazoned in colourful flames at the rear of the *trotro* was the axiom 'knowledge is power'. For my part, I was glad to witness that tribalism – the singular most common stereotype sinisterly attributed to Africans by the West – was given no room to breathe.

Alighting at *Kejetia,* one of the busiest commercial districts in Kumasi, the capital town of the Ashanti empire, I was overwhelmed by the surge of people briskly passing one another with haste and purpose. A far cry from Polish journalist Ryszard Kapuscinski's lethargic Africa of docile bodies under acacia trees, lodging in the stillness of time. The atmosphere was saturated with noises from all corners of the earth. The cry of the street vendors and market women, the howl of porters ushering people out of their way as they haul heavy loads of wholesale goods. Dishevelled Sudanese and Somalian child refugees with broken smiles, a tender five years of age, aggressively harassing pedestrians for money. Both motorists and pedestrians flood onto the main highway competing for space to travel. The horns never stop hooting in anger, the cursing and kisses of teeth fought back. Charismatic proselytisers blast their message from hi-tech base speakers, courtesy of China. Chorused by the call to afternoon prayers echoed in the far distance. The view, where the Imam's voice could be heard, showed crowded settlements of wooden makeshift structures and corrugated buildings stacked onto each other. I am told by the plump lady at the small Vodafone stand selling mobile top ups and vouchers, that, that part of the city is called Zongo.

The presence of Islam in Ashanti reads like a 'Once upon a time' legend. The story, as passed down generations, begins in the hinterlands of Ashanti, somewhere yonder in the brushes of the sun-baked northern Savannah lands. So be still as we follow the caravan trail of the trans Saharan trade, that runs through the awe-inspiring city of Timbuktu along the jungle routes of present Ghana. Islamic presence in Ghana took two major forms, beginning with the early waves of Dyula or Wangara, Berber and Arabic traders from the Sahel region to the northern parts of present Ghana between the sixteenth to nineteenth centuries. The downward spread of Islam from the Sahel to the Savannah engendered a hybrid practice that combined existing traditions with Sufi elements. Followed by the formation of Hausa communities along the southern regions of West Africa, spurred by the Islamist movement of Uthman Dan Fodio, which emphasised Sunni orthodox traditions, culminating in the foundation of the Sokoto Caliphate in the nineteenth century.

These migrations into Ghana, brought with it distinct brands of Islam, specific to the interactions between the Muslim community and existing political and social traditions. During the height of the Asante empire, roughly in the 1700s, Sahelian caravans moved southward along the Black volta from Jenne through transitional zones like Bonduku in present day Côte d'Ivoire to Begho, north west of Ashanti in the Brong Ahafo region to trade in salt, beads, clothes, brassware, and much more. Meanwhile, gold and highly valued red kola-nuts passed northward through Nkoranza to Begho from the forest kingdom of Ashanti.

This was not the only route where caravans from the Islamic regions travelled to Ghana. The slave market of Salaga, also brought Asante traders in regular contact with Mande and Fulani traders from the Futa Jallon highlands of present-day Guinea, who embraced Islam around the thirteen and sixteenth century. The movement of goods was also accompanied by the dissemination of knowledge by Muslim clerics. Muslim presence was more felt within local political structures, rather than society as a whole, a fact richly dramatised in the 2018 historical novel by Ghanaian writer Ayesha Haruna Attah *The Hundred Wells of Salaga*. Set against the backdrop of civil wars in Yendi (1868 and 1898), she paints an evocative portrait of Salaga, where concerns around trade overshadowed the desire for religious conversion.

European accounts and records from Muslim scholars show that, by the nineteenth century, Muslim influence on indigenous populations was mostly confined to clothing and popular fashion. And though Muslim leaders did wield considerable political influence in the courts of native rulers, the population at large remained rooted in their traditional beliefs and customs. Thus, conversion into Islam along the Sahelian expanse contrasts slightly from the Savannah regions of northern Ghana. Popular wisdom holds that in the case of the former, Islamisation came about through the process of accommodation as opposed to conquest. The spread of Islam across the regions of Mali, Guinea, Gambia, Senegal and Sierra Leone, is depicted through the ruler's recognition of Islam as the religion of the state, followed by a gradual or in some cases radical introduction of Islam to the rest of the population, such as in the case of the Muslim empires of Mansa Musa (Mali) and Samori Ture (Wassoulou Empire). However, this does not rule out the use of state coercion through the introduction of sharia law and Islamic jurisprudence to engender conformity. In regions where a more purist and orthodox form of Islamic tradition took hold, under Sunni dominance similar to the Uthman Don Fodio Sokoto caliphate, jihadist movements were commonplace.

Spreading across the Sahel to the Voltaic basin of Ghana, adherents to Sufi Islam are believed to have encouraged rather less friction between the minority Muslim community and the *dar al-kufr* (un-believing) majority. Sheikh Hajj Suwara, Sufi scholar, marabout and saint from the Muslim town of Dioala in Mali, is reported to have formulated a theological basis for the peaceful coexistence between Muslims and the non-Muslim ruling classes, with the aim to promote trade between Dyula merchants and the native population. The exact period of Hajj Suwari's existence is highly contested amongst historians. Some claim that he lived around the thirteenth century whilst others maintain that he was active in the fifteen century. Notwithstanding the facts of birth and life, the Suwarian tradition as it latterly came to be known took a *real politik* approach to Islam, by adapting its practices to the conditions and needs of a small Muslim migrant group living amongst a predominant 'pagan' host community. His teachings were spread by disciples in the Sahel to the voltaic stretch of Northern Ghana, roughly around the sixteenth and seventeenth century. Historians describes Sheikh Al-Hajj Salim Suwari as 'pacifistic and quietist in content', alluding to the establishment of an Islamic tradition based on a culture of tolerance and respect towards non- Muslims.

As trade relations deepened between the northern areas of West Africa and the South, so did the influence of Islam. By the eighteenth to nineteenth century, Islam had gained a strong foothold in the north of present-day Ghana, in places such as Mossi, Dagomba, Dagara, Mamprusi, Gonja, interacting and shaping indigenous cultural structures in substantive ways. This resulted in the widespread perception of the north as a Muslim country. In the south the impact of Islam remained marginal, nonetheless, during crucial historic moments Muslims enjoyed considerable political influence in the administration of the state.

The Ashanti Kingdom founded by King (Asantehene) Osei Tutu and his demiurgic priest Okomfo Anokye around 1670 and 1690, expanded its reach through conquest, assisted by the creation of a sophisticated political machinery. The formation of decentralised political structures under a confederation of chiefs connected outlying chiefdoms to the central administration. The confederacy allowed for democratic decision-making processes and a united body of representation expressed through the office of the King as the *inter pares primus*. Emissaries were stationed across captured states as the organ of central government, representing the very authority of the King. By 1750 the Asante empire was the largest and most powerful state in the region. It had defeated the states of Gonja and Dagbon, placing considerable lands and populations in the north at the disposal of the Asantehene. The Ashanti sphere of influence extended beyond the whole of present-day Ghana, covering parts of Ivory Coast to the west and Togo to the East. During the reign of Asantehene Osei Kwadwo Kwoawia (1764–1777), also referred to as the 'lion of the Savannah' the Ashanti witnessed the first Muslim travellers to the Kings

Palace. He is reported to be the principal Ashanti King to have associated with Muslims.

Ashanti incursion to the north, brought to the King's attention the knowledge of Islamic charms and cures. As his interest in the potency of Islamic 'magic' grew, he immediately recruited several Muslim clerics and scribes into his administration to provide auxiliary services to the military wing through the office of the Gyaseehene (head of central administration). Muslims were called upon to provide advice to the ruler and record important events in the capacity of councillors and scribes. Unlike the northern and voltaic states, Ashanti state formation did not include residential Muslims in political roles. State policy stopped short of creating a permanent Muslim resident, and mainly treated them as guests living and enjoying the privileges of the court at the pleasure of his majesty. As such they were keenly aware of their precarious position. That they could be easily expelled from the land once they fell out of favour or grace with the King. The state was constructed around the absolute control of the monarch over the forces of economic production, whilst the political spheres conform to democratic dispensation, through a two-tier system of jural corporateness: *aman mu* (immemorial customs not subject to legislative changes) and *aman bre* (jural custom subjected to legislative acts). The Ashanti King acted as the guarantor of all lands and wealth controlling economic production and distribution of wealth. As a result, the Asantehene was able to fend off social revolutions, by constraining the rise of an indigenous commercial class through favouring non-resident Muslim merchants over Ashanti traders.

The ascension of Nana Osei Tutu Kwame to the golden stool ushered in from 1777 to 1803 dramatic shifts in state policy towards Muslims. Osei Kwame's liberal economic policies encouraged an influx of Muslims into the capital of Ashanti, Kumasi, establishing a Muslim residence close to the Kings Palace, Manhyia. Whilst there are no definite records of the size of the Muslim population during this period, it is fair to assume that their numbers were within the thousands. Muslim clerics exercised important state functions as ambassadors and emissaries of the King and there is considerable evidence that shows that state correspondence between Ashanti, European and foreign states was conducted in Arabic. The King also permitted religious proselytisation, which oversaw a modest number of converts, since Muslim relations with Ashanti remained confined to court politics, war and trade. In this regard Muslim traders due to their knowledge of the geography gained dominance of the cross-country caravan trade, rendering them an asset to the state.

Asantehene Osei Kwame has been described as a 'Muslim at heart', who showed great interest in the Qur'an. His patronage towards the followers of the faith in Kumasi has caused commentators to claim that he was the first Muslim King. This may not be far from the truth, given that the underlying premise of Asante *grund norms* was predicated on a system of conformity and accommodation, allowing for the instrumental incorporation of other belief systems into the pre-existing framework of indigenous structures. Islam was therefore acceptable provided that its adherents conformed to the State's demands and interests. In the words of the distinguished Africanist historian on Ashanti, Tom McCaskie, the public lives of Muslims in Ashanti 'extended along a spectrum from compromise to apostasy'.

Ashanti reverence for Muslim talisman, charms and amulets along with the belief that the Qur'an and Islamic inscriptions held great power, helped maintain and deepen cordial relations between the state and the Muslim community. Successive regimes stuck to this pro-Muslim policy, with Osei Kwame Asibe Bonsu, who reigned from 1804-1823, opening up new vistas of opportunities for Muslims to ascend to high positions in government. In particular, Sheikh Muhamma al-Ghamba, commonly known as Baba, from Wangara became the first officially recognised head of the Muslim community. He settled in Kumasi in 1807 and adhered to the Suwarain tradition, integrating Islam and indigenous belief while firmly rejecting the propagation of Islam through force or violence. He considered himself to be a favoured servant of the King, and perhaps he was right, as he enjoyed high rank at court. In the war against Gyaman and its northern borders in 1818, he commanded a force of 7000 strong Muslim soldiers on behalf of the Ashanti Kingdom. In preparation for the war the King invoked both pagan gods and Allah to intercede on his behalf.

Ultimately, though, Sheikh Baba's allegiances would disappoint the King, when he refused to face the Kong and Gonja people in the Gyaman war, declaring that he could not fight against fellow Muslims. Despite his bitterness at the perceived betrayal, the King would pardon his life on the account of him being a holy man. Such largesse and kindness of heart from the Commander in Chief of the Ashanti army was rare and perhaps a testament to the genuine affection between the men. Had he been an Ashanti General, Baba would have certainly paid with his life. Baba's influence was such that it is thought that the term *kramo* was coined during this period in reference to him. The word is of a Wangara derivation instead of the language of the Ashanti, twi, and is commonly used to denote a knowledgeable person.

Sheikh Baba was not the only Muslim cleric who enjoyed nobility and high rank. One Uthman Kamaghatay who founded the first Immamate in Kumasi in 1844 served the King as a close confidant and highly valued councillor, playing an important role in negotiations over the Anglo-Ashanti treaty of 1820. Both Kamaghatay and Baba sat in the Kings close senate, or privy council and advised on matters regarding the state's relations with its northern subjects, as well as vetted European visitors. The French and English travellers Jean Dupuis and Thomas Edward Bowdich, respectively recount that during their visit to Ashanti they came across many Muslims of influence, rank and repute in the capital, who they identified as either Turks or Moors. They also described having to swear on the Qur'an to avow their goodwill towards the King. Several other high-profile Muslims from that period such as Kramo Ali and Kramo Suleyman are celebrated in oral tradition for their service to the King as spiritual mentors. According to folklore they are believed to have helped the King defeat his enemies through their knowledge of the supernatural and practice of magic.

Not all Muslims dabbled in the mystic and esoteric, or even approved of fraternisation with pagan customs and practices. Sharif Ibrahim left the Niger for Kumasi, in or around 1815, and after sojourning for two years he quickly left for Mecca, incensed by the interaction between Kumasi Muslims and pagan customs. He belonged to a strict Sunni order and advocated a clear distinction between Dar-al-Islam and Dar-al-Harb. In his view 'the Government of the country is the Government of its King without question. If the King is a Muslim, his land is Muslim: If he is an unbeliever his land is a land of unbelievers'. Sharif harshly condemned Kumasi Muslims as apostates and strongly disagreed with the making of amulets or use of magic to support the pagan objectives of Ashanti. He renounced all forms of interaction between Muslims and pagans in every area of public life, even including trade.

Whatever tensions emerged within the Muslim community, the Islamisation of Ashanti as a whole seemed unlikely. First the Ashanti state policy kept Muslims closely attached to the Kings court, providing them limited access to the population at large. Trade with Ashanti was largely conducted by the state as opposed to ordinary citizens. The state also allocated spaces for Muslim settlement, which further allowed for close surveillance of Muslim migrants. In this context, the Muslim population had very little choice but to adopt a more pragmatic approach that emphasised peaceful coexistence and accommodation rather than risk conflict with the majority population.

Between 1874 and 1896 marked the beginning of the end of a golden era. The British army, under the command of Lieutenant Colonel Willcocks sacked the city of Kumasi with the support of 1000 Hausa troops from Nigeria and Sierra Leone. Subsequent to the arrest and exile of the Asantehene Prempeh I, Kumasi was set ablaze along with the Asantehene's palace. Yaa Asantewaa, the intrepid and fierce queen mother of Ejisu staged a historic uprising, which for a brief moment turned the tide in favour of the Ashanti forces. Sadly, the British repelled the Ashanti advantage, finally bringing the empire to its knees. Yaa Asantewaa and her rebellious rabble were shipped off to the Seychelles to join their exiled King, as prisoners of war. These were truly dark days for the residents of Kumasi. The whole town was covered in a mournful smog of smoke punctuated by the stench of blood and corpses. That said, trouble had been long brewing. Prior to the final defeat of the Ashanti in the 1900s, the capital experienced protracted conflicts and antagonism between the power holders in Kumasi. These conflicts developed largely around succession disputes, which found state officials in a maelstrom of violent skirmishes as emerging factions vied to install their candidate of choice in office. The civil war created a hostile environment which saw a massive deterioration of trade relations between the state and Muslim traders. The Ashanti state put an embargo on foreign citizens to Ashanti resulting in a rapid decline of the presence of Muslims in court and state affairs. The brutal crackdown on Ashanti dissent at the hands of the British, resulted in a new political dispensation and configuration of the public space.

Amidst this backdrop, the British seized their opportunity and, in 1902, declared Ashanti a British protectorate with a resident district commissioner tasked with the daily administration of the region. 700 Hausa troops out of the 1000 stayed behind, buoyed by the British removal of the embargo on the influx of foreign nationals. Colonial policies sought to boost commerce and economic growth in Ashanti, driving large numbers of Muslim traders and other ethnic groups from the Northern territories, Burkina Faso, Mali, Nigeria and Niger to the capital. However, the Hausa residents remained the largest single group and the first foreign occupants to enjoy British protection. The British administration reconfigured the colonial space along ethnic and racial lines, establishing the precedent for urban segregation through zoning. This reinforced Ashanti antipathy towards foreign subjects as interlopers or illegitimate tenants. The foreign quarter came to be known as Hausa Zongo, given the predominance of Hausa groups. The tenets of Ummah played a prominent role in altering the social and cultural complexion of these quarters. It attracted Muslims of different theological strands and cultural influences to the Zongos and this unofficially established the Islamic faith as a prerequisite for occupancy in the Zongos. Muslim landlords were accused of preferring to rent out or lease their properties only to Muslim tenants. Meanwhile, Ashanti residents considered the Zongos to be a Muslim neighbourhood, an illegitimate dwelling of squatters kept on their land through colonial subjugation, rather than a peaceful accommodation of popular consent.

During my recent visit to the Zongos at Aboabo and Yenyawoso, in Kumasi, as I spoke to tenants it became clear to me that these quarters, though with a large Muslim population, also housed Ashantis and residents from other ethnic divisions. Whilst the term *Asante Nkramo* reflects a long and fruitful relationship that Ashanti has had with Muslim societies, the colonial spatial ordering has had a fundamental impact on the perception of Muslims in Ashanti, eventually engendering and hardening xenophobic attitudes towards them. As we chat, an Ashanti respondent and resident of the Zongo furiously gesticulates his arms in the air delivering an angry tirade against the appalling and squalid conditions in which he is forced to live, noticeable through the lack of infrastructure and basic sanitation. He condemned the government for the systemic marginalisation of Zongo residents but in an unexpected turn, seizes upon Muslim residents as the reason behind the government's apathy. Poverty often provokes the marginalised and disaffected to scapegoat easy targets, and this is no exception. He claims that Zongos are a cesspool of illicit foreigners, whose cultural way of life is antithetical to Ashanti values and customs. Interestingly, prejudice towards Zongo residents is often passed off as cultural difference and not religious antipathy. Yet in recent times, the rise of groups like Boko Haram has perpetuated the othering of Muslims or in the case of Zongo residents a patina of religious prejudice. As another Ashanti resident living just off the fringes told me, 'they are all recruits for boko haram in the waiting', pointing in the direction of the mosque.

Islamophobia is on the rise in this part of West Africa, intensifying existing tensions as it finds new forms of expression. Yet underlying such sentiment is the legacy of colonial residential segregation that has found Muslims living separate but parallel lives alongside Ashanti citizens. This has deeply altered the relationship between the Ashanti traditional state and Islam, conjuring up negative images of Muslims within the Ashanti historic imagination, from one of invited guests and friends of the state to that of illegitimate squatters. The situation has not been helped by the preservation of the architecture of colonial urban policies under post-colonial regimes. Within Muslim circles in Ghana, *Asante Nkramo* is either a muted expression or emblematic of the Islamic presence in precolonial Asante. When invoked, strong emphasis is placed on the cultural difference of *Asante Nkramo* from other Islamic groups. Consequently, Islam, as a binding force is subjected to reinterpretation, where secular norms are celebrated and extolled. This marks a dramatic shift in the negotiation of Muslim identity as practiced by the former Asante Nkramo attached to the Kings court. The former adopted a pragmatic response to the material circumstances surrounding their presence in Asante, and thus sought to integrate into the superstructure of Ashanti polity as a unitary body bound by the concept of Ummah. The latter, as a result of colonial spatial ordering of identity that designated groups to a fixed physical location, is deracinated from its historic genealogy and socially displaced. Compelled to refashion novel forms of identity formation by evoking new symbolic sites of self-expression, in accordance with prevailing norms.

Asante Nkramo, once reminiscent of the fluid and social mixing between Ashantis and Muslim communities reconstructs Islam in a secular idiom that mobilises Suwarian principles towards a syncretised ethic, albeit, within a hostile environment. In practice, must the *Asante Nkramo* temporarily opt out of the Ummah to insist on his cultural difference from the *other* Muslims - the foreigners? He must also allow his faith an air of malleability and worldly aura. It is not surprising to encounter individuals in Ghana who identify as *Asante Nkramo* and possess an Islamic name but do not practice the faith, raising questions around the popular view of peaceful coexistence between Muslims and the rest of society. Colonialism has undoubtedly played its role in shaping Africa's social geography and cultural demographic, but it cannot be held responsible for all the ills of contemporary West Africa. We all remember the scramble for Africa, where African lands and its people were carved out and served on a political smorgasbord to satisfy the appetite and greed of European nations. Who can forget the haunted ghost of decapitated Congolese children that trails the horrors of King Leopold's cotton industry. Sadly, not much has changed. Children are still sent to their death by the thousands in the production of coltan within the postcolonial estate. Just as the precolonial Asante state and colonial state fashioned different sets of arrangements with the Muslim population, to meet their specific interest, so has the postcolonial state in Ghana. The postcolonial state promotes the idea of coexistence on the national theatres through the incorporation of Muslim cultural aesthetics and strategic presence in the representation of the nation state. The celebration of Ramadan as a national holiday, the presence of high state officials such as the president or his vice at Muslim durbars, which is often televised and the intimate courtship between the state and dominant Muslim territories as fundamental to the maintenance and consolidation of the nation state. The star-crossed romance between the Ghanaian state and Muslim population is more pronounced in political party affiliation with supposed Muslim territories in the north as important voting blocs, expressed through the tradition of reserving important seats in government for a Muslim candidate. The current ruling party in Ghana, the New Patriotic Party (NPP), has gone to great lengths to give vice presidency to a northern Muslim - Mahamudu Bawumia - partly to repair its image as a party of southern Ashanti elites.

Ironically in the 1940s the NPP in its evolution was known as the Northern Peoples Party, and largely represented the interest of the Northern region. In the presidential address to the nation in 2019, for the first time in history, Nana Addo Dankwa Akufo-Addo announced that the celebration of Independence Day commemoration on 6 March 2019, is held in the northern capitals. Clearly, the theme of peaceful coexistence advanced by the state assumes a singular coherent narrative that repackages Muslim identities within the appeal of the nation state. A deliberate political manoeuvre that seeks to conceal discontinuous and divergent narratives like the *Asante Nkramo*, by overemphasising syncretisation as a unique cultural ethics and value, specific to a singular rendition of Islamisation in Ghana and to some extent Africa in general. *Asante Nkramo* is reinterpreted and (re)produced out of the tensions and conflicts over the invocation of Muslim identities as a homogenous community against contested narratives of Muslim identities as historic categories subjected to change.

Waiting for a taxi to convey me from the silence of hostility normalised as part of the flow of life in the Zongo, an elderly lady asks me for the time. She stares pensively into my face, giving me a surreal feeling of my fate being read out loud. She shuffles closer, casts a doubtful smile and asks, my son do you live here? No mama I answered, I was just passing through. Be careful, this place is not safe, and may God be with you. She did not have to spell it out, since we both understood her meaning: the Muslims are no longer a friend of the Ashanti.

GRIOTS

Jean-Ann Ndow

Griots hold the memory and history of a community. They are the storytellers, musicians and singers of songs of praise. They are the archives. They are the historians. They speak the history of our people. They are our oral historians.

Growing up in Gambia in the eighties, I have vivid memories of listening to the songs and poetry of Griots as they sang with melodic voices. I recall their nimble fingers plucking the cords of a Kora as they chorused with emotion. I was fascinated by the scale and power of their presence and performance, compounded by their Grand Buba outfits, one of our traditional garments comprising a long shirt made of reams of material gathered up and draped over the shoulders, with trousers and a matching hat. The Griot would balance what from my vantage point as a small child appeared to be a huge Kora, longer than their torso. They would then masterfully weave their fingers up and down the cords to attentive ears. My awe was shared by many, for Griots commanded the respect of the people and occupied the same space as the head of the family, community leaders, noblemen and dignitaries.

Gambia, Senegal and Mali are three countries located next to each other in the West of Africa, and home to the descendants of the Mende people, who are considered one of the earliest civilisations in the region. The Mende were responsible for the formation of many empires including the Ghana (not to be confused with the country Ghana) and Songhay Empires. Prior to European colonisation in West Africa, the three countries formed part of the illustrious Malian empire from 1230 to 1630. Founded by Sundiata Keita, it boasted immense wealth and culture that flowed outward to impact the West African region and beyond. Hugely prosperous, it covered a considerable stretch, spanning current-day Senegal, Gambia, Guinea, Niger, Nigeria, Chad, and Mauritania, including Mali.

The renowned King Mansa Musa ruled the Malian Empire during the fourteenth century and has been named in historic records as the richest person in history, and by moderate accounts his wealth is estimated to be roughly around the equivalent of $400 billion in today's money, at the time of his death. Nonetheless, it is almost impossible to quantify Mansa Musa's vast riches during his lifetime. Scholars maintain that his wealth is unmatched by any other figure in history. As a devout Muslim, during his pilgrimage to Mecca to perform Hajj, Musa is reputed to have travelled with a caravan that included 'tens of thousands of soldiers, slaves and heralds, draped in Persian silk and carrying golden staffs'. Upon passing through Egypt, Musa littered the streets, cities and villages in Egypt with so much gold, that the precious metal, once in short supply, dramatically depreciated in value, plunging the Egyptian economy into recession for almost twelve years.

It was under Musa's rule that the great Mosque of Timbuktu, locally referred to as Djinguerereber or Djingareyber, was built in 1327. Musa paid the architect Abu Es Haq es Saheil 200kg of gold dust (40,000 *mithqals* of gold). Such was the grandeur and spectacle that accompanied Musa's reign, that by the late fourteenth century, he was featured on the 1375 Catalan Atlas. The Atlas was an important resource for navigators and showed a towering Musa, planted on a golden stool, adorned with a gold crown and sceptre, whilst balancing in in his palm a gold nugget. The splendour and unrestrained opulence, with which the Spanish cartographer Abraham Cresques, the author of the Catalan Altas depicts Musa, goes to show the awe and bewilderment of European travellers upon learning of this great African King.

Word of King Musa's great riches spread far and wide and not long after his death the mission to colonise Africa began. In the fifteenth century the Portuguese were the first to arrive, followed by the French and then the British, in search of the West African Eldorado. During the colonisation of Africa, the region, was carved out like an *a la carte* menu, into Gambia, Senegal and Mali. Senegal gained its independence from the French on 4 April 1960, Mali from the French on 20 June 1960, and The Gambia from the British on 18 February 1965.

Despite the violent and brutal period of colonisation and the cruel exploitation of the wealth of the continent; the fracturing of Mende society and culture; and the enslavement of the healthy and strong, the resilient culture of the people endured, through the tradition of the Griot. Thus, the Griot served as a vital force for the preservation of history and culture, located at the very heart of the community.

The practice of Griot spans over seven centuries. Throughout this period of time, Griots have been tasked with recounting the lineage of families and histories of communities. They are genealogists keeping record of births, deaths, marriages and notable cultural practices of a community. They compose and sing songs of reverence and adoration, sorrow and pain and are often called on during significant occasions in the community. They recount the stories of great heroes, kings and queens and of victorious battles.

Traditionally born into families that have been Griots for many generations, they carry the responsibility of committing to memory the history of a community. This knowledge is passed down through family members and although usually male, there are many females today practising the art of Griot known as Griottes. Given the huge volume of information that Griot must absorb, training starts at a young age. Immersion in verbal storytelling, training in playing musical instruments and familiarising themselves with the arts and culture of the community begins at a young age. Students spend their time travelling and listening to Master Griots to hone their skills as well as spending precious hours practicing in order to excel at the art form. They are masterful orators and musicians skilled in weaving together stories and songs of emotion, power and history.

Voice has played a critical role in storytelling in many cultures but particularly in the Griot tradition where voice and words are used to impart knowledge and wisdom. Orature, as described by Ngugi wa Thiong'o, a writer from Kenya, is the use of utterance as an aesthetic means of expression, requiring no validation from the literary. The language of the Griot is the language of their people with songs sung in the medium of the cultural group to which they belong. In this way, communication in native tongue rather than the speech of the coloniser has enabled Griots to serve an important function in the preservation of language and identity before, during, and after the colonisation of Africa.

Seckou Keita is a Senegalese musician born and trained in a Griot family. He describes it as his 'responsibility as a member of my family to pass on what I was taught so that our stories may never be lost or forgotten. The most beautiful thing about our music is that you don't need to understand the words in order to understand the language of a song. Some songs are sung from the belly and some from the heart or head. Meaning comes with the feeling that the voice and the music create together'.

Besides the voice, the instruments of a Griot are the kora, balafon and ngoni. The kora belongs to the harp family, emitting sound through the plucking of strings. Made out of a large calabash that has been cut in half and covered with the skin of a cow, a long wooden neck is then added to support the twenty-one-string instrument. The balafon originates from Mali and is a long xylophone that can consist of over sixteen keys. Similar to a Kora, the Ngoni is an instrument that is made from a Calabash with animal skin stretched over it and consists of a single string. Other versions of the Ngoni have included the six-string Dondo Ngoni that was reported to be played in Gambia as early as the 1620s.

West African music has its own unique sound and energy that has come from our use of rhythmic instruments like the djembe drum. Djembe drums belong to the Mande tribe, originating from Gambia, Senegal, Cote d'Ivoire and most of the other countries in the region. The djembe forms the bass line and rhythms that create the West African sound. Djembe's are made from one piece of wood with the skin stretched on top. Djembe drummers are notorious for their strong hard hands due to the force and pace with which they beat the drums to signal their presence as the heart of any occasion or performance.

Sabar is also a very popular instrument. A small drum, it is played with a stick and a single hand and is linked to a form of music in Senegal known as Mbalax. It is accompanied by one of the most vibrant forms of dance I have witnessed in Africa with use of one's entire body, arms, legs, hips... everything, down to facial expression. It requires the lifting of the legs in circular motions, accompanied by the swaying of the arms to create movements that resemble trees in the midst of a gust of wind. There is an interplay and flirtation with the drummer punctuated by exaggerated gyration of the hips and groin.

One of my personal favourite instruments is the talking drum, also known as the Tama. Small enough to be placed under the arm, the drummer beats it with one hand and a stick. The Tama is often used to punctuate sentences, show approval and converse with other drums present. It has its own unique character with pitches that can go from very high to low with rapid speed and placement of the stick and hands. The Tama has the ability to convey the emotion of the player and the people, generating laughter, dance and understanding. Another percussion instrument frequently used is the Dunun, a group of bass drums. The drum takes the shape of a cylinder with two heads – one on either side. Played on its side at both ends or placed on the floor and played from one end.

These instruments all form the basis of what is a very distinctive West African sound. Often described as being polyrhythmic, since it features two or more conflicting rhythms that are layered to form discordant yet congenial melodies.

Over the years, Griot men and women have been able to take their music from the community to international stages, sharing the art form and cultural practice. Artists like Sona Jobarteh born into one of the main Griot families in Gambia has found fame as a professional musician playing the Kora and other stringed instruments to audiences around the world. Her sound is a fusion of the new and the old, sharing the beauty of traditional sounds whilst bringing a fresh perspective and interpretation of style. Baaba Mall, Youssou N'Dour and Amadou and Mariam have found mainstream success with their music reaching global audiences. They have been nominated for prestigious awards and can be heard on film scores like the Marvel movie Black Panther.

In recent times there has been increased flexibility with the opportunity for those not born into Griot families to undertake the training given to Griots and perform to audiences. The non-hereditary tenor of Griot practice today is a sign of shifting times as Griot music and sounds move more towards the mainstream, becoming increasingly accessible to new audiences. Schools have opened in West Africa, US and Europe to teach the skill and some of the repertoire of Griot music.

Outside of the practice of Griot storytelling, oral traditions play a big part in Senegambian families. I have often sat through aunts, uncles and grandparents recounting the complex connection of Aunty this, to cousin that, who married cousin that, and had cousin other, who then lived with Uncle that and had children with so and so, who is now living in xyz... Despite eventually being totally confused and none the wiser as to how I am connected to these individuals, I enjoy the opportunity to listen to them and revel in their ability to educate me on who we are, and where we come from, and their pride in occupying the role of living archive. I also enjoy their slight frustration and annoyance that this information is not already stored somewhere in my bank of knowledge. The relationship then becomes one of teacher and student.

Beyond stories of our lineage there are often folktales, proverbs and sayings that Griots deliver with almost comic expectation and timing. Sayings like:

Way u nyams white, cover am – when things are going well for you keep quiet don't go around publicising it.

Okra shall never long pass im master – however big you are, however tall you are, however old you are you can never be wiser than your mother because she will always have more wisdom than you.

Dat water wey na for you e no go run pass you – what God has destined for you nobody can take it away.

Truckey wan box, e hand no reach – you want to achieve or do something but do not have the means or cannot afford it.

I dey take yeye ker you go – I'm guiding you where you go, my eyes are on you to guide and protect you wherever you go.

These sayings are passed from one generation to the next and have stood the test of time and transcended geographical location. Hearing and understanding sayings like this from my family, from childhood to present day, I have been able to retain close links to my culture and identity despite being part of the global community of Africans living in the diaspora. These oral traditions have enabled me to be firmly rooted in my identity as a Serer, Wolof, Gambian woman.

Storytelling calls for more than just words. Facial expressions, physical movements and gestures all form part of the story captivating the listener. Weaved into these oral traditions is the art of performance that is often used for the delivery of stories with impact. Storytelling is a method of cultural preservation that has long existed in our communities. Although there are records of written text from West Africa prior to colonisation, storytelling and oral traditions have far outweighed written text as a way to pass knowledge from one generation to the next. Much of West Africa's written history was in Arabic but with the violent disruption of colonialism, the ability of Africans to write our own narrative was abruptly interrupted. Thankfully, over time this has begun to shift with the success of writers like Chinua Achebe and Chimamanda Ngozi Adichie. These writers paint a picture of African life through African words and stories that resonate with both those on the continent and outside of it. They provide a space and opportunity for recognition of the value of our culture and the universal nature of the human experience despite differences in upbringing and location. That said, the written word cannot be a substitute for oral traditions or orature. Invariably, it fails to capture the spontaneity and magic of storytelling.

It will be remiss of me not to recount the great epic of Sunjata, the founder of the great ancient Mali Empire. A wondrous sight to behold is that of the Griot as he seductively strings the travails of Sunjata. With his kora delicately balanced between his legs he sends his audience in the stupor of time, to a distant land. At the stroke of a hunter's prophesy, King Maghan begot a son on Sogolon, his name was Sunjata. Sogolon, was known as the 'Buffalo woman' for she was bereft of any redeeming qualities. Legend has it that she was a hunchback with monstrous eyes. Born crippled, Sunjata took after his mother in his grotesque bearing. His head was unusually large, which he could barely support with his scrawny neck. For seven years, he did not walk nor speak. With fiery round savage eyes, he crawled on all fours like a man cub. The crowd chimes in laughter. A woman interjects, tell it well, he was handsome, another groans, devilry! It is true he was not of this world. The timbres of the kora painfully shriek a change in chord, the Griot howls, darkness cast a long shadow over the land of the Mende. For seven years the teats of the earth mother run dried, whilst hunger and drought feasted on the living. King Maghan laid on his sick bed with the prophesy of the hunter throbbing in his heart. He called his son to his bedside, and gently stroked the tears of his lurid eyes and said, 'take heart, be not afraid, when I go, you will be king. You are destined for greatness, my boy!' Taking his last breath Maghan parted with the living to meet the ancestors.

Upon learning of the dead King's wish, Maghan's first wife Sassouma set out to make her son Dankaran King. Messengers, concubines, slaves and servants were assembled and dispatched across the land to spread vicious rumours about Sunjata and Sogolon. Some said that since birth the boy drew strength by feasting on his father's blood. Others claimed that at the rise of the full moon the dark lord exposed himself to Sogolon, caressing her in a naked embrace. And so, they believed that is how Sunjata was born. Stricken by fear, the people were unsettled. The council of elders nod in confusion but agreed that the only way to avoid unrest and save the land from eternal doom was to make Dankaran King.

The Kora weeps, the days that followed were dark, indeed, sings the Griot. Mother and Child were banished to a foreign land. Misery and grief overcame Sogolon that one day she said to her son, 'Sunjata, you are destined for greatness, but I am worried about your future. You are a strong boy and have a great heart, but your legs have allowed Sassouma to take control. We cannot let Dankaran be chief – it is against your father's wishes!' Hearing the pain in his mother's words, Sunjata grabbed a branch from the S'ra tree, an African baobab or Adansonian tree. With courage and great determination he pulled himself up and started to walk. The crowd cheered in applause. Oh! A man shakes his head, muttering, 'Nobody knows the beginning of a great man'. The kora rumbles a velvety blues, the tempo cuts and swings, interlacing the griots drawl.

Sunjata grew to be a strong hunter, known for his athletic feats and bravery. By then he had gained many admirers, all spoke well of him. He had shed of his ugly looks to emerge as a handsome man, with a regal mien and sagacious disposition. The Kingdom of the Mandinka, however had fallen under the spell of an evil sorcerer, Soumaoro. Soumaoro ousted King Dankaran and enslaved half the population. He even displayed the skins and skulls of his enemies as treasures in his chamber. Hearing this from an eyewitness, Sunjata was reminded of the prophesy his father told him on his sick bed. He sought the advice of an old friend, Balle Fasseke, who revealed to him that Soumaoro can only be defeated with a magical arrow. Balle Fasseke for years had known of the coming of the evil sorcerer through the vision of the gods. Forty nights and days he laboured in the gorges of the gods, forging a magical arrow for the young warrior. Wasting no time Sunjata raised an army to face Soumaoro.

The battle was long and arduous, with no side gaining the advantage. For months Sunjata advanced on his enemy with no avail since he could not breach their defence. Suomaoro had fortified the walls of the city with a protective charm. Taking advantage of the restless mood and declining morale within his men, Suomaoro lead a deadly assault, slaughtering half of

Sunjata's army. Victory still remained hidden out of sight. With great forbearance and patience, Sunjata spotted a weakness in his opponents' tactics. On the next assault, he rode from rear flank of the cavalry allowing his men to engage Soumaoro's close bodyguards, leaving him open for attack. Sunjata charging his horse at his enemy at a greater pace shot his arrow directly through the aperture of clashing swords and bodies making a fatal contact with Suomaoro, who suddenly fell off his horse with dread in his eyes. In fear of his life, his men quickly formed a human shield around him allowing the wicked wizard to flee the battle, never to be seen again. For his bravery in battle, Sunjata was finally crowned King, winning the loyalty of his people and fulfilling the hunter's prophesy. They called him the Lion King of Mali because of his strength and courage. He was also given the title Mansa meaning King of Kings, becoming the first ruler of the Malian Empire. His reign was long and prosperous, and he became one the greatest kings ever to rule the kingdom of Mali. The Griot's voice shrills a jubilant call 'Sunjata the Great'. The people respond, 'truly he was great'. The Kora sonorously meanders, assembling together intricate melodies of a thousand syncopated turns. The Griot drives the recitation to a close, tenderly plucking the strings to a final whisper. 'Allah is Great!', he chants.

It was during the reign of Sunjata, in the 1300s, that Mali first became an important economic and agricultural force amongst the West African Empires. Some academics have compared Sunjata's exploits to that of Alexander the Great. It is believed that Walt Disney's 1994 animation *The Lion King* was inspired by the story of Sunjata, although the Disney corporation cites Shakespeare's *Hamlet* as its source material. Yet the closeness of narrative, events and themes between *The Lion King* and Sunjata, also referred to in Mende legend as the Lion King, cannot be overstressed.

Each Griot tells the story differently but must remain faithful to the overarching narrative: order of events, name of characters and other details that are traditionally considered to be the bare facts. Improvisation in the playing of the recitation is also encouraged. The audience are at liberty to interrupt, to correct, or challenge the Griot or even include their version of events, views and opinions. As such the Griot must have a meticulous memory and eloquence to avoid their displeasure. In a way both the Griot and audience participate in the creating and shaping of the story. This form of cultural production, namely orature, contrasts remarkably from literature. It is neither alienated from its audience nor crafted by an isolated detached writer, embedded within impersonal relations of production. Instead it is a product of the community, part of its identity, where it emerged and will be persevered through the handing down of the tradition from one generation to the other. It defies time, though limited to temporal existence but not in the linear or historical sense. Unlike, a complete and immutable body of work, each time the story is told it is instantiated in the now, bound to the context in which it is produced.

However, as we move further into the digital age the challenge that we face as Africans with long and rich histories, is how best to preserve our culture and ensure that traditional practices like having a Griot in the community retain their importance and prominence. I was recently challenged by a Gambian filmmaker to question the manner in which we as Africans create archives of our history or rather the lack of archiving that exists. Some weeks later the same question was posed by an Angolan musician on a mission to create an archive of the sounds and rhythms of Angola. These conversations prompted me to think about the rich archives that exist in the minds of our Griots and to question the sustainability of the practice as the technological boom continues to sweep across Africa reaching young minds far and wide. Is our culture and heritage strong enough to continue the legacy of Griot?

Much of our African history has been lost or relies on the telling and retelling of stories orally. This is subject to adaptation and embellishment, therefore the sooner we recognise Griots as repositories of knowledge and holders of our archives, the more imperative it seems to adapt their practice to modern modes of preservation. Though remaining faithful to the tradition of indigenous knowledge production, in my view the adoption of digital and modern techniques to traditional forms of production should not be seen as a perversion but rather an opportunity to preserve tradition for posterity, whilst enlarging participation on a global scale. This will further allow for a reconstruction of an African history and culture that reinforces African authorship. Just imagine how magnificent it will be if the Sundiata epic was performed on a virtual platform where audiences from around the world could tune in and participate. Or a holographic performance that one can access in one's living room. However, we must definitely stop at robots. I can't possibly imagine a brass shell crooning and shuffling like the Griot.

SEEING AFRICAN CITIES

Peter Griffiths

In 1950, roughly half the world's urban population lived in Europe and North America. A few decades on, Asia has eclipsed Europe and is today home to half the world's city dwellers. As Europe enters deeper into an ageing society, Africa will soon overtake it for second position behind Asia. The United Nations Department for Economic and Social Affairs (UNDESA) recently claimed that 42 per cent of Africans are urban dwellers, about 500 million people. In the next few decades this number is set to swell over 1.4 billion, with twelve million young people entering the labour market every year. This incredible growth puts Africa and her cities on the global agenda in a way that hasn't been the case before.

The rapidly growing urban areas in Africa and Asia may soon set the global urban agenda on everything from climate change and social inclusion to productivity and transport innovation, given the relatively larger populations and significant need for constructing spaces, connecting people and supporting livelihoods. Nigeria's cities alone, of which Lagos is Africa's largest, will accommodate 189 million more people by 2050. Ethiopia, one of the world's least urban nations, is fast moving from being a predominantly rural economy to an urban one, with Addis Ababa growing at an annual rate of about 4 per cent – twice the rate of Beijing or Jakarta. In the rush to deliver cities, critical infrastructure needs may be overwhelming. Two-thirds of the investments in urban infrastructure needed between now and 2050 have yet to be made, and extensive informal housing will require some form of upgrading. The housing requirements are so large that demolishing, and rebuilding will simply take too long. But can the grace of an incremental growth narrative be afforded to African cities?

It took London over 150 years to grow its metro rail network, which it is still tinkering with, whilst Shanghai built the world's longest metro in little over fifteen years. In a more technologically advanced world than Victorian England, the question of how to design and plan cities may never have been so important. The pressure is also on Africa's leaders, with global expectations to deliver 'sustainable', 'liveable' and 'productive' cities more quickly than in countries that urbanised in previous centuries or risk being cast as a failure. And yet the infrastructure (and governance) challenges African cities face are not necessarily unique. In the *Paradoxes of African Urbanism*, Edward Glaeser reminds us that since 'many of the wealthy cities of the Global North dealt with these by-products of urban crowding so long ago, they may have forgotten how difficult it was to make Paris or New York liveable.'

From the start of the millennium there has been renewed interest in building high rises in cities as diverse as Cairo, Maputo, Abuja, Kampala, Cape Town, Durban, Addis Ababa, Dar es Salaam, Luanda and Port Louis. A building in Johannesburg's financial district has just become the new tallest building in Africa after 45 years, highlighting a growing optimism in Africa's cities. Plans for even taller towers in Casablanca, Nairobi, Accra and Abuja are on the way. While reaching for the sky doesn't define city-ness (Barcelona and Paris seldom go above eight storeys), it does suggest the eyes of global investors are on African cities. At the same time, these cities are focused on reinventing themselves. This real estate euphoria is, however, frequently met with coordination challenges, with markets and planning authorities finding it difficult to strategically direct growth. Johannesburg's new tower is two blocks away from Sandton station, yet around and above the station, possibly some of the most well-placed development opportunities remain unexercised.

The state-led development model in Addis Ababa is perhaps atypical of the African story. Green and yellow corrugated-iron sheets enclose demolished areas like bandages, highlighting a scale of change occurring in many cities across the continent: some positive, some not. The plethora of experiments across Africa's divergent cities suggests that Africa may perhaps give birth to new forms of city-making and find bold ways of responding to rapid growth, environmental sustainability and reconfiguring cities to be spatially more inclusive in a context of urbanisation without industrialisation.

A potential benefit of the continent's current phase of urbanisation is that development models have already been tested sufficiently across the globe. Those developing Africa's urban *futures* can learn from what worked and, perhaps more important, what didn't. But the evidence on the ground is, at best, mixed. Congestion, sprawl and inadequate infrastructure prevail as city leaders attempt to modernise and retrofit overstressed urban systems. Jean-Louis Missika, Paris' deputy mayor, and staunch critic of free market urban development, believes some of the focus on 'modern' development may be depriving Africa from benefitting from local knowledge: 'In Paris we are abandoning concrete. Addis Ababa seems to be going in the opposite direction despite having a rich local understanding of using sustainable building materials.' Yet policymakers, investors and entrepreneurs are operating in a context where according to the International Labour Organisation (ILO) the informal economy accounts for 50–80 per cent of the continent's GDP, 60–80 per cent of employment and 90 per cent of new jobs. Thus, the motivation to import what seems to be global best practice into local situations that appear not to work is substantial. The prevailing form of growth in many African cities of varying size is ad-hoc and incremental.

As a continent, Africa's infrastructure patterns have historically focused on connecting resources and commodities to global markets, rather than people and ideas. This process has become more complex in the twenty-first century, with China playing a critical – and controversial – role in creating a new generation of infrastructure with potentially transformative impact. Among other forms of investment, the growing superpower is replacing and extending some of the railways built by British, French and Portuguese colonial governments to connect places in Nigeria, Kenya and Ethiopia. This infrastructure may allow cities in the world's most unified regional union (the African Union covers the entire continent) to link not just to the outside world, but also internally.

Intra-regional trade in Africa is only 15 per cent of total exports versus 58 per cent and 67 per cent for Asia and Europe (African Export-Import Bank, 2018). As African cities connect to each other and share ideas, opportunities to negotiate more favourable trade terms increase. Africa's changing flight patterns illustrate this: growth has not only been directed at China and India – flights within Africa have also doubled in the last 15 years. Increasing air connectivity with the Americas provides the potential to reposition Africa more centrally in global trade networks, something Addis Ababa has particularly benefited from. With 108 non-stop routes, Ethiopia's gateway airport is Africa's most connected. Trade figures over a similar period mirror this trend, with export and import growth between Africa and China and India almost doubling. And, as China taught the English to drink tea, Ethiopia is taking coffee to China, with one entrepreneur betting on an empire of 100 cafes by 2022, highlighting how culture continues to flow from African shores. Africa's unique contribution to the world is significant: as internal, regional and global connectivity expands in its cities, this will become increasingly clear.

However, this growth is not evenly spread between cities or consumers. Flying between Cape Town and Johannesburg – one of the world's busiest routes – you could sit next to almost anyone given the range of available ticketing and schedule options. Many other intra-African routes are serviced by only one carrier, meaning you're more likely to sit next to a businessman, an aid worker sponsored on a strong foreign currency or even a pilot than people more representative of Africa's young population, for whom the skies are generally not open. It can often be more expensive and more difficult to fly within Africa than further afield, undermining opportunity for African cities to develop strategic relationships between each other. As with the fibre-optic connectivity that recently proliferated Africa's coastline, it is the last-mile connectivity that is the most difficult to build.

An Urban Age perspective

For two years (2017-2018), the Urban Age research project at the London School of Economics undertook an investigation into increasing the visibility of African cities. This included an extensive data collection and visualisation process, culminating in a report. After several research trips, and commissioning expert commentaries and photography, we were able to present key aspects of African urbanisation in a global context. With several texts, like UNICEF's *Generation 2030 / Africa* or J J Bish's *Population growth in Africa: grasping the scale of the challenge*, often negatively documenting Africa's population 'explosion'. Shlomo Angel, author of

Planet of Cities, shows that, globally, it isn't necessarily rapid population growth (while a significant contributor) that is driving urban expansion, but sprawl, with cities taking up more space per person than ever before, a condition known to make cities less productive, less sustainable and less inclusive. Since 1990, a basket of 200 cities has expanded five times, but their populations have only doubled. This, and the economist Nicholas Stern's caution that the next few decades are a once-in-history opportunity to build sustainable cities, frames the challenge of developing new urban futures that are resilient to technological, economic and climate change, and inclusive.

Even so, all the research into understanding Africa's existing popular transport networks, the challenge of connecting people and opportunities and how best to govern urban informality also suggests that at least some of what might need to be built in Africa has already been built. Lagos and Cairo already have populations as large as some of the world's largest mega-cities: New York City, Shanghai and Mexico City. In the quest to have a story that is more connected to a modern and global narrative, it is important to appreciate and preserve the past, not only in symbolic architecture, but also in the texture of connection on the streets. These are qualities that, once lost, can never be designed back in. As such, citizen participation experiments, like in Nigeria's Port Harcourt, could be part of the solution to retrofitting existing pieces of city instead of rebuilding them from scratch. In the Nigerian case, an extensive community mapping project plugged a gap in available data, enabling the possibility of delivering urban infrastructures in informally planned areas rather than demolishing, displacing and rebuilding.

A significant challenge in understanding Africa's urban conditions is its vast complexity. While some areas are among the least urbanised globally, African urbanisation can be traced further back than much of Europe. Language barriers in Anglo-, Franco- and Lusophone knowledge production, and a tendency to simplify the African story given limited and inaccessible locally produced content, has increased the challenge of comparing African cities to each other and to global examples. In my research experience I found that almost half of all cities in Africa do not have a recent census and accessing data at sufficient quality for study required substantial resources except in a few examples. At the same time, many 'African' experts have knowledge of only a handful of countries, leading to a conflated discussion of what urban African is. We need to disrupt the idea that there is a single Africa or a single African Planning Model. Africa has over 200 cities larger than 300,000 people with significant diversity of urban form, governance, mobility and lived experiences. Europe has fewer cities of this size.

Many of the African cities investigated by the Urban Age simply cannot be known at the same level of detail as more developed cities. To put this into perspective: someone studying say London, Paris and Moscow at the same level of detail available for many African cities might erroneously conclude that they are effectively the *same* city. With knowledge production about cities still concentrated in the Global North, the risk is that Africa's urban success stories remain hidden. But there are exceptions. Cape Town, for instance, encourages the use of city data by universities, entrepreneurs and the public to drive innovation. There is considerable work to be done, though, to satisfy the tongue-in-cheek exhortation: 'In God we trust. Everyone else bring data.'

In an effort to understand the local story, *Urban Age* commissioned a series of commentaries on cities across Africa. Some came back overwhelmingly negative. The comparative data collected by the Urban Age project – an international investigation into the future of cities – shows that African cities do not necessarily perform worst-of-the-worst. In many instances African cities – for now – perform far better than cities elsewhere, particularly in resource use. The high percentage of people who walk or use public transport provide many of the most sustainable modal splits globally. This can offer some reason to hope. It is also clear that African countries with the highest human development are also the most urbanised, mirroring a trend found across the world. As Africa urbanises, it seems likely that measures of education, health and wellbeing will increase too, as will democratic accountability.

Drawing urban narratives

The impact of being able to visualise what's happening in cities is illustrated by Charles Boothe's famous maps of deprivation in Victorian London. These maps provided the impetus for the introduction of old age pensions, and directly influenced the subsequent analysis of poverty. By visualising the link between urban poverty and age, these maps further contributed to the establishment of the welfare state. Booth's surveys provided narrative snapshots, increasing the richness of his maps and adding weight to welfare advocacy. His annotating slum areas, however, as 'vicious, semi-criminal' also passed an unhelpful moral judgement on the poor that planners today are still trying to shrug off.

In Nairobi, the Open Public Spaces Assessment and Inventory make available the city's first Geographic Information System (GIS) database of public space. This is a significant step towards understanding, maintaining and expanding public space in the city. However, Nairobi's central streets – by far the largest share of public space in most cities – are highly contested. Streets are often excluded from what we consider to be public space, but they are significant public goods – making up 11.5 per cent of Nairobi's land and 36 per cent in New York. Stated differently – streets (including pavements) make up almost 70 per cent of New York's public space, confirming the importance of designing road design for all residents. The success of Times Square's pedestrianisation project, which raised the ire of car-pro lobbyists and was only possible because of a remarkably plucky planning team, has raised the profile of New York City's efforts to expand its cycle network and add more pedestrian plazas to make streets safer. Transport planners in Nairobi have been criticised for the exact opposite reason – not designing 'streets for all', by neglecting pedestrians, cyclists and street vendors. Almost half of residents in Nairobi walk as their main way of getting around, yet pavement design providing safe passage isn't prioritised. Where pavements do exist, it isn't uncommon for them to abruptly end, creating even more competition with cars, or for the road surface quality to be so much better that people have little choice but to share it with cars. In fairness, this is a challenge many cities around the world face, with Bogotá taking extreme measures by demolishing private property to re-establish public pathways and Paris has imagined covering its *Boulevard Périphérique* – a 35 kilometre ring road – with a green park to reconnect the city. An exercise in mapping Nairobi's public space may, therefore, not be sufficient to make it public.

On my research trip in 2017, I was temporarily detained by police in Nairobi. This further highlighted the sense that Nairobi's streets are not

places of significant personal freedom. Police have responded to the very
real threat of terrorism in Nairobi, as in many other parts of the world by
defining 'protected areas' of which photography is prohibited. After being
told that I had taken photos with the intent of causing harm and being
questioned by a plainclothes police officer to confirm my university
credentials, I was released with all my photos intact. (For the avoidance of
doubt, the photo I took did not break any law I know of and an almost
identical image is available on Google Street View.) Without understanding
the politics and cultural practices, and implementing design solutions with
this in mind, Nairobi's efforts to improve access to public space – despite
the importance of the mapping exercise – will likely fall short.
Johannesburg has a similar challenge: the pavements around new privately-
operated train stations, a system designed to increase accessibility, are
spaces where personal freedoms are significantly curtailed by private
security. In Colombia, Medellín's 'social urbanism' uses design
interventions (including public space) to change the culture of unequal
access in the city in a context of extreme violence and informality, helping
to veil the prominence of violence in everyday politics. In other words, the
physical architectural interventions of better public transport, public space
and educational facilities was part of redrafting not only social access in
Medellín, but also political power and citizenship.

It may not be possible to understand the impact cultural practices have
on urban infrastructure, but a better link between culture and policy
intervention seems to increase the potential for sustainable development.
We may not be able to identify causality, but it is curious that Ethiopia,
with its tradition of shared eating where several people enjoy a large injera
'pancake', is able to deliver one of the continent's most ambitious housing
programmes and has built a light rail public transport network far ahead of
what might be expected in a predominantly rural country. While other
African nations have opened (Algeria) or are constructing (Nigeria) light
rail, Ethiopia is unusual in that, at 22 per cent urbanised, it has done so far
earlier in its urbanisation curve than other nations on the planet. In
Kampala – where very little shared infrastructure is being developed – the
perimeter of our Ugandan hosts' plates were swiftly defended when it was
suggested we could enjoy more flavours if we shared. In much the same

way, Kampala – like Accra – has a distinctly suburban feel where properties are surrounded by private islands of unutilised land.

Despite the increased gating of Addis Ababa, the city feels more urban in character, with a greater concentration of buildings touching each other and set right against pavements. Mixed use with shops on the ground floor are also common across the city. The recent addition of skyscrapers – including the under construction 198m Commercial Bank of Ethiopia Headquarters – does not, however, necessarily add to the city's urban character. Ethiopian architects worry that the quality and capacity of local design has suffered by buildings delivered almost entirely by Chinese hands, while they argue their city has lost touch with its past. The city's ambitious housing project, which since 2006 has delivered over 230,000 flats mostly on the urban periphery, has also resulted in the demolition of thousands of inner-city homes not seen to be of suitable quality by the government. In many instances, speculative real estate projects have popped up where dense networks of homes and businesses once existed.

Focusing on West Africa

Lagos and Addis Ababa, in many ways representing a West Africa with a longer urban tradition and an East Africa earlier in the process of urbanisation, are both investing in major urban projects that break from existing patterns, cultures and histories. Eko Atlantic, a prime real estate covering 10 million square metres in Nigeria dubbed as 'a beacon for international business and tourism', like much of Africa's colonial infrastructure, is aimed at connecting externally rather than internally.

Lagos's ambitious Eko Atlantic does little to enhance or connect with the established urban quality of the city. To the north of the city's central areas of Lagos Island and Victoria Island, the water communities hug the mainland. Over 1,000 people enter Lagos every day, many ending up in informal settlements like that of Makoko, popularised in global media after waves of violent evictions. Built on stilts, the de facto self-governing fishing village is also a significant source of cut timber. These areas are also not included in the census; Lagos may well be larger than the estimate of 21.5 million. To the south of the central islands is Eko Altantic. Like Makoko, it sits on reclaimed land. Its residents, should the project succeed in building enough accommodation and attracting the anticipated 250,000 people, will be counted. While Makoko shows an organic connection to the street pattern where it connects to land, Eko Atlantic's masterplan and architectural renders, mostly sketched up in London, show little sensitivity to the project's physical association to Africa's largest city. Despite referencing the city's historic name, there is little in the scheme to situate a past which likely stretches earlier than the fifteenth century.

Lagos is, however, a bit of an anomaly in West Africa, indeed Africa. Growing at fifty-six people per hour, it is one of the continent's most rapidly expanding cities. Accra, Cape Town and Kampala are all growing at rates comparable to London (around ten people per hour). Generally, a number of factors, including access to health services, nutrition, education and economic opportunity, and exposure to risk, as well as gender equity bias, have seen fertility rates drop in cities in comparison to rural populations across the globe. Lagos, which has 43 per cent of people under twenty, is one of a few cities in Africa where fertility rates are higher than for the country. The competition for space has significant impact on the shape of the city: it is one of the few cities globally that has become more densely populated. Nearby Accra, where quickly erecting a structure is seen as the most effective way to secure land tenure, is at the opposite end of the scale, taking up five times more space than in 1990. In the same period, the population of both tripled.

To better manage congestion in both cities, a range of public transport interventions are being programmed. In Lagos 'the roads are full of cars while the water is empty' so the city is developing water infrastructure and ferries to unload some of the pressure. Currently, only 1.5 per cent of commuters use ferries to get around. Investments in inter-city and light rail as well as bus rapid transit may help the city retain its impressive active and public transport mode share: 85 per cent of residents walk, cycle or take public transport to get around. By contrast Copenhagen, hailed as having one of the world's most sustainable cities achieves only 60 per cent active and public transport use. Accra's mode share is equally impressive, although the city's pilot bus rapid transit project has done little to slow motorisation. The city's privately-operated fleet of shared minibus taxis *tro-tros* is slowly losing market share to single-use vehicles and cheaper motorbike taxis *okadas*. A typical journey cost in Accra and the percentage of household income spent on public transport is not particularly high compared to a basket of African and international examples, so the move may reflect more on convenience given the city's increasing congestion. Between 1985 and 2002, average morning traffic speeds decreased by roughly 20 per cent.

A bit further down the coast, Abidjan's Cocody Bay project, like Eko Atlantic, also aims to repurpose the relationship between water and city while increasing flood resilience. Both cities have similar geographic features; a mix of islands, mainland and lagoons. Financially supported by Morocco, the plan has all the infrastructure associated with international development and tourism: hotels, a trade centre, a convention centre and a centre promoting Ivorian culture (but not necessarily as part of the architecture). However, the proposal also includes providing public space and restabilising fishing along the bay and a corridor to the city's most import green space: the Banco forest.

The under construction Métro d'Abidjan, funded by France, may redefine the city's public transport network when it opens. Accessing data on these projects – and the city as a whole – proved a challenge, limiting the extent to which the city could be analysed. An opportunity to rewrite the narrative of Côte d'Ivoire's economic capital as projects unfold may also be missed, especially as these projects will likely take longer to deliver than expected. However, the unusual focus on using public space and transport interventions to reimagine how the city connects not just globally but also to itself will likely not only result in agglomeration benefits, but also in allowing the city to share its unique urbanity. This uniqueness isn't only physical. Hosting institutions like the African Development Bank gives Abidjan access to a global financial network in the way cities like Addis Ababa, despite being Africa's diplomatic heart, simply cannot.

Conclusion

The Urban Age has investigated models of sustainable development in other parts of the world where urbanisation is largely complete. Will Africa produce new models, rendering them more inclusive, productive and liveable? The evidence, in part, suggests this is possible. Greater connectivity and trade between cities, which could soon be part of the largest free trade area in terms of participating countries since the formation of the World Trade Organization, may also result in a far less fragmented urban landscape. Perhaps the biggest challenge facing Africa's urban future is not the magnitude of problems, but the urgency of implementing solutions and finding a language to communicate a richer and more complex urban story.

TIMBUKTU

Hafeez Burhan Khan

Like dust devils in the Sahara, they came from the north in beat up 4 x 4s and sped across the desert. Hundreds of men in fatigues and battle garb emerged from the vehicles laden with weapons and guns. Some had their faces covered, shielding themselves from the harsh glare of the sun and the blast of the sand-speckled wind. They had heard of the fabled city of books, of song and dance, of loose morals. A land of debauchery that the ramshackle motley crew were to descend upon; firm in the belief they had been ordained to reinstate morality. And in April 2012, they arrived. Al-Qaida in the Maghreb (AQIM) had reached the West African city of Timbuktu, bringing with them a harsh and puritanical interpretation of Shariah law and imposing an alien rule of intolerance in stark contrast to the city's lauded origins.

How had it come to this? After all, the very name, Timbuktu, evokes a mystique that has existed for centuries. A name fired through the European psyche. Conjuring up an impenetrable exotic city in the middle of 'nowhere', harbouring vast treasures of gold and promising a daring sense of adventure. The phrase 'as far as Timbuktu' denotes the farthest reaches of the Earth and although that award goes to Kashgar in China's Xianjang region, it is true that Timbuktu is a notoriously difficult place to reach, perhaps contributing to its allure. Lying at the southern end of the Sahara Desert, surrounded by sand dunes and a few miles north of the Niger River, the climate is hot, dry and arid. Add to this, what little rainfall occurs is now affected by shifting patterns of precipitation due to climate change. This has increased the scarcity of water, which wreaks havoc with agriculture and irrigation. In addition, there is the added crisis of desert creep. Corruption and underdevelopment only exacerbate the situation, leaving this part of Mali riven with conflicts over territory, resources and ideology. A perfect storm into which AQIM swooped.

The enchantment of Timbuktu belies so much more, however. For centuries, white Europeans loftily informed Africans that no evidence of ancient civilisations or a text-based history exists for their people. In the eighteenth century, the philosophers David Hume and Immanuel Kant both argued that black people were inferior to whites as they had no written culture. As recently as 1963 the historian Hugh Trevor Roper claimed there was no reason to teach African history as it was similar to pre-European and pre-Christopher Columbus American history. In sharp contrast to such assertions, the region around Timbuktu was proven to be an important intellectual and cultural centre for hundreds if not thousands of years, and was commensurate to other contemporary societies.

The story of Timbuktu's significance began around 500BC. The expanse around the River Niger between Djenne and Timbuktu had become one of the most densely populated areas in the world. Hundreds of settlements were dotted along the river and a civilisation that was contemporary with Near Eastern civilisations of the time soon emerged. Recent archaeological excavations around Timbuktu uncovered an urban landscape where the distribution of pottery, radiocarbon dated to around 500BC, covered an area greater than 100 hectares. This would make the ancient city twice the size of present-day Timbuktu at its height in the mid-fifteenth century, which in turn was nearly twice as large as Elizabethan London.

The sophistication of Timbuktu society was established by the anthropologist Douglas Park. His research showed the region was forested mainly with hardwood trees 2,500 years ago, with the timber being used in the generation of iron, as iron slags, which are the residue of iron production, were excavated by archaeologists. Smelting iron demanded extremely high temperatures and the number of hardwood trees required for this process was immense. The evidence for iron smelting showed that people were engaged in specific occupations characteristic of more complex urbanised societies, like fishermen or forest clearers. Material evidence also highlighted some hierarchical social grouping but deviated from the classical ancient civilisations as there was very little evidence of warfare. This showed that Timbuktu society did not follow traditional power hierarchies of the Near East and the community borne around the banks of the Niger River was extremely unique in its formation. As archaeological work is still in its infancy, future excavations will uncover a wealth of information that, until now, lies undiscovered.

With its evolved society, it is no surprise that by the ninth and tenth centuries, Timbuktu was a prominent trade centre, capitalising upon the bend of the River Niger. Camel trains flooded in from the northeast and northwest loaded with salt, fabrics, glass, jewellery, dates, spices, incense and fabric from as far away as England, spending weeks crossing the Sahara. Caravan merchants would bring gold to buy salt from nearby mines, while boats from the south brought honey, cereals, gold and slaves, ivory, cotton, nuts and shea butter. It is no coincidence that the name Timbuktu derived from Bouctou's (which translates as one with the large navel) well. Bouctou, who owned the well that was named after her, was a female slave who was responsible for looking after nomadic Tuareg's belongings as they utilised her well. It became a permanent settlement around 1100 for the Kel Tamasheq - nomads, who roamed the desert in search of grazing land for their camels. Due to its distinct geographical position with the Niger River flowing northwards from Nigeria into the Southern edge of the Sahara before bending southwest, Timbuktu became a meeting point for numerous races and cultures such as the Tuareg, Fulani, Wangara, Songhai

Dromedary camels, loaded with slabs of salt, on caravan route, Timbuktu, Mali, 1971, Photograph by Eliot Elisofon. Eliot Elisofon Photographic Archives, National Museum of African Art, Smithsonian Institution, Washington DC, EEPA EECL 14130.

and the Arabs occupying the point where the Maghreb and sub Saharan Africa met.

Timbuktu's importance also grew with the spread of Islam and the Arabic language, now the written language for international trade, and was by now a major hub for manuscripts and books. In the late thirteenth century, some of the richest people in the city owned libraries and having a library or a retinue of books was an acknowledgement of status and prestige. Such was the demand for manuscripts and books that calligraphers became some of the highest paid citizens. This ascent grew with the creation of the Malian Empire by the end of the thirteenth century. The Emperor, Musa Keita, had made the pilgrimage to Mecca with a caravan of over 60,000 men and carrying 15 tonnes of gold. Upon arrival in Cairo, he handed out so much gold that it prompted a collapse in the price of gold in Arabia for over a decade. Local historian al Maqrizi remarked that the price of the precious metal in Arabia had dropped by as much as six dirhams. His repute was such that traveller Ibn Battuta wrote that he was initially unimpressed, calling the emperor miserly, although this may have been a grumbling on his part due to failing health and the fact he had not yet been invited to meet the emperor. When Musa gave him gold, an allowance and a place to stay, he was quick to change his mind.

By now nearly two thirds of all the gold in the world was from the Malian Empire, and along with its trade in salt and books, Timbuktu was celebrated as a place of international renown. Musa was the richest man of all time with an estimated wealth calculated today at $400 billion, and his fame swept through Europe, mesmerising the Holy Roman Emperor who commissioned Abraham Cresques to construct a map featuring an illustration of a black monarch on a gold throne with Timbuktu as the capital of the Empire. On his return from Mecca in 1426, with a multitude of Arab scholars in tow, Musa proceeded to build mosques, schools and libraries as well as the prestigious Sankore University, regarded as one of the knowledge centres of the world. Islamic Studies was its focus, although other courses such as the sciences, history, geography, philosophy and art were also taught. In addition to academic endeavours, students were encouraged to learn a trade and invited to enrol on construction, business, carpentry and agriculture classes. Various types of degrees were offered, including the superior degree of which an equivalent is the PhD, taking up

Atlas of Maritime Charts (The Catalan Atlas) [detail of Mansa Musa], Abraham
Cresque (1325–1387), 1375, Mallorca. Parchment mounted on six wood panels,
illuminated. Bibliothèque nationale de France.

to ten years to acquire. The level of attainment was reflected in special
turbans signifying the prestige of these scholars in a city where learning was
already the highest goal for any Muslim.

By the mid sixteenth century, Timbuktu was a flourishing city of 100,000
of which 25,000 were scholars. It was the championing of scholarship that
drove the economy to its zenith. Not only was it a wealthy city but it was a
hive of intellectual curiosity, research and discovery. The French explorer
and journalist Felix Dubois remarked in 1896 that black African scholars
surpassed Arab scholars in their depth of knowledge, holding esteemed
professorships throughout the Islamic world. It was under the Songhai
Empire in the fifteenth and sixteenth century that Timbuktu reached its
peak. Larger than Western Europe, its capital was Gao, some 200 miles to
the east, to which European traders flocked.

Such was the growing fame of Timbuktu that the curiosity of Pope Leo X
was piqued, inspiring him to commission El Hasan Mohamed Al Wazzan Al
Zayyati, or Leo Africanus as he is better known, to write a survey of Africa.
The fruition of his efforts was a book, published in 1550, that became a
best seller around Europe and was thought to have influenced Shakespeare's

depiction of the 'learned negro' in Othello. What's more, it augmented Timbuktu's reputation as an inaccessible yet captivating exotic domain. Africanus observed that the city housed huts made from clay with thatched roofs and with a limestone palace for the king dominating the centre. Inhabitants had slaves and dressed impeccably due to the numerous cloth shops, which also sold European fabrics. Water was diverted by canals from the nearby Niger and plenty of wells had been dug. He spoke admiringly of the royal court and the King's zeal for learning, ensuring that book-selling remained a vitally important economic enterprise. He detailed lively music and dancing throughout the night, but also mentioned less palatable aspects of the kingdom such as the King's banishment of the Jewish population.

This was despite the fact that an arguably tolerant strand of Sufi Islam was practised among Timbuktu society and the Maliki school of jurisprudence was the dominant legal system. A thriving, cosmopolitan city with regular influxes of people from around the world, it represented the medieval information highway of its time where ideas and knowledge from diverging traditions were examined and synthesised by scholars and enthusiasts to create dynamic and original patterns of intellectual thought. Along every alleyway scribes and calligraphers would be painstakingly translating and copying books and manuscripts into Arabic and Ajami scripts, and into West African languages such as Tamasheq, Hausa, Bambara and Soninke. The city was a magnet for scientists and saw the publication of books on astronomy, physics, maths, chemistry and observations on the movement of the stars in relation to the seasons. Texts of ancient Greek philosophers were translated into Arabic and manuscripts on medicine and surgery, poetry, history and nutrition were much sought after. Theological debates on the morality of slavery, money-lending and polygamy were committed to paper with one volume discussing aphrodisiacs and infertility remedies for men and advice on how to enhance the pleasure women have a right to enjoy during sexual intercourse. Qur'anic verses and hadith were quoted at a time when any sign of a woman's sexuality was deemed an expression of witchcraft in Europe.

Manuscripts relating to fiqh and fatwas were provided on all issues of concern to the population at the time. These included a fatwa supporting a woman's decision not to sleep in her husband's bed and the distribution of inheritance among family members. Socially progressive ideas coincided with this era of scientific discovery, artistic expression, open mindedness and tolerance with Ahmad Baba regarded as the greatest of all scholars of the period. A black African polymath who lived in the late sixteenth century, he wrote sixty books on subjects as diverse as conflict resolution to questioning the ethics of slavery. Not only were manuscripts prized for their scholarly work, they were also sought after for their aesthetics.

Ahmad Ba¯ba¯ al-Tinbuktı¯, as dictated to Yu¯suf al-Isı¯, The Uttermost Hope in the Preference of Sincere Intention over Action, Timbuktu, Mali, 1592. Ink on paper, 20 x 15.5 cm. Melville J. Herskovits Library of African Studies, Northwestern University Library, Hunwick 541. Photograph by Clare Britt.

Unique pigments derived from materials such as gelatine, aluminium and calcium salts were used to create a higher grade ink with complex geometric patterns overlaid with gold leaf for the finest texts.

As innovative, relatively liberal and diverse as Timbuktu was, flashes of intolerance and brutality would be sporadically unleashed. In 1495, King Askia Mohammed abruptly imprisoned and banished Jews on the advice of a Maghrebi scholar and known anti-semite, Mohammed Al Maghili. He later reversed that ruling when a delegation of Qadis from Timbuktu arrived at his palace in Gao to change his mind and it is this king that Leo Africanus alludes to in discussion of his treatment of Jews.

Timbuktu's golden age finally faltered in 1591, when an invading army from Morocco tore into the city and looted numerous manuscripts stored in mosques and libraries. Countless scholars were abducted and taken back to Morocco or forcibly dispersed throughout the Islamic world. The demand for gold also decreased around this time as Europe plundered South America. The Malian civilisation declined but its fame as an 'African El Dorado' continued to intrigue the world for centuries to come. European explorers risked life and limb to 'discover' this city imagined to have streets paved with gold, located in the middle of 'nowhere'. Myth became embedded in folklore as Europe's relationship with Islam grew ever more complex as a consequence of empire and colonialism. The thought of a magical city existing in the realms of a blurry line between reality and fantasy captivated the imaginations of explorers and imperialists. Writer Bruce Chatwin wrote that there were two Timbuktus: 'One a real place, a tired caravan town; the other is altogether more fabulous, a legendary city in a never-never land, the Timbuktu of the mind.'

By the end of the nineteenth century Timbuktu was just another backwater under French colonial rule. However, before too long its tumultuous past would be revisited with violent disruption courtesy of AQIM. On 28 January, 2013, the Mayor of Timbuktu announced that jihadists had destroyed Timbuktu's priceless literary heritage. To the world, this was an act of cultural vandalism on an epic scale and a source of immeasurable anguish. It is true that a few thousand manuscripts in the Ahmad Baba Institute were ruined but, what was not known at the time was that nearly a hundred times that number had been smuggled out of the city in what was called 'an Indiana Jones moment in real life'.

This highly organised, secret and desperately dangerous operation involved hundreds of ordinary people from Timbuktu and across Mali who risked their lives to save some of the most precious manuscripts dating from the medieval world. Abdel Kaider Haidara who holds the largest non-private collection in the city and is founder of Savama, an NGO which safeguards private libraries, was the brainchild of the breath-taking mission. In the 1980s and 1990s Haidara rescued and restored many thousands of manuscripts in poor condition by using grant money from the West and Gulf Arab states to buy them. The manuscripts were then kept at the Ahmad Baba Institute where he worked. In a labour of love, he devoted himself to the preservation of manuscripts and spearheaded the restoration and creation of forty-five libraries in Timbuktu alone, which eventually boasted a total of 377,000 manuscripts. The conservation and digitisation facilities in some of the institutions rivalled even the west, with the revamped Ahmad Baba Institute comprising an $8 million dollar complex funded by the South African government and his own Mamma Haidara Commemorative library housing thousands of manuscripts, many of which still await translation.

Rewind one year earlier to 2012, and the President of Mali, Amadou Toure was ousted by army officers furious at his inability to stop a coalition AQIM, who were advancing into Northern Mali from bases in Libya and Algeria, having made their money from drug smuggling and capturing western hostages for ransom. An insurrection by Ansar Dine, another Salafi jihadist group, and the secular Tuareg nationalists who dreamed of an 'Azawad' or a national Tuareg home also fuelled instability and chaos across the region. Many Tuareg fighters had returned from Libya pumped with weapons looted after the fall of Gadaffi. The poorly equipped and demoralised Malian army was no match for these battle-hardened veterans of Afghanistan and Iraq who showed little or no mercy to their prisoners, and Timbuktu easily fell. The new rulers of this ancient city of learning imposed their puritanical brand of Shariah Law and imposed strict curfews on inhabitants. Music, for which Timbuktu is renowned, poetry and dancing were banned. Soon people were being flogged for smoking or for worshipping at the plethora of tombs of Sufi saints. Couples seen together risked punishment or even being stoned to death for 'adultery'. Timbuktu needed to be purified after centuries of un-Islamic practices had infected the city, the extremists convinced themselves. Thousands fled south as the regime consolidated its power in Northern Mali and began wreaking its vandalism on the intellectual symbols of its literary past.

By July 2012, the fifteenth century Sidi Yahye mosque, a world heritage site, was damaged as the jihadis destroyed the mausoleum of the Sufi saints. UNESCO declared an emergency but the world was powerless to stop the destruction. Amidst the chaos and anarchy, many owners of manuscripts already knew they urgently needed to protect their precious artefacts and had hidden some away in the desert or in the walls of their houses. Haidara, who had been in Bamako earlier in the year when the jihadists first struck, was warned it would be suicide to return home. But he did return, in

March 2012, driving back to Timbuktu covertly aided by family and countless contacts. He made it back and desperately devised an elaborate plan to evacuate all the manuscripts from Timbuktu. There wasn't much time, the extremists knew the reverence surrounding the manuscripts and it would not be long before they would turn their attention to texts they considered utterly blasphemous.

Haidara secretly gathered his colleagues and put his plan into action. First they were to take all the manuscripts out of libraries and disperse them in family homes across the city. This in itself was a risky move as anyone caught would be subjected to the severest of punishments. Thus, it was agreed the operation had to be so confidential that they could not disclose anything to even their families, only those actively involved could know. For such an enterprise, the logistics were seemingly intractable. How would they move the manuscripts and when would they do this? Where would the money come from? Haidara had been due to commence studies in English at Oxford University later that year and had been awarded a $12,000 grant by the Ford Foundation. He emailed the foundation about his predicament and persuaded them to release the funds. Soon, librarians, archivists, tour guides and trusted family members began to buy metal trunks and then wooden trunks. This was done as discreetly as possible and the trunks were converted into chests, which were dispersed among the city's libraries.

At night and under the cover of darkness, dozens of the team armed only with small torches crept into the libraries and moved the manuscripts into the chests. The next night, the chests were covered in blankets and transported by mules across the city to various safe houses. They decided to then sit tight and wait until a chance arose to move the chests out of the city to Bamako which was 600 miles to the south. However, the destruction of the shrines of Sufi Saints changed everything. Haidara, having escaped back to Bamako after overseeing the hiding of the manuscripts, knew they could no longer delay. Over the years, he had built up contacts amongst NGO and government organisations and began contacting anyone he could think of to help. He knew that smuggling the manuscripts out of Timbuktu would cost hundreds of thousands of dollars due to paying couriers to travel with each shipment of chests. There also would be the cost of renting trucks and four wheel drives, safe houses, equipment, not to mention the inevitable bribes. Heeding Haidara's pleas, benefactors such as the Prince

Claus fund in the Netherlands, Dubai's Juma Al Majid Centre and a kickstarter campaign to name but a few, stepped up.

The operation to smuggle out the manuscripts was terribly perilous. One evening, as Haidara's nephew Mohammed Toure was moving a metal chest out of a library, he was arrested by the jihadis for stealing. Knowing that justice would be swift and severe, Toure stated that the library belonged to his family and so he was not technically stealing. Quoting Qur'anic texts and hadiths, to the astonishment of his captors, he said that proof was needed before they could implement any punishment. He informed them that the elders and imams of the local quarter would confirm his story the next morning. Haidara soon learned about his nephew's imprisonment and using his contacts in the city managed to mobilise imams and elders as well as producing documents substantiating Toure's claims. The next morning, with the evidence provided, Toure was set free. Now more than ever, the young man knew the manuscripts had to be moved to safe houses as soon as possible.

The task was an unenviable one. Ahmad Baba Institute had been turned into a weapons store guarded by twenty fighters, and there was the small matter of the 24,000 manuscripts which remained hidden inside the building. At first, the librarians were hesitant to take decisive action, fearful that they would be blamed if anything would happen to the manuscripts, but Haidara eventually persuaded the director of the Institute that drastic action was the only option. Over two weeks and under the noses of the jihadis, all the manuscripts were spirited away to safety. These were among the last of the manuscripts to be moved. Once that was done, the next phase was to move them out of the city.

Wheels were quite literally set in motion and the volunteers were told what they had to do. Most of the couriers and drivers were trusted members of the librarians' families and knew the valuable legacy of the manuscripts and what these texts meant to the wider world. The first shipment left on 18 October 2012 with thirty-five lockers on donkey carts, where they were moved to a depot outside Timbuktu. They travelled on to Bamako with the couriers in trucks and buses to appear as inconspicuous as possible. There were AQIM checkpoints along the way and sometimes the jihadis poked at the chests. Everyone held their breath but their cargo was never discovered. This, however, was the least of their worries. Government controlled territory was no less fraught. If the chests were opened and the soldiers saw the manuscripts, the couriers would be accused of being thieves or smugglers in cahoots with the jihadis. They could even be arrested. On one occasion, this did happen, a bribe or frantic phone calls from Haidara to someone in authority to get things back on track was needed. So secretive was the mission, the army wasn't even told about it, as any information could get back to the jihadis guaranteeing a rampage searching out hidden manuscripts. There were other problems too. Due to the chaos and power vacuum, bandits seized some of the chests and held them for ransom until they were paid. Some couriers were so traumatised after their ordeal they would, understandably, be unable to carry on, but most continued with the mission.

By the end of 2012, nearly 270,000 manuscripts had received safe haven after being smuggled out of Timbuktu, but things would become more dangerous in 2013. The French military, sensing that Mali was in danger of being overrun by extremists, turned their attention towards Bamako. Fearful that the whole of West Africa plus the Sahel would become unstable and threaten French interests in the region, France was determined to drive out AQIM from francophone West Africa. French military resolutely attacked the fighters with airpower and switched their advance into a full on retreat. This may have sounded like good news but any vehicles on roads south of Timbuktu were the target of French missiles raining hellfire on them. Furthermore, in retreat, jihadists would attempt to destroy any cultural sites in acts of rage and vandalism. The couriers were trapped, unable to use the roads and liable to being bombed equally by friend or foe. The manuscripts left in Timbuktu were now in danger of being decimated. Knowing that road use was out of bounds Haidara turned to the boatmen of the River Niger. The plan was to transport the chests by boat to Djenne, some 220 miles and two days away. Once there, they would be unloaded onto trucks and taxis where they would be taken to the capital in a journey of an additional 330 miles. Once again, money was needed and the Dutch government released 320,000 euros. As before, everything was shrouded in absolute secrecy so that only a few people knew.

Firstly, the chests were transported the twelve miles from the city to the river by mule cart through rice paddies and fields. Local village chiefs who knew Haidara let him use their huts for storage as there were still AQIM patrols nearby. Local fishermen helped to get the chests onto the boats. But there were hazards in transporting them on the river. What about the fast moving currents and what if the boats overturned? On a test run, the pinasse, a motorised boat, was ordered by a French attack helicopter to open the chests, suspicious that they contained weapons. Once opened, there was nothing but paper. The helicopter left, much to the relief of the couriers and the boatmen. To avoid any further incident the pinasse travelled in small convoys so as not to arouse suspicion. Everything was planned to the nth degree. One such convoy of boats was stopped by bandits and when they opened the chests and saw the manuscripts they decided to take them. The couriers tried to offer watches and jewellery but to no avail. The bandits then contacted Haidara, who informed them he had no money but promised that he would pay them eventually. After a lengthy discussion, the bandits agreed and were subsequently paid.

Meanwhile, Timbuktu was being attacked by French jets and AQIM leaders prepared to evacuate the city, but not before turning their attention to the manuscripts. 4,202 manuscripts from the Ahmad Baba Institute were set alight. Rare fourteenth and fifteenth century works on algebra, physics, astronomy and molecular diagrams went up in smoke as the dry fragile pages combusted instantaneously. Manuscripts by some of the greatest scientists of the age that had survived invasions and other natural and man-made calamities were lost forever. It was this destruction that the Mayor of Timbuktu decried. Like nearly everyone, he had not known that almost all the rest of the manuscripts had been saved in an act so underground that the Malian government had no knowledge of it.

In Bamako, a representative from the Dutch embassy went to see if the 500 chests that the Dutch had paid for were actually there. To Tjoelker entered a room with about 600 chests, each box proudly labelled with the name of a funder. To be sure that there were manuscripts in the chests, he pointed to a chest and asked Haidara to open it. The chest was, indeed, full of manuscripts. The seemingly impossible had been achieved. Altogether, nearly 373,000 manuscripts had been saved. What was remarkable was that not one manuscript had been lost during transport. Had the manuscripts been destroyed, the world would have lost some of the greatest treasures known to mankind.

Even to this day significant numbers of manuscripts await translation as the situation in Timbuktu remains tense. But this is a resolute city with a resolute population. A city no longer shrouded in the mystery of European imaginations but with a dynamic lived and documented history and vibrant heritage, a city that, over time, evolved into one of the greatest intellectual centres of the Middle Ages. Timbuktu's love for the written word was almost extinguished, repeatedly, in preceding centuries but continues to defy even its most unscrupulous foes. Had it not been for the fearless inhabitants of Timbuktu its priceless artefacts would have been lost into the desert sand. Slowly, and vitally, its secrets are being revealed, disproving the dominant narrative that framed discussion of Africa up until even a few decades ago, that this was a continent devoid of historical or literary culture. In the words of African-American academic Henry Louis Gates Jr, when he saw Haidara's manuscripts in Timbuktu: 'If translated, they might completely rewrite the history of Black Africa.'

OUSMANE SEMBÈNE'S CINEMA

Estrella Sendra

The work of prolific Senegalese writer and filmmaker Ousmane Sembène is strongly linked to the decolonisation and liberation of African countries from the 1960s onwards. The son of a Lébou father – a fisherman from a community originally from the Cap Vert peninsula – and a Serer mother, an ethnic group among the last in Senegal to convert to Islam or Christianity, this pioneer of African film still lacks the recognition he is rightfully due in global cinema.

In 1942 Sembène joined the Senegalese *tirailleurs* and following the Second World War returned to Senegal to participate in the railworkers' strike in Dakar, which would inspire the writing of his novella *Bouts de bois de Dieu* (*God's Bits of Wood*) in 1960. He had moved to Marseilles in France in 1948, where he worked as a docker and became a union worker. By 1960, when Senegal gained independence from France, Sembène returned to his home country, and aware of the importance of oral traditions and the high rate of illiteracy in West Africa, decided to become a filmmaker. Initiating his career through a funded training at Gorky Studios in Moscow, he returned a year later with an old camera from the Soviet Union and adapted five of his novels to film.

A leading advocate of *cinema engagé,* and a Marxist militant, whose films critique colonial and imperial history, and postcolony, Sembène regarded cinema as a 'medium… to teach the masses'. He further understood film as a means of political action, partisan and militant, that would invite audiences to reflect and generate questions. If former films by colonisers had contributed to the establishment of colonial rule and to the misrepresentation of Africa and African people as seen through an alienating gaze, Sembène saw film as a medium to restore African dignity. It is this common aim that leads to comparisons with the first president of the independent republic of Senegal, Léopold Sédar Senghor, who was also one of the proponents of the Négritude philosophical movement.

Senghor understood Négritude as a weapon for decolonisation, composed of 'the ensemble of cultural values from the black world'. The concept was first developed by Aimé Césaire in the 1930s in Paris, which sought to restore black African dignity through a return to local sources, placing black African cultural heritage at the very centre of decolonisation. However, Négritude was often criticised for its emplacement in an idealised and romanticised African past, misrepresentative of the variety of cultural practices in postcolonial Senegal. Sékou Touré, first president of post-independent Guinea, even claimed that Négritude was fatal to pan-Africanism and should therefore be destroyed. Nigerian writer Wole Soyinka was also a critic, comparing the absurdity of Négritude to that of tigritude – 'must a tiger declare its tigritude?' In a sense, Negritude remained a philosophical movement which repackaged, remodified and rearticulated earlier European notions of Africa and its people. Sembène found this movement obfuscating and unable to respond to a continent where countries like Senegal for over five centuries have been fighting for liberation from European influence.

Despite their differences in the modes of expression and representation, both Sembène and Senghor shared the view of culture as central to the process of decolonising postcolonial Africa. When Dakar, capital of Senegal, celebrated the First World Festival of Negro Arts in 1966, under the patronage of Senghor and as an embodiment of Négritude, Ousmane Sembène received two awards. One was for his novella, *Le Mandat* (*The Money Order*), a work that was staunchly critical of the independence era in Senegal. The second award was for his first feature-length film, *Black Girl*, which also engaged in fierce criticism of the continuing influence and status of France in postcolonial Senegal. Sembène's success in the 1966 Festival is reflective of the contested dimension of culture and its role in the (re)building of a national and pan-African consciousness as a reaction against centuries of colonial destruction of African culture. Beyond its conceptualisation of African culture as a romanticised past and of raw emotion, with rhythm, as its 'architecture of being', Negritude seems to exclude a large number of non-black Africans. In fact, in 1969, Algiers, the capital of Algeria, hosted the second of four pan-African festivals celebrated in the 1960s and 1970s. The *Premier Festival Cultural Panafricain* (First Cultural Pan-African Festival), also known as PANAF, was, however, not framed as a continuation of the First World Festival of Negro Arts, but rather, as a reaction to it.

Malian thinker and filmmaker Manthia Diawara has classified West African film into three categories: social realism, postmodernism and 'return to the source'. He strongly associates Sembène's artform with social realism, developing a narrative focussed on sociocultural issues. By adopting a critical perspective to modernity and necolonialism, often seen as opposed to tradition, which is frequently represented by traditional dance, music and 'griots', African culture emerges as veritable forms of expression *par excellence*. An example is *Borom Sarret*, Ousmane Sembène's first short film, made in 1963, which translates as *The Owner of the Cart* and follows a day in the life of an ordinary individual in post-independence Senegal. It opens with a scene depicting the sound of prayer over a black background, which fades into the image of a mosque. The weary Borom Sarret faces the mosque while praying, as his wife lingers in the background, cooking with a mortar. This is flanked by an image of a regular road in Dakar, the capital, with cars, motorcycles, and human transit. Such contrasting images seamlessly run throughout the film, simultaneously conveying a sense of conflict and coexistence. A shot of the cathedral in Dakar over orchestral music is harmonised with Borom Sarret's voice, invoking protection from his dear marabout (spiritual guide).

After a short interaction with his wife, we follow the Borom Sarret going about his everyday routine, picking up a series of customers with his reflections resonating in a voice-over. The use of the voice-over constitutes an aesthetic resource to express resistance. As Cameroonian filmmaker, Jean-Pierre Bekolo argues, 'no one ever hears what Africans say or what they think', noting that, by extension, one could conclude that 'Africans don't think at all'. The first-person voice-over places viewers in the main character's perspective, through an intradiegetic narrative, that of *Borom Sarret*. Similarly, in Sembène's first feature-length film, *Black Girl*, the voice character is acted by a young woman, Diouana. She features prominently, offering a first-person reflection on Diouana's internal crises and insecurities. Diouana is a young Senegalese woman who is recruited by a French family to work as a maid, first in Senegal, and then, in France. The positive image that people in independent Senegal have of the former colony, France, is challenged. The film opens with the image of a travelling boat, in the port, with a smartly and modern dressed young Senegalese woman, excited to board in the direction of *La France*.

A hectic market, a physically impaired man begging for money, a pregnant lady about to give birth who needs to be taken to hospital, traffic lights, the Sandaga market in the financial centre of Dakar... *Borom Sarret* offers a realist social account of life in Senegal for the marginalised navigating the challenges of modernity. *Borom Sarret*, while listening to a griot singing, laments in the voice-over: 'It's this modern life that has reduced me to a working slave.' Several mishaps on his way home leave him with no money to feed his family. Capturing the pecuniary living conditions of the hard working poor, Sembène makes subtle critique of the social injustice of postcolonial Senegal. He brings into sharp focus the exclusion of ordinary individuals like Borrom Sarret from the postcolonial vision of independent Senegal.

Sembène views Africa through African lenses, which departs from colonial representations of the continent, as negated, essentialised and stereotyped through 'alien lenses'. Cinema is a rejection of Eurocentrism, a bold denunciation of narratives based on European standards. Such narratives often offered a paternalistic view of the country and justified colonialism since it was primarily aimed at non-African viewers. In contrast, films like *Borom Sarret* and *Black Girl* are the result of an inward gaze, vital to the liberation struggle, contrasting it with what Françoise Pfaff calls the 'Tarzanistic', picturesque, dark, exoticised and othered images of Africa. It portrays a country where, in Sembène's words, '[our] daily acts are regulated by our culture'.

Sembène considered himself 'a modern-day griot', a story-teller, concerned with disseminating African stories for African audiences, to better understand the present and future through a critical look or throw-back. He suggests that the filmmaker must live within his society and comment on the goings on of that society. In addition to his rejection of Eurocentrism in his films, he also turns his attention to the role of religion, language and women in modern-day Senegal. They serve as critical and aesthetic resources to engage his audience on the oppressive tendencies of the existing social and political structures in Senegal.

Senegal is, by Constitution, a secular country. However, today over 90 per cent of the population practice Islam mainly through Sufi orders, known as tariqas. Its long history and impact in Senegal and its culture has meant that very few people see Islam as an alien religion. While the exact date when Islam reached Senegal is difficult to determine, some scholars claim that it could have been at the end of the seventh or beginning of eight century, but achieved its greatest impact in the fifteenth century. With the arrival of European colonisers, Christianity would be implemented as a tool to reinforce the establishment of the colonial authority. Today, roughly five per cent of the population adheres to Christianity, while the other five per cent follows other spiritual beliefs.

As a Muslim, Sembène became aware of the way in which religion was used instrumentally by both colonisers and corrupt politicians in post-independence Senegal to manipulate and exploit the masses. His films address religious, social and political tensions, and call for a return to the fundamental social and spiritual values shared by Africans. Both his writing and cinema shed light on the heterodoxy of Islam and the way in which it is evoked differently for diverse purposes, depending on the conditions and power relations of the characters. Islam and religion, more broadly, appear as contradictory driving forces of a postcolonial and modern country, where people find themselves negotiating its meanings and values, becoming aware of its openness of interpretation. The kind of conflicts that arise, as a result, invite viewers to challenge the power attributed to religion, as another form of resisting the colonisation of the mind. When asked if his 1977 film *Ceddo* is an anti-clerical film, Sembène explains that it is a depiction of the way Islam penetrated Senegal: 'Despite the fact that we are Muslim or Christian, we remain deeply rooted in the universe of the *ceddo*. This is of paramount importance, for it means that our culture is very much alive, very strong. We can absorb other cultures, use them, adapt ourselves without any loss'. *Ceddo* is a Wolofisation of a Pulaar word, which refers to both a social subclass in Pulaar society and to Mandinko-speaking people. In the Pulaar society, the Sebbe were the king warriors who resisted Islamisation. However, in the film, the *ceddo* are those who fight off such foreign forces. It refers rather to a state of mind resisting the status quo and any form of subjugation, claiming a return to tradition. Ceddo are those who refuse.

The multi-layered dimension of religion is portrayed by Sembène in his films by drawing attention to the false impression of tolerance that is often taken for granted in postcolonial Senegal. His films invite viewers to (re) value the immaterial cultural heritage present before the arrival of both Islam and Christianity. Its critical approach to religion is a form of resisting alienation, and a call to understand this within the cultural and postcolonial framework of a country whose geographical boundaries have been established by a colonial regime. Inter-generational dialogue, where mothers and daughters hold different views on religious traditions convey this, as is the case in *Xala,* where Rama confronts her mother, accusing her of passively accepting her husband's third marriage: 'Never will I share my man with another woman.'

A culturally diverse country with a wide repertoire of languages, it is the norm in Senegal to engage in multilingual conversations. There is no institutional support to the large repertoire of languages spoken and Sembène's films resist hegemonic linguistic structure with characters speaking in their own tongue, mainly Wolof and Joola, particularly in his later productions. However, French is also used strategically, as associated to specific contexts, often in relation to the political elite, education, snobbery, or further forms of power. Sembène acknowledges that sometimes French operates as a unifying language among speakers of different languages: 'linguistic liberation in Africa may not necessarily mean downright abandoning of the colonial language'. Instead, he advocates for the promotion of African languages.

Diversity is not confined to language in Sembène's works. His representation of women as powerful, even when initially depicted as victims, has caused critics and scholars to label him a feminist, despite his continuous efforts to avoid such classification. Women are portrayed as agents of resistance in their expression of refusal. They are courageous and instigators of social change. Each of his films challenges, to a certain extent, male domination. Women are seen as everyday heroines against a backdrop of men concerned about losing their privilege.

His films feature the voices of leading Senegalese *griottes*. Wolof-speaking Fatou Kassé is described as possessing one of the most beautiful voices from *Cercle de la Jeunesse,* in Louga and famed for her lullabies, which can be heard in the short drama film *Niaye*; and Serer-speaking Yandé Codou

Sène, who was Senghor's official griot, is the entrancing voice in *Faat Kiné*. Women often lead the narrative, for example in *Emitaï* it is the women who hide the rice so that the white colonisers, do not see it, and steal it from them. Rice becomes a symbol of the struggle for dignity. With his depiction of women, Sembène adds complexity to the reality represented, acknowledges the important historic role of women, their current everyday struggle and invokes the need to consider women in thinking about Africa's *avenir*.

Female power and heroism reach a climax in Sembène's last film, *Moolade*. Collé Ardo Gallo Sy, Cire's much older second wife has one daughter, Amsatou, who Collé gives birth to through caesarean. She also miscarried twice due to undergoing Female Genital Mutilation (FGM). The scar left by Amsatou's delivery features prominently in the film and her struggle, embodying her resistance through connecting a past experience with the present and the near-future that is yet to be achieved. She points at it to explain to her daughter why she should not be afraid of being a 'bilakoro', the word used to refer to those women who have not gone through excision, and who are consequently warned that no men will marry them. In the film, four young girls seek Collé's protection against FGM. This leads to a revolution against the practice, led by Collé and increasingly joined by Ciré's first wife and the rest of the women in the village. The culmination of Collé's resistance also appears as an embodied form of resistance – resistance to pain, which will lead to further permanent scars on her body. Instigated by Amath, Ciré's elder brother, Ciré flagellates Collé in public, ordering her to utter the word that would bring an end to the *moolade*, the protection she is giving to the girls. Collé refuses. While men gather around to encourage Ciré to beat her even stronger, the women support Collé asking her not to say it. It is, however, a young man, the shopkeeper, who stops Ciré from continuing to inflict violence on his own wife, an act for which he will face grave consequences. Later in the film, more men join the resistance against the practice, suggesting that men must unite with women in the fight for female emancipation.

Ousmane Sembène's prolific film career is imbued with stark realism. It depicts a pluralistic Senegalese population grappling with a complex and contradictory array of values shaped by continuing structures of colonisation. Sembène sought to create cinema that would speak to African audiences, calling for self-reflection and critical awareness of societal issues. 'Sembènian cinema' continues to reflect the way in which contemporary Africa needs to manage contradicting tensions between modernity and tradition.

AFROBEATS

Kalaf Epalanga

Born in the triangle of Lagos – Accra – London, Afrobeats is an irresistible blend of Afro-Pop, R&B and Funky House that in less than a decade has become a musical genre with incredible potential for growth, only rivalled in its dynamism by the likes of reggaeton in Latin America. Both musical genres owe plenty to the rise of the internet, in particular YouTube and we must recognise today that if video killed the radio star, YouTube came to incinerate what was left of his remains. Never before in the history of popular music, and not since the invention of the cassette tape, the 33 rpm disc and FM radio broadcasting, had we found a tool as useful for creating and spreading music as YouTube. Without it, half of the niche musical styles such as Azonto, Electro–Cumbia, which have emerged on the fringes of mainstream music and under the acronym Global Dance Music, would not have had the slightest chance of entering the mainstream. Today, fame and success means having millions of views, almost as if the only way to legitimise the existence of a song or musical genre, whether using the barometer of the internet, or some digital analytics, is the number of views on YouTube.

However, I prefer to enjoy these cultural movements on the street. There is no better city or scene to experience such musical genres than London's club culture. Perhaps that's why Afrobeats gained the prominence that it now enjoys by having the UK and its African diaspora as one place of incubation. To understand the impact of club culture on the UK capital, let's revert back to Mayor Sadiq Khan's comments. When questioned about the decline of nightlife in London, the then Labour candidate did not stutter: 'I do not want young and creative Londoners to leave our city to go to Amsterdam, Berlin or Prague where clubs are supported and where they are allowed to grow'. A moment of rare lucidity on the part of a

politician, but Sadiq Khan, son of Pakistani immigrants, is not just any
politician. He went on to say: 'I want to be able to celebrate what they love
in the city they love, instead of punishing or marginalising what they do,
or forcing them into exodus.'

It was with these words that Mayor Sadiq Khan managed to melt the hearts
of the creative community, young people and revellers of all kinds,
convincing them to vote and make history, by electing him, the first Muslim
Mayor of London. A handsome speech that many have considered audacious
for London today. A city that in recent years has not resisted the pressure of
large real estate investors who, in the name of profit, have halved the number
of nightlife spaces and venues. Among the extinct are Plastic People, Power
Lunches, and Dance Tunnel: faithful institutions that introduced artists to the
world and solidified musical genres. Plastic People in Shoreditch, for
example, has forever changed my relationship with electronic music. It was
there, on Co-Op nights promoted by Bugz in The Attic, 4Hero and IG
Culture, that I heard, at the height of Broken Beat, DJs introduce Afro–Latin
rhythms to London's dance music scene taking the crowd to a frenzy. Those
nights also served as inspiration for the events that we would create with my
band, Buraka Som Sistema, in Lisbon. I'm confident that this culture also
inspired other musical visionaries like DJ Abrantee – host of the popular
Afrobeats radio show on British radio station Choice FM. He coined the term
Afrobeats and publicised the genre at parties he hosted. These parties with
urban music from Ghana and Nigeria were the perfect recipe for connecting
the new generation of Afro-descendents in London with the music of their
parents' countries.

I have a certain envy of this current internet generation. The relationship
they have with music is completely different from mine. I still remember
when YouTube appeared in our lives. It altered everything. Suddenly I had
access to the largest music library in the world. Music from across the
globe that made me fall in love with dance culture, that shaped me and the
places where it happens. The clubs and warehouses turned into dance
floors, we elevated it to sanctuary status; these were the spaces that
contributed most to my musical training.

Electronic music is the new world order, a revolution that does not
depend on anything to happen. This artistic awareness arises from the need
to find a distinctive tone that, instead of separating, fuses all the sounds

present in the grand metropolis. Africa is no different. In Western African cities like Lagos and Accra, there is today a youthful Pan-African urban music movement that has made use of technology, transformed the local scene, gained new designations and established new stars who have taken the world by storm with the throbbing rhythms of Afrobeats.

The biggest musical revolution to come from the continent after South Africa's Miriam Makeba and Nigeria's Fela Kuti – unlike music from Mali and Senegal – did not need the 'World Music' label nor the French co-sign. It just took YouTube, thrilling dance steps and the youth of the diaspora living in Europe and the United States to spread the joy. Afrobeats is perhaps the first musical genre to come from West Africa that only needed African consumers to grow into a global phenomenon. No other demographic had to tell us that 'Oliver Twist' by Nigerian Oladapo Daniel Oyebanjo aka D'Banj is a great song. We were the African listeners who adopted it as our anthem in the summer of 2012, an unprecedented feat that made it rise to the Top 10 in the UK, peaking at No.2 on the UK R&B chart. To the point that US global superstar Kanye West could not resist the hype around D'Banj and producer Don Jazzy and presented them a record deal with his GOOD Music label. The same happened with Wizkid, P-Square and Innocent Ujah Idibia aka 2Baba. Other great names of the Afrobeats universe were signed by the former musician and self-made business tycoon Akon, the son of Senegalese immigrants to the United States, famously known to have introduced to the hip hop world the likes of Lady Gaga and T-Pain.

For many people, Afrobeats entered their lives unnoticed. Drake, the Canadian rap ambassador and millennial crooner, toasted us with the memorable verses 'Oti, oti, there's never much love when we go OT' in the already classic, 'One Dance' featuring Wizkid & Kyla in the summer of 2016. The song was a huge hit, thanks to Wizkid, the Nigerian starboy who lent some of his style and signing to the song. Wizkid also sang one of the biggest anthems of Afrobeats, 'Ojuelegba', the song that put him on Drake's radar; and after a DM exchange on Instagram, the remix of Ojuelegba featuring Drake & Skepta, the latter being the son of Nigerian parents and one of the biggest voices of British Grime, was born.

Can Afrobeats truly reinvent the future of African culture? One of the most catchy slogans when we talk about the potential that exists on the continent and in the context of Afrobeats, Fuse ODG aka Nana Richard Abiona placed half the country under the mesmerising spell of Azonto in 2013. Fuse is British but of Ghanaian parentage. He burst onto the scene with loud colourful clothing and accessories, emblazoned with the word TINA, an acronym for 'This Is New Africa'.

According to him TINA is a manifesto that aims to elevate Afrobeats from a musical genre in clubs to a movement with a message:

> For me, everything is about getting the message across. This movement will shed a positive light on Africa and focus on how we can improve Africa. It's not about just plying your trade in the Western world; it's about going back home and helping Africa. The same way I believe you cannot forget your roots in music, you can not forget your roots in life – where you are from. It is our duty to make noise about the positive things that are happening in Africa. It's on to make noise about the good things that happen and spread the word.

These kinds of statements bring to mind thinkers such as Frantz Fanon, the psychiatrist, philosopher and Marxist essayist born in Martinique. One of the most influential thinkers of the twentieth century who sparked discussions about decolonisation, inspiring many of the fathers of African revolutions in the 1960s and 1970s. It is within that same period that musician and political activist Fela Kuti and his band Africa 70 created militant and revolutionary Afrobeats, in the Kalakuta Republic commune founded on the outskirts of Lagos. Fela's political and social influence is undeniable when discussing Afrobeats' impact on today's new generation of African musicians.

I often find myself involved in discussions about the content and message contained in today's Afrobeats. The fact that these musicians choose not to challenge their current political leaders as Fela Kuti did with Olusegun Obasanjo, does not mean that today's music is not nourishing. This current generation proposes to change the perception that we have of African culture, perhaps without great analysis or intellectual speeches according to Western norms. The truth is that music although indulgent is also a cry of resistance. Resistance to being tagged a victim, passive and at the mercy of Western charity. Resistance to being labelled an immigrant when many of these musicians were born in Europe and carry two or more nationalities. As it arrives, this music restores the dignity of African cultural production like never seen before. And that's liberating, right?

How can we not be moved by the exuberance and optimism that this new West African music exudes? Seeing them occupy spaces such as stadiums and sports pavilions, arenas and entertainment venues that we thought were prohibited or only within the reach of African–American artists has been heartening. Imagine what the next generation of Davido, Tiwa Savage, Mr Eazi and Yemi Alade, Sarkodie and Niniola will do? These and many other culture makers. I do not know them all, but I am deeply interested in their attempts, innovations and discoveries of new paths to popular music. I know they are cool, because as far as I can understand, being cool is just being, without effort, by knowing how to get the best out of every experience, no matter how banal. It is to let everything around us pulse and vibrate according to its own intensity.

Somehow, everywhere, including West Africa, the role of congregational spaces such as concert halls, clubs, art galleries has undergone drastic change. The challenges are new, and the poles of culture and thought have entered a process of requalification. Assuming that the traditional limits that defined the functions of art have changed, today the stage has become the very extension of the will and spirit of the artist, juxtaposed with the pulse and dynamism of the society into which they are embedded. The fact that mainstream festivals in the West include African countries in their concert line-ups, shows that these African musicians have scaled the heights of global pop charts. However, we must not forget that they are part of a large musical ecosystem with fans across the African continent, in Mozambique, Angola, Botswana, Zimbabwe, that sustained these artists before they crossed the Atlantic. And if there is something in common among the peoples that produce this music is that more than ever its audience wants to dance to their beat.

I suppose being African was never easy. All of us, from our collective and individual experiences have something to say about it. The story is relatively well documented, and we must not be indifferent to it. In all periods of our history and unfortunately until the present day – without taking into account the advances and achievements of all the children of the earth – there have been moments of true despair. Nevertheless, it seems that more than ever, the appeal of the identity that unites us is so crucial for the future.

We came to dance. Tell me what you hear and dance and I'll tell you who you are. On July 15 2018, after twenty years, the world watched the French team win the biggest sporting event on the planet – the World Cup. At a time when all of France rejoiced at the 4–2 against Croatia, we Africans from the continent and from the vast diaspora let out equally euphoric cries of joy, as that triumph was ours too. Khaled A Beydoun, one of the leading scholars on Islamophobia, national security, anti-terrorism laws and civil liberties, posted a tweet that went viral, minutes before the final whistle blow at the Luzhniki stadium in Moscow:

> Dear France,
> Congratulations on winning the #WorldCup.
> 80% of your team is African, cut out the racism and xenophobia.
> 50% of your team are Muslims, cut out the Islamophobia.
> Africans and Muslims delivered you a second World Cup, now deliver them justice

South African comedian and *Daily Show* host Trevor Noah quoted Professor Beydoun's tweet in his opening monologue making the joke, 'Africa won the World Cup,' sparking the ire of French ambassador to the United States, Gerard Araud, who sent a letter of indignation to Trevor Noah. Someone should have shown him the celebration videos that French players had been posting on social media immediately after each win, from the group stage to the semi-finals. Someone should have sent him a playlist for Presnel Kimpembe, the official Les Bleus DJ, featuring genres ranging from Kompa to Hip Hop, Coupe-Décale to Reggaeton, Afrobeats to Soukous. Without leaving out the mandatory Zouk, the genre made popular by the iconic Kassav in the early 1980s, and put the French West Indies on the Francophone musical map, infecting other Africans and influencing musicians and inspiring the creation of other genres that would shape modern African music, such as the Kizomba that is heard and consumed in the Cape Verde-Angola axis.

Someone should have warned the ambassador that unlike the 1998 team, social media opened a window for conviviality in the team managed by Didier Deschamps. We got to know their musical tastes, and what better way to know the soul of an individual than to know the songs he listens to?

From the letter that was available on the French embassy's official Facebook page, a few such passages were highlighted:

> all but two of the 23, players were born in France, educated in France, learned to play football in France, are French citizens... They are proud of their country, France... The rich and diverse backgrounds of these players is a reflection of the diversity of France... Unlike the United States of America, France does not refer to its citizens based on their race , religion or origin. For us, there is no hyphenated identity.

The French ambassador was offended by an African comedian's joke, which does not deny that any of those players, like the 1998 selection, were as French as croissants and Roquefort. Trevor Noah's intentions as well as of those of many of us believers in the ideals of pan-Africanism, was to put into context this win in a world where immigration is a divisive issue for liberal societies that still do not know how to discuss diversity and racism.

If we do not reach any conclusion, do not despair. We can always stop and listen to the playlist that inspired French players to win the FIFA World Cup for a second time. Identity is nothing more than a bureaucratic invention, useful for the conservative rhetoric of politicians who insist on denying that diversity is the only possible miracle to save Europe.

Let us understand that saving Europe, to a large extent, means Africa the ancient wellspring of 'civilisations' must save herself first. Afrobeats is the soundtrack to this revived optimism.

We hear A-list artists surf the Afrobeats wave, such as Alicia Keys with the single 'In Common', French Montana with 'Unforgettable' featuring Swae Lee or Janet Jackson 'Made For Now' featuring Daddy Yankee, 'Wale – My Love' featuring Major Lazer, WizKid & Dua Lipa. And of course, Drake, out of all the biggest pop stars at the moment, has plunged deeper into the Afro universe by giving us gems like 'Too Good' featuring Rihanna, 'Madiba Riddim', and a collaboration with Wizkid in Afrobeats meets Dancehall hit 'Come Closer'. Of all these hits, none compares to Davido's vast repertoire of smash hits like 'Fall' and 'If' produced by Tekno, who gave us the classic 'Pana'. Or, Maleek Berry with 'Kontrol' and Mr Eazi who signed to Mad Decent, the record label of Diplo and Major Lazer, with the hypnotising 'Leg Over'. Yemi Alade's 'Johnny' with over 90 million views is the most viewed song by an African female singer as well as Korede Bello's 'Do Like That' with its 100 million views on YouTube, leading as the song title with the most streams across the internet.

Although we are still far from achieving the status that Latin American pop has in the world, the presence and numbers that Afrobeats has conquered year after year, are promising. We can't yet dream of an African Grammys, but the fact is that the North American television network BET has turned its attention to what African artists are doing. In the last three years, The Best International Act category of the BET Awards has been won by DJ Black Coffee (2016), Wizkid (2017), and Davido (2018). The latter took the occasion to address the Hip Hop elites in the room: 'My continent has been so blessed to influence other cultures. Let's collaborate everybody'. Showing that the second most populous continent in the world can not be overlooked.

In my view, this is not the only way to understand Africa and its diaspora and the continent. It has been manifesting itself through the music that is being produced on the continent: Azonto, Afro-House, Kwaito, GQOM, the style of striking, percussive, house-adjacent club music that originated in South Africa or the Kuduro of Angola which mixes Techno with traditional Angolan rhythms. The truth is that dance music is teaching us to look at Africa from a new perspective. Although far from an ideal situation, we have witnessed a decline in the number of conflicts in Africa. The rise of a cultural middle class along with creative industries invites us to look at the continent in a different context. Beyond the syndrome of the ex-colonised, and the paternalism and condescension to which Africa is often subjected.

And so I come back to the question: how can West Africans invent the future? We could begin by identifying and stimulating those who have Africa as their greatest source of inspiration. Those who mobilise the physical and emotional geographies of the continent to highlight the different Africas with their unique identities and sensitivities.

The new West African creators, across music, film, literature, science and technology, working with and from this space, are inventing a future that has already begun. What they create is a kind of magnifying glass, the instruments that allow us to look a little closer, a little deeper into ourselves. They know that for any cultural manifestation to make sense in the fifty-four countries that make up the cradle of humankind, needs the transcendent impact reminiscent of a slap or an unexpected kiss.

AFRICAN YUAN

Hang Zhou

China's presence in West Africa is shrouded in myth, misconception, and often comical misinformation, invoking simplistic tendencies to present each region as a monolithic entity. I remember the China-Africa Beijing Summit in 2006, the largest ever conference on Africa held outside the continent, and the hysterical headlines it provoked, characterising the China-Africa equation as if there is one 'China' and one 'Africa'. The narrative of 'The Chinese are Coming' has ominously gathered momentum and belies an underlying assumption that African politicians are not smart enough to protect their interests when negotiating deals. China has been cast as yet another exploitative neo-colonial force, stripping the African continent of its wealth and diverting resources for its own gain. Anyone who has spent time in these two parts of world, as I have, knows that this two-dimensional assumption should be treated with caution, as the realities are far more complex, nuanced and multi-layered.

I was born and raised in Guangzhou in southern China, a city with a proud tradition of overseas trading, and it is some coincidence that my home city boasts the largest population of Africans residing in China. The contemporary presence of African migrants dates back to the late 1990s when the Asian financial crisis prompted many African merchants to leave Southeast Asia in search of opportunities elsewhere. China's economic resilience during the crisis and its accession to the World Trade Organisation in 2001 presented it as an ideal alternative. Its attractiveness was further boosted by the launch of the tri-annual Forum on China-Africa Cooperation (FOCAC) in 2000, an institutionalised platform for Chinese and African leaders to meet regularly and identify areas of co-operation. What followed was more than a decade of steady increase in bilateral trade.

It was against this economic backdrop that Guangzhou witnessed the increasing arrival of Africans, and before long a thriving African neighbourhood emerged, nicknamed somewhat unfortunately by the locals as 'Qiaokeli Cheng' – Chocolate City. Estimates put the population between 20,000 and 100,000 and at the forefront of this human movement were stories of resilience, creativity, and entrepreneurship, but also hardship, disappointments and tragedy experienced by migrants from West Africa, particularly Nigerians, Senegalese, Malians, Guineans and Ghanaians. It was likely the first time people from contemporary mainland China would have direct and quotidian interactions with Africans on such a scale.

It would be easy to assume that my interest in Africa was piqued by this transnational migration occurring in my own home town. However, I left Guangzhou in 2005 – too early to fully appreciate such an unprecedented level of migration, because it was only after 2005 that this human presence and its enclave in Guangzhou became more established, embedded, and felt. Looking back now, my initial interest in Africa, or China-Africa, arose about three years later. It was 2008, and I had travelled abroad for the first time to continue my undergraduate study in Paris. Unsurprisingly, I experienced many 'first times' during that period, including racial diversity. It was the first time I became conscious of my skin colour. I was living in a particularly cosmopolitan city and I newly encountered people from different places of origin, from West and North Africa, the Antilles, and Southern Indian Ocean. I vaguely knew of these places and their peoples when I had been back in China, but to have a lived experience of interacting with immigrant communities, from West Africa and elsewhere, was truly enriching.

What connects the dots between my new vibrant reality and my interest in Chinese affairs in Africa was the moment when a book cover randomly caught my attention. It depicted a scene in front of a line of newly-built, two-story villas on a sandy ground. A local, uniformed African security guard clutched a rifle in his left hand and was holding an umbrella in his right over a Chinese business man. The Chinese man was dressed in a black polo top and blue cargo pants, his one hand akimbo and the other holding a phone to his ear. Perhaps he was negotiating a deal or some sort of important business? *Chinafrique* is the name of this book, a neologism coined to echo the expression *Françafrique*, which nowadays alludes to the complicated and murky relationship between France and its former west and central African colonies. On glimpsing this book cover, many thoughts immediately flooded my mind. What are the messages behind it? What does the photographer, who was Western, wish to convey? What is in his mind while taking this photo? Who is this Chinese businessman? What is in his mind while being photographed? And what about the local African security guard? What is his emotion and feeling in this power dynamic? To date, I can still vividly recall to my mind this cover and I continue to be intrigued by this image. The questions it once led me to ask myself still perplex me, because I am still pursuing answers to them, and because all the questions I asked actually boil down to what the burgeoning encounter means for China, Africa, the West and beyond, and the people from all walks of life involved personally in this encounter, wittingly or unwittingly.

The year of 2008 also witnessed another important event in China – the Beijing Olympics, which China envisioned as a sort of coming-of-age party to showcase its rejuvenation. Back in 2001 I had been sitting in front of the TV at home with my parents anxiously waiting for the announcement of the decision and we felt the joy in the images of ecstatic Beijingers and revellers across the country taking to the streets to celebrate our win. It was indeed an exultation for us and for me – a high school student back then, which only makes my experience seven years later in Paris of the Olympic torch relay much more contrasting and unsettling. I skipped my French class with some friends to go to the Champs-Élysées, hoping to see the torch, only to be told that the relay had been disrupted by pro-Tibetan protesters and would be cut short. We dashed to the Hotel de Ville (City Hall), where a celebration ceremony was planned, but it too was cancelled, and instead I was confronted by a tumultuous scene – the plaza in front of the City Hall was divided into two camps, differentiated by people holding opposing flags: the Chinese national flag and the Tibetan snow lion flag. This scene troubled me greatly.

The protests did not only disrupt the Paris leg of the relay, but also those in London, in San Francisco and provided an international platform and public space for activists to criticise Beijing's records on human rights, particularly relating to its crackdown on the unrest in Tibet which took place in March 2008, only days before the torch reached Europe. It occurred to me that these protests were not solely targeted at what Beijing considers its internal affairs, which is how it perceives Tibet, but also at its role on the global stage. Protests were being directed at China's intervention in Africa, particularly its relationship with Khartoum and inaction in Darfur. Civil war was re-ignited in Sudan in 2003, and Beijing's close economic, political, and military relationship with Khartoum came under increasing global scrutiny with the approaching Beijing Olympics. China was confronted with enormous international pressure from foreign leaders, athletes, activists, and Hollywood celebrities calling for China to be a 'responsible stakeholder/citizen' in international affairs and to use its diplomatic leverage with Sudan to help curtail the violence in Darfur. There were intense efforts by Darfur sympathisers to emphasise Beijing's connivance in the conflict through a visual and textual discourse, leading to what might be called a Darfur Olympic narrative - the jarring image of the Olympic rings being replaced by interlocking handcuffs. This is why, alongside a Tibetan flag, I also saw a black banner depicting the handcuffs-like rings hung from the City Hall. Some years later, when I started to research China-Africa, I realised I had witnessed in 2008 scenes that were a prelude to an important turning point in China's foreign policy engagement in Africa.

Under international pressure and also out of concern for its global image, reputation, economic investment in Sudan and preparations for the Olympics, Beijing adjusted its long-held principle of non-interference and shifted its attitude from indifference to taking action to persuade Khartoum to accept the joint African Union and United Nations peacekeeping mission. China also appointed its first Special Envoy for African Affairs Liu Guijin in 2007, whose main task was overseeing the Darfur peace process. Liu engaged in conversation not only with the ruling elites in Khartoum, but more importantly and symbolically, with leaders of Darfur rebel groups, albeit on an ad-hoc and informal basis. This diverged from Beijing's deep-seated non-interference principle and demonstrates its increasing difficulty in putting into practice this principle when its own interests were rapidly globalised. The expansion of China's overseas interest, in fact, became a significant factor contributing to Beijing's more proactive foreign policy posture across the globe, including in Africa from then till now.

The 2008 global financial crisis and its relatively rapid recovery enabled China to take a dominant position in global trade and finance, particularly in the emerging economies of Africa, where it soon surpassed the US as the largest trading partner in the region. Geopolitically, however, the occurrence of the Arab Spring and the Libya crisis posed significant risks to China's overseas interest in the region, with China undertaking its largest evacuation operation in Libya in 2011 of 35,860 Chinese nationals. This further encouraged Beijing to re-think its foreign and security policy towards the continent. The announcement of a China-Africa Cooperative Partnership for Peace and Security at the 2012 FOCAC epitomises this process of revaluating and indicates that peace and security issues have been integrated as an integral pillar of the FOCAC discussion. Beijing had come to realise that a meaningful security element commensurate with its economic policy should be included in its bilateral engagements with the continent, and became an important channel for China to engage in African peace and security issues.

Looking back now, China's growing role in UN peacekeeping missions best epitomises its expanding peace and security footprint in Africa. It currently ranks as the tenth largest contributor with 2,515 peacekeepers on the ground in 2018, a 25-fold increase since 2000. Over 80% of these peacekeepers are deployed in Africa. It has also surpassed Japan to become the second largest contributor to the UN peacekeeping budget in 2016, only behind the USA. Peacekeeping missions remain an ideal and internationally-acceptable platform for Beijing to protect its ever-growing overseas trade and economic interests, particularly in conflict-prone regions, without deflecting much – at least discursively – from its non-interference foreign policy principle. Additionally, Beijing actively resorts to peacekeeping to build up its image and reputation as a responsible global stakeholder. This holds particular relevance within the context of China-Africa relations, given the wide criticism China often receives particularly from the West against its allegedly 'mercantilist' approach to Africa. There have been no other areas better than peacekeeping, which symbolise China's increasingly pervasive presence in African peace and security. And this growing role is only likely to increase with Xi Jinping firmly at the helm, eager to project a more proactive diplomatic and military posture overseas.

More specifically in West Africa, China has participated in all the UN peacekeeping missions that have ever been established in this sub-region, including UNOSMIL in Sierra Leone, UNOCI in Cote d'Ivoire, UNMIL in Liberia, and MINUSMA in Mali. This latter mission offers a particularly interesting case for our understanding of China's growing role. China currently sends 403 peacekeepers to MINUSMA, making up 16% of the total number of Chinese peacekeepers under deployment. When France initiated Operation Serval to prevent Bamako from being captured by Islamist rebels in Jan 2013, Beijing offered a reserved response without overtly criticising or explicitly supporting it. However, many prominent Chinese analysts strongly criticised the French intervention and viewed it as a sign of neo-interventionism and neo-colonialism, initiated by Paris to maintain its sphere of influence in the Sahel region. Yet, three months later, Beijing endorsed the UN resolution No 2100, which appreciated the action of the French forces and approved their cooperation with MINUSMA. The mission is also established with a strong mandate to restore peace and assist the Malian transitional authorities to extend its administration across the country.

Beijing's changing attitudes from tepidness to offering clear support to French intervention through its endorsement of the UN resolution can be, to a large degree, attributed to the fact that the French operation was invited by the Malian transitional authority and both the Economic Community of West African States (ECOWAS) and African Union officially welcomed the deployment. This is also consistent with the prerequisites under which Beijing endorses any peacekeeping mission: the consent of host country and relevant organisations. Nevertheless, what is interesting to note in the establishment of MINUSMA is that this mission is not a neutral and impartial actor to keep peace, but to side with the government to combat domestic and foreign opponents and to restore the status quo in the name of peace.

Other conditions also play a role in Beijing's pragmatism with regards to the Malian crisis. With the still fresh memory of significant economic loss that Beijing and its enterprises suffered from the Libyan crisis in 2011, Beijing was concerned about the aftermath of Gaddafi's fall in Libya, which saw a movement of Islamist insurgency and its spill-over effects across the Sahel region, in particular through the porous Libyan borders. The imminent risk of Bamako being captured by terrorist groups and leaving another security vacuum in the Sahel also resonates with the top leadership in Beijing. The Chinese government has been preoccupied, particularly since the last decade, with its far-west Xinjiang region, which it claims is unstable and volatile due to the alleged activities of Muslim Uyghur and separatist groups. The ongoing controversy engendered by the significant number of Uyghurs being held in what Beijing describes as 're-education camps' again testifies to the volatility in the region and China's approach with security uppermost in its mind.

Additionally, Chinese participation in UN peacekeeping missions had been characterised by dispatching non-combatant troops, mainly police, logistics, engineering, and medical contingents until in January 2012 when Beijing discreetly deployed for the first time a small infantry platoon to South Sudan to protect its engineer and medical staff operating in the UN peacekeeping mission there. Beijing showed extra prudence in publicising this first ever deployment of combat troops. Moreover, in Mali, for the first time in its history of participation, the Chinese troops assigned to the region are responsible for the security of other foreign forces. Retrospectively, China's participation in MINUSMA with its increased willingness to bend its traditional foreign policy principles and decision to send combat troops in 2013 is probably one of the earliest indications of Xi Jinping's diplomatic activism since his arrival at the pinnacle of power in 2012. One of the key reasons why China is determined to deepen its relations with Africa appears to be to secure Africa's support of China's political agenda and foreign policies regionally and globally, prompted by the increasingly urgent need to protect its ever-growing overseas economic interests.

The political significance that Beijing continues to attach to China-Africa relations has a further historical root. Beijing believes that it is their 'African brothers' who helped it to replace Taipei to regain the permanent seat in the United Nations in 1971, a significant reference point in Beijing's official portrayal and memory of China-Africa friendship up to now. Since then, Beijing has secured Africa as a natural ally in international affairs and actively constructs a shared identity of developing countries and a shared history and grievances towards the West, so that it can garner support from African countries to increase the legitimacy and credibility of its positions in different bilateral and multilateral settings. This political support appears to be even more meaningful, necessary and crucial for

Beijing in the current political climate as US-China rivalry shows no sign of abating in light of the Trump administration. China has never been at a better position to rally this support as now, given its current economic heft in Africa and the most recent switch of allegiance to Beijing from Taipei by three Western and Central African capitals – Banjul and São Tomé in 2016 and Ouagadougou in 2018 – are a result of the renewed diplomatic competition for recognition since the arrival of a pro-independence president in Taiwan in 2016.

Another case in point relating to China's security engagement in West Africa is her response to China's response to the 2014 outbreak of Ebola in West Africa amounted to the largest scale in its history of health assistance provisions. China offered 750 million Yuan (US$123 million) worth of humanitarian aid by the end of 2014 and deployed more than 1,200 medical and public health staff to the three most affected countries: Liberia, Sierra Leone, and Guinea. China's response has created multiple 'firsts' in the history of its health diplomacy in Africa and across the globe. It was the first time that China built a Biosafety Level 3 laboratory overseas, in Sierra Leone, and an infectious disease treatment centre overseas, in Liberia.

However, what is more interesting is the role the Chinese military played in Beijing's response. It was the first time that the People's Liberation Army (PLA) sent military medical staff units abroad: more than 500 staff were deployed to Sierra Leone and Liberia. This episode of intense engagement has important implications for its health cooperation with the African continent in the post-Ebola era. To begin with, the PLA, through its experience with Ebola, continues to strengthen its role in China's health cooperation with Africa. In Sierra Leone, as a post-Ebola initiative, an infectious disease prevention centre started operations in 2018 in Freetown – one of the first built by the PLA and currently managed by its medical staff. The PLA also recognised that the absence of an overseas logistics chain and base posed significant challenges to its medical cooperation. During the Ebola crisis, the first medical team sent by the PLA needed to equip itself with a two-month supply, whereas the second and third teams had to ship their medical supplies two months in advance before they set off. It is reasonable to speculate that this lesson further reinforced the PLA's determination to establish its first overseas base in Djibouti, officially inaugurated in 2017. It is able to provide logistical support to any future Chinese military medical operations in Africa.

Chinese health assistance was primarily bilateral in its delivery, provided by Beijing to respective African countries in the forms of dispatching medical teams, building hospitals, training of medical staff, and donations of medical supplies and funds. However, with more frequent interaction with traditional donors, particularly the USA, France, UK and international organisations during the Ebola crisis in West Africa, Beijing realised that global concerted and coordinated effort is indispensable in the occurrence of a public health crisis like Ebola and therefore has taken a more open-minded position in pursuing trilateral or multilateral cooperation in its health cooperation with Africa. In May 2014 China and the WHO agreed upon a pilot schistosomiasis elimination programme in Zanzibar, the first time China engaged with an international organisation to undertake health cooperation in Africa. In 2015, China and the US agreed to jointly support the African Union to establish the first African Centre for Disease Control. The China-UK-Tanzania tripartite pilot project on malaria control was also kicked off in April 2015.

The tangible reality of my evocative journey into Africa was realised when I first landed in Dar es Salaam in July 2014 in the midst of the dry season, wandering and exploring like any regular backpacker. I had previously been unable to enjoy a lived experience in and with the continent, undertaking research on China in Africa especially peace and security issues, that sometimes felt abstract, distanced, even elitist. It was at this time that I turned to African literature to help ground myself more in the cultural, social, and political texture of the continent – a decision I never regret, a habit I keep now, and a new world that continuously astonishes me after every read.

Much African literature remains inaccessible to Chinese readers because of the unavailability of Chinese translation. Often I try to recommend African novels to my friends and they ask me, 'why African writers?'. This leaves me feeling that much remains to be done in China to attain a more nuanced and multidimensional understanding of Africa. While China is proactively constructing the 'win-win' discourse of its all-round cooperation with Africa and paying greater attention to its soft power and cultural diplomacy across the continent, we might also wonder what China is 'importing' and 'learning' from Africa? What cultural and literary treasures can be unearthed? What greater cohesion can be attained through continued, mutual illumination of the complexities of China and Africa?

PAN-AFRICANISM

Nouria Bah

I was ten years old when I became aware of Ahmed Sékou Touré's death. My dad and his friends were huddled in our living room on a Sunday morning. It was a typical scene consisting of booming voices that reminisced, debated and plunged into silences filled with shaking heads. Then finally, the same refrain: 'Oh La Guinée!'. I was eating cereal in the kitchen when I overheard someone say, 'When Sékou Touré died...' To my young ears this was shocking and I immediately asked in surprise 'He's dead?' Hearing his name so frequently, not once did I ever think that he could have already passed. His legacy obviously still haunted my father, his friends and their families across the Atlantic Ocean – in Maryland or wherever the Guinean diaspora now called home. In response to my reaction they laughed before being plunged into silence once again.

Unbeknown to me, Ahmed Sékou Touré, one of the many leaders of the Pan-Africanist movement, had indeed passed away five years before I was born, in 1984. For a variety of historical reasons, Touré alongside Amical Cabral, Kwame Nkrumah and others, remain very much alive in living rooms, coffee shops, lectures and conferences around the world. Whenever Pan-Africanism is mentioned these names come to mind. But as I reflect on Pan-Africanism's impact today many questions occur to me. What were Touré, Cabral and Nkrumah's roles? And how could their individual legacies be differentiated?

Analysing the Pan-African movement requires looking at the way it relates to its political 'pioneers' as well as examining its philosophical and ideological foundations. It goes without saying that there are many definitions of Pan-Africanism. Historian Hakim Adi describes it as 'one river with many streams and currents'. Within the various definitions, there are two main strands: the former stemming from achieving unity after slavery and the latter based in the anti-colonial struggle after the

1940s. Each point to the notion of uniting Africans around the world to achieve social, economic and political emancipation from colonial power, taking on multiple forms, visible in the spheres of anti-racism, politics, and artistic expression.

There is no doubt that Pan-Africanism's response to segregation and slavery remains complex. Legislative tools of oppression used by French colonialists such as the Code Noir (Black Code), the Code of indigénat (Code of the indigenous) and Jim Crow in the United States are examples of this. The Code Noir was a sixty-article treaty created in the seventeenth and eighteenth century addressing the treatment of African slaves by France's colonies in North America. Its main purpose was to ensure that there was no possibility of revolution, no access to any form of rights, and the enforcement upon the population of Roman Catholicism. By the nineteenth century, the Code of the indiginate and Jim Crow laws had been introduced. Originally created in Algeria, the Code of the indiginate was drafted and used by the French to encourage assimilation while propagating indirect rule. In slight contrast, Jim Crow was a racial caste system that cemented African Americans as second-class citizens and propagated anti-black law. It did so through guiding beliefs and rationalisations of the superiority of white people.

Responding to these oppressive and dehumanising laws was the imperative task undertaken by the Civil Rights and Black Power movement, sustained by the rise of African consciousness. Heavily influenced by the Civil Rights Movement, Black Power placed black identity at the core of its ideology and demanded that the community have power and control over schools, universities, welfare rights, prison reform, and the job market. The African Independence movement helped heavily in upholding these forms of re-vindication and their values. Key figures in the Black Power movement became closely allied to African Pan-Africanist leaders, Stokely Carmichael was eventually exiled by the United States to Ghana, before moving to Guinea and subsequently changing his name to Kwame Ture (after Nkrumah and Touré).

Another key figure in the development of African consciousness and Pan-Africanism abroad was Marcus Garvey, from whom the Civil Rights movement and its Pan-Africanist collaboration borrowed heavily. A Jamaican-born black and civil rights nationalist leader in the movement,

Garvey advocated for a model of separation, in which people of African heritage would live under the 'separate but equal' status. Garvey pushed the separation theory to advocate the return of African descendants in America to Africa and worked fiercely to establish Liberia as one of the first independent black states. Both Garvey and Ture became targets of the former director of the Federal Bureau of Investigation (FBI) J Edgar Hoover's efforts to thwart Pan-Africanism and black freedom.

Beyond politics, the cultural world was also awakening to the influence of Pan-Africanism. Various approaches from literary authors such as Leopold Sédar Senghor, Aimé Césaire and Leon Dumas embraced the movement. Senghor would go on to become the first president of Senegal after its independence in 1960 and along with French Caribbean poet and playwright Aimé Césaire and French Guinean poet Léon Damas, he championed the concept of Négritude through the first publication of *L'Étudiant noir* (The Black Student) in Paris in 1935.

The Négritude concept was rooted in defining and establishing characteristics and principles of Africans within the diaspora. It was a rejection of the legacy of Code Noir and Code of L'indigénat which erased any concept of African culture and advocated assimilation to the 'superior' French culture. Senghor, Césaire, and Damas, while coming from different countries, were connected by the very system of assimilation they would struggle against. It brought them together as students in Paris and they connected in their struggles against colonialist powers that encouraged unilateral French assimilation. *L'Étudiant noir*, previously titled the *L'Étudiant Martiniquais* (Student from Martinique) set about writing from a perspective that was unique to the situation of the African student and elites. Denouncing colonialism and the bourgeois world, they were influenced by the writers of the Harlem Renaissance, particularly by Claude McKay. They sought to develop new Antillean literature that was another response to the sense of alienation faced by the Francophone African diaspora resident in France.

This common pathos in fighting for the plight of Africans and African descendants was emphasised during the emancipation movement after World War Two. Racial discrimination was abolished in the military by former President Harry Truman and Jim Crow was finally expunged as civil rights legislation was passed as a result of the hard work of

organisations including the NAACP and the Congress of Racial Equality
(CORE). With the onset of the Cold War, the role of communism also
became significant, with Marxist values permeating the Pan African
narrative. Lenin's early analysis of imperialism denounced the oppression
of those living under colonialism, rendering him a natural ally.

Communist International (Comintern), as cited by Pan-Africanist and
Black Marxist George Padmore, recognised that Africans and the African
diaspora faced similar problems to those in the communist party. This was
labelled as The Negro-Question and eventually led to the establishment of
an International Trade Union Committee of Negro Workers by Comintern.
This institution was led by Padmore himself. Sympathy to communism and
socialism was notable but did not overtake the notion that Pan Africanism
was bound as a response to a specific history: the history of slavery,
violence, and oppression by imperialists of Africans in the continent and
the diaspora. The Non-Aligned Movement included the Initiative of Five:
Kwame Nkrumah of Ghana, Josip Broz Tito of Socialist Yugoslavia,
Jawaharlal Nehru of India, Sukarno of Indonesia, Gamal Abdel Nasser of
Egypt. They carried the name Non-Aligned to emphasise that their
countries would work with the principles of independence, promotion of
peace and non-interference in internal affairs.

It was in 1955 that the Bandung Conference saw the gathering of Asian
and African states including the Non-Aligned Movement. The conference
was vocal on the topic of Western countries meddling in internal affairs
and put forward an agenda of peaceful resolution of world conflict and
decolonisation. The two movements contributed to the acceleration of the
independence movement of African countries in the 1960s and Pan-
Africanism served as a powerful ideological support. The Year of Africa in
1960, as it is sometimes referred to, saw the political independence of
seventeen countries from their colonial rulers: France, Belgium, and the
United Kingdom. The pathos of unity demonstrated in the Non-Aligned
Movement and the Bandung Conference, elevated the value of African
unity and independence from Eastern and Western ideologies. It was also
during this time that President Nkrumah addressed the United Nations
calling for an end to white supremacy and injustice. He emphasised there
would be no revenge but rather a focus on freedom for all African people.

The Year of Africa in 1960 also marked the second All African People's Conference. The first had covered themes surrounding the struggle to achieve independence and demanding the end to the exploitation of Africans. Further efforts to attain freedom, especially economic freedom, were called for as more and more countries declared independence. However, behind the facade of Pan-Africanism, there was the creation of multi-nation communities such as the Casablanca Group and the Brazzaville Group and from their very beginning, these groups differed sharply.

Ahmed Sékou Touré and Kwame Nkrumah belonged to The Casablanca Group that was formed a year after the euphoria of independence of the 1960s. Comprised of a group of diverse 'radical' states that included Egypt, Ghana, Guinea, Mali, Morocco, and Algeria, the group advocated the creation of a United African State. In contrast, the Brazzaville Group advocated cooperation with the West, particularly France. In addition, the Monrovia Group was credited with the early establishment of the Organization of African Unity (OAU). The Monrovia Group championed the idea of a common market and a permanent tribunal, which the Brazzaville Group was more aligned to, eventually joining the Monrovia Group when all three met in Liberia. The split between these groups was a result of one side leaning to the left while the other moved towards the right.

Two years later, in 1963, with a compromise among the Brazzaville, Monrovia, Casablanca groups of African nations, the OAU was created in Ethiopia. Its founding figures included Haile Selassie, Mohamed V, Ben Bella, Kwame Nkrumah, and Sekou Touré. The OAU's main aims were inspired by Pan-Africanism, advocating the strategic defence of African states and the disintegration of all countries still operating under the rule of colonialism. While it was unanimous in the creation of the African Development Bank, the groups held conflicting views on any alliance with the West. This would stall decision making, rendering the OAU paralysed from the onset. The institution would have no real power and their claimed goals would just remain slogans; even if many of its figures championed these mantras and messages.

Kwame Nkrumah, Ahmed Sékou Touré and Amical Cabral were instrumental in the differing outcomes of independence for the three West African powerhouses they headed. Two of the leaders, Nkrumah and Sékou Touré struggled with the reality of governing fledgling administrations after proclaiming independence. Cabral would face the challenge of fighting the remaining colonial European country, Portugal; that was far from being a democracy. Pan-Africanism in practice for these leaders would mean different approaches. Despite advocating interdependency and unity, the historical and political realities would lead to ruthless calculations of survival and ultimately to blatant betrayals.

Nkrumah was the first prime minister of Ghana in 1952, and after independence from Britain, the first president of Ghana. He had studied in the US where he became acquainted with Marxism and Socialism before travelling to the United Kingdom to organise the Fifth Pan African Congress. Nkrumah's life in the West and the casual and institutional racism he observed and experienced profoundly affected the development of his Pan-Africanism. It was in London that he befriended George Padmore with whom he attended the Pan African Congress in Manchester, upon his return to the Gold Coast, using his teachings and interest in politics to become general secretary of the United Gold Coast Convention (UGCC). While organising a splinter movement, riots occurred and Nkrumah and others were arrested and imprisoned. Upon his release, Nkrumah formed the Convention Peoples' Party (CPP) and led an initiative of peaceful protests and activism against colonial authorities known as positive action. The positive action campaign led to a peaceful strike but that too erupted into violence. Nkrumah was imprisoned once more but this did not prevent him from standing as a candidate for the legislative election. He easily won and upon his release was to play a key role in creating a new government.

Employing his Pan-Africanist views in various ways after Independence, Nkrumah renamed his country Ghana, after the old empire that was destroyed by the Almoravids in the eleventh century. He believed in the pathos relating to a stable and pre-colonial Africa and sought to use this history as a means to help rebuild and form the country. In doing so he sought to eliminate the notion of tribalism and engagement based on racial and religious communities. This was met with opposition from various ethnic groups who did not believe a form of nationalism without recognising ethnic pasts could be possible. Nkrumah encouraged Pan-African culture through teachings of history and culture and the opening of a research library, museum, and council of arts, education, and culture.

Women were encouraged to pursue an education and increasingly attended universities, joined in the military and became doctors or other key players in international business.

During his presidency, Nkrumah struggled to balance his continued campaign to unify Africans with the immediate pressing issues that the country of Ghana was facing. This, unfortunately, resulted in a descent into debt, and the disintegration of national projects addressing these issues. While on a business trip to China, Nkrumah was toppled by a military coup orchestrated by the National Liberation Council. Forced to seek asylum in Guinea he would languish in exile for the rest of his life.

Failure to engage the Ghanaian population and cement his vision was Nkrumah's main shortcoming. His tenure was marked by economic disappointment and lack of policies engaging neighbouring countries. A repressive reign and narrow focus on a visionary ideology at the expense of economic improvement made his downfall inevitable. However, Nkrumah's legacy remains. Perceived to be one of the first leaders fervently committed to the Pan-Africanist movement, he was among many leaders of his time to push forward the idea of a single continental government. While his goals were never realised, his writings continue to be studied and discussed. He is, after all, credited with the advancement of Pan-Africanism with the formation of OAU and in the cultural and arts front, his legacy is still alive.

Similarly, Ahmed Sékou Touré was also influenced by Marxism and Leninism. He joined a small group of French leftists living in Guinea and belonged to the French communist party and its affiliated trade-union, the CGT. He would later become one of the founders of the Post and Telecommunications Workers' Union, previously having been active on the political scene during the creation of the African Democratic Rally, which held close ties with others in Francophone and Equatorial Africa. The rally was an umbrella group with local affiliation in each of the eight French colonies in West Africa. In the 1950s, Touré became one of the trade union leaders and during a strike in 1952 was jailed for three months. This would propel him in the political arena with the help of Houphouet-Boigny, the communist-leaning trade-unionist, combined with the privileged relations he had with Governor Cornut-Gentile and Francois Mitterrand.

At the forefront of the decolonisation of Africa via the Democratic Party of Guinea, which was the Guinean branch of the African Democratic Rally, Touré played a key role in the rejection of France's new referendum proposed by President Charles de Gaulle in 1958. Political opponents even joined his party to create a national united front, leaving only one party to govern the country. The Guinean vote for independence propelled Touré as a prominent African figure as he cultivated close ties with President Eisenhower and John F Kennedy. Their aim was to pull Guinea away from Soviet influence, causing temporary tensions with his allies in the Soviet Union. Touré also had ties with Malcolm X and Kwame Ture, leaders of the African diaspora and he used his personal aura to advocate for the civil right movement in the United States.

Sékou Touré's activism in the Pan-African movement was intense. His close ties with Nkrumah and the first president of Mali, Modibo Keita, meant that as early as 1960, the three leaders decided to create an embryo of the African Union. The largely symbolic Guinea-Ghana-Mali union orchestrated the appointment of Nkrumah, one of the founding fathers of the OAU, as co-president of Guinea when he was toppled as president of Ghana in 1966. Diallo Telli, a prominent Guinean decolonisation activist, was elected as its first general secretary, and would be instrumental in achieving one of the most important roles of the OAU: ridding the continent of colonial dominance. Undoubtedly one of the key leaders of the independence movement, Touré's legacy in Pan-Africanism is heavily tainted by his tribal politics and repressive regime. He quickly moved after independence to eliminate democratic rule and the optimism that gripped Guinea after 1958, soon dissipated. Many intellectuals from the African diaspora who relocated to Guinea to assist and experience the first French colony to gain independence in Africa left within four years. Economic development stalled and a large portion of the Guinean population took refuge in neighbouring countries. Opponents and former allies were detained and executed, citizens were arrested indiscriminately and sent to concentration camps. The largest and most prominent was Camp Boiro in Conakry, Guinea where prisoners were tortured, starved to death and executed. Touré the Pan-Africanist had become Touré the dictator and is believed to have killed up to 50,000 people.

In 1976, four years after the end of Diallo Telli's tenure at the helm of the OAU, Sékou Touré had him arrested, tortured and left him to die of starvation. Touré would then subject the Fulani ethnic group to the same treatment. This was the climax of ethnic politics he had used in his rise to power and Guinea has yet to recover. As economic hardship continued, the dictator decided to trade with the West, visiting the United States in the 1980s asking for further private investment in minerals and opening up a dialogue with France.

Meanwhile, during the war for independence it was Cabral who led the African Party for the Independence of Guinea and Cape Verde (PAIGC). The guerilla movement was dedicated to resisting the Portuguese government and he became its leader. Utilising his studies as an agronomist he created a system of training camps set up in Ghana that were supported by Nkrumah. Troops were taught to be self-sustainable, and other than providing military service for the country, soldiers also became farmers helping to work the land. A trading system was developed along with medical supply care with materials provided by the USSR and Sweden. In addition, Cabral benefitted from the support of the OAU, which put a mandate on neighbouring countries to offer logistical and military assistance to all remaining Portuguese colonies in Africa. Sékou Touré hosted the headquarters of Cabral's party, the PAIGC, in Conakry, enabling him to rise to international prominence. He tried to maintain a balance between the two contesting camps juggling financial freedom and political power post-independence. This helped him gain a reputation as a peacekeeper between feuding heads of African states. However, his Pan-Africanism could not fill the gap in balancing Cap-Vert, Guinea and his own party. This caused tensions and as the People's Assembly was beginning to be formed, pre-empting the independence of Guinea-Bissau, Cabral was assassinated by rival PAIGC leader Inocêncio Kani.

The friendship that had been enjoyed by Nkrumah, Cabral and Touré, along with their Pan-Africanism idealisms receded against a backdrop of western influences and complicities, economic turmoil and angst from their own people. Ousted from Ghana and subsequently named co-president of Guinea, the intense propaganda surrounding Nkrumah's promises to use force to return to power in his home country exacerbated the rift between Guinea and the Ivory-Coast. The military junta that toppled Nkrumah presented a united front against the coalition leaving Touré and Nkrumah, in a sign of a fragile African unity, only with each other, their governments more concerned with survival at any cost.

In 1970, a group of Portuguese militaries, accompanied by opponents to Sékou Touré's regime, made an incursion into Conakry. An absent Cabral enabled Touré and PAIGC dissidents to recapture Portuguese war prisoners held by the PAIGC. Touré would go on to use the international outcry created by the Portuguese invasion to liquidate all his opponents and obtain a permanent grip on the state apparatus with his family members. Cabral felt bitterly betrayed. His relationship with Touré became irrevocably strained and the resulting bad blood is widely believed to have led Touré to encourage dissenting factions in the PAICG to eliminate Cabral.

The demise of these leaders, forever mourned, celebrated and resented, remains a powerful symbol of all that Pan-Africanism could have achieved but failed. Just as in 1960, West Africa is still threatened by political instability, with repressive leadership that garners support from powerful international interests, stifling true freedom. The sad truth is that rampant corruption has led to many failures in economic growth and lack of rule of law, basic infrastructure and sound education. Multiple regional bodies, created with the aim to promote economic cooperation and maintain stability among neighbouring countries, are powerless and largely funded by ex-colonial powers.

EVERYTHING I AM

Zahrah Nesbitt-Ahmed

Mid-July 2018. I am dressed in black – ripped jeans, a sleeveless loose top and black sandals. I am on my way to see a friend who is in town from Nigeria for work. Running late, I request an Uber. I know where the conversation is going the second the Uber driver says 'you have a pretty name – Zahrah'. I had not even put my seatbelt on. 'It looks more like Arabic'. The driver continues to speak as I battle with the very tricky contraption. I am finally strapped in. I am now also ready – aware the driver has more questions for me now that my seatbelt is safely secured. We begin our journey. It is only then I reply. 'It is'.

I had arrived in Washington, DC six weeks prior. This was not the first time in my very short tenure in the US capital that an Uber driver struck up a conversation with me solely on the basis of my first name. Prior to this journey, Uber drivers from Afghanistan, Bangladesh, Iran and Pakistan have asked me about my name. This tends to happen either within a few minutes into my journey if I am in an Uber X, or after a passenger exits the vehicle, if I am in an Uber pool.

The first time it happened, the driver – who may have been of South Asian descent (I did not ask his country of origin) – started a conversation once the other passenger in the Uber pool had arrived at their destination. 'My brother's wife's name is Zahra'. I assume it was spelt that way based on the way he pronounced it. 'It's Muslim name? You Muslim?'

His remarks, as with the other Uber drivers, do not offend me or make me uncomfortable. I have come to expect this. Not just with male Uber drivers in Washington, DC. Although I must admit, the frequency with which men who drive Ubers in DC have asked me the same thing veiled in different questions is somewhat amusing.

I have come to expect this question around my name, because really it is more a question around my religious identity. I am an obviously black woman with an overtly Arabic name. So these men — who identify as Muslim — are really trying to determine if I am Muslim or not.

I was born on a Saturday — either quarter to two or quarter after two in the afternoon. My mother forgets which of us between my sister and I was born at which time.

I digress.

I was born on a Saturday afternoon in June. I was eventually named Zahrah Dominique Nesbitt-Ahmed.

Zahrah — derived from Arabic meaning (desert) flower. Dominique — derived from French meaning of the Lord. Nesbitt — my mother's maiden name. Ahmed — my father's last name.

The product of a union between a Christian British-Caribbean mother and a Muslim Nigerian father, my name is a clear indication of my identity that sometimes I feel I do not need to explain myself.

'Are you Muslim?' is a question I get asked a lot. I always think to myself — take away Dominique and Nesbitt, and you are left with a Muslim-sounding name. The question need not even be asked. A response should not even be required. Still, I have needed to explain myself for as long as I can remember. The problem is, it has always been quite complicated to do so.

I was born at the intersection of multiple identities. Girl. Black. West African. Nigerian. Hausa. Caribbean. Kittian. British. Black British. Muslim. Christian. 'Labels' assigned to me before I was even conceived. From birth until seventeen, my life in Lagos was a medley of these different aspects of me. Simultaneously everything and nothing is how I always felt growing up.

Islamiyya classes to learn how to read the Qu'ran, memorise Suras, to read and write Arabic, do ablution and pray. When I was old enough, fasting during Ramadan. Celebrating Eid al-Fitr and Eid al-Adha, or what I knew it as growing up — Sallah. As I got older, I re-read the Qur'an, picked up texts on Islam and read the Bible — informing myself on both religions, ensuring I learned as much as I could about Prophet Muhammad *Sallallahu alayhi wa Salam* (Peace be upon him) and Jesus Christ.

There were Easter and Christmas celebrations. Decorating our family home, wrapping gifts and then waking up Christmas morning — first to Christmas carols, then gospel songs, and then Calypso — are some of the fondest memories of my childhood. It is also why Christmas remains one of my favourite time of the year. As a family, we still make Ackee and Saltfish with Johnny Cakes as we wake for breakfast on 25 December. My mother makes the traditional dishes, or sometimes, okra and saltfish, but the ritual of making Johnny Cakes on Christmas morning was absolutely passed down. It has been my contribution to the festive season ever since I was fourteen.

Then the 'West Indian' carnival at Tafawa Balewa Square in Lagos, Nigeria – I think it used to be in April, but I forget.

Finally, the best of both worlds – the cuisine. There were meat pies, *moin-moin* (steamed bean cake), rice and stew, jollof rice, fried rice, pounded yam, *egusi* soup made from ground melon seeds, okro (never okra) soup. There was also fried bean cake called *kosai* (*akara* for my Southern Nigerian counterparts), *tuwo skinkafa* a dish from Northern Nigeria made from rice, fermented rice cake also from Northern Nigeria named *masa, fura da nunu*, which is a drink made of millet and fermented milk, kunu – another drink made from millet, sorghum or corn, and of course the hibiscus flower drink *zobo*. There was plan-*tain* and plan-*tin*. There was also rice and peas, curried goat, stewed chicken, oxtail with boiled dumplings and butter beans, patties. There was certainly a Caribbean twist on many Nigerian dishes, which made them even better. Sundays was all about roasts – roast chicken, Yorkshire pudding, roast potatoes, rice and peas, gravy and pudding.

Navigating the world – my world – those first seventeen years in Nigeria was precarious. I experienced confusion similar to (sometimes even more than) that of Uber drivers in DC, from Nigerians – including people within my own ethnic and religious group. I constantly felt I was not authentic enough, too culturally and religiously ambiguous to be fully accepted. This resulted in me choosing sides. Consciously, being Nigerian, Hausa, Muslim. I kept the other parts of me quiet, hidden, invisible. It was easier that way. It was simpler. Describing myself to others was complicated and always led to even more questions.

Today I walk my path with a little more ease. I am now Woman. Black. West African. Nigerian. Hausa. Caribbean. Kittian. British. Black British. Muslim. Christian. Those 'labels' assigned to me before I was even born, none of which I chose, are no longer a burden that I must keep secret.

I still classify myself as simultaneously everything and nothing. Yet, one thing is certain. I was born into Islam. I am not a revert. It is this which the

Uber drivers – and most people that come across me – though they never say it – really try to ascertain when they first meet this Black woman with an Arabic – and Muslim – name.

That a Black, West African Muslim exists in the world today should not come as a surprise. The spread of Islam into Africa dates as far back as the middle of the seventh century with the faith spreading to West African regions that now comprise modern day Burkina Faso, Gambia, Ghana, Guinea, Ivory Coast, Mali, Niger, Nigeria and Senegal. Traders were major actors in introducing Islam to West Africa, with several trade routes, such as the cities of Gao, a medieval city near the Niger River, and Ghadames, an oasis town now in present-day Libya, connecting North Africa to Sub-Saharan African. Although trade between the Mediterranean and West African regions predated Islam, North African Muslims – mainly Berbers – intensified this when they began to travel in trading caravans across the trans-Saharan trade routes from North Africa across the Sahara to Western Sudan, for merchant transactions with West Africans. The trans-Saharan trade, and the contact between North African Muslims and sub-Saharan Africans, was important in the spreading of Islam through the exchange of goods because the concept of the ummah and adherence to sharia law fostered mutual trust.

Merchant-scholars also played a large role in the spread of Islam, including the Jakhanke merchant scholars in the Senegambia region, the Jula merchants in Mali and the Ivory Coast and the Hausa merchants during the nineteenth century in Guinea, Nigeria and Ghana. Their ability to read and write made them valuable to West African kings as they performed religious and diplomatic services and administrative tasks useful to the kingdoms. Beyond the administrative needs of the ruling class, West African kings also sought spiritual protection from Islamic scholars. The influence of Muslim traders and merchant-scholars went beyond those that converted to Islam because of the value of the services they offered not only for the nobility, but also for the larger population in urban centres. In empires like Mali and the Hausa city states, such as Gobir (most northern), Katsina, Kano, Zazzau (the most southern), Zamfara and Kebbi, most of the kings were Muslim or had embraced Islam, while others did not convert, but supported the presence of Islamic culture and institutions.

The majority of the people in West Africa that adopted Islam did not do so until the late seventeenth century and early eighteenth century, with a large number of conversions in Hausa Muslim States occurring when a series of jihads were launched by the Fulbe, tired of the corrupt ways of the ruling elite. This was accomplished under the leadership of religious scholar, jurist, ascetic, reformer, revolutionary, Shehu Usmān dan Fodīo, also known as 'Uthman b. Fudi, under which Sokoto Caliphate was established. Until then, the rest of the population often still practiced indigenous religions, leading to the blending of Islamic beliefs and traditional West African practices establishing a form of Islam that maintained the fundamental tenets of the faith, but was also specific to the region.

Despite the plethora of research and scholarship on Islam in West Africa, there is one glaring omission – women are often said to be marginal or absent in the literature due to the overwhelming focus on male leaders. While the mere mention of women and Islam often conjures up clichés of veiling and oppression, discussions tend to oscillate between women's subordination in Islam and whether the religion empowers women. The African Muslim woman is often located on the periphery of the periphery.

However, women are not bit-players in the story of Islam in West Africa. Consider how women in Kano succeeded in gaining autonomy despite the constraints imposed upon them, or in Dogondoutchi, Niger, where efforts by women to affirm their involvement in society were viewed as an agentive capacity. There were also Muslim women in positions of authority, such as Queen Amina of Zazzau (modern day Zaria in Kaduna State, Nigeria) – one of the first women to become *Sarauniya* (queen) in a male-dominated society. Queen Amina expanded the territory of Zazzau beyond its initial borders in the early to mid-fifteenth century – prior to the establishment of the Sokoto Caliphate. Her kingdom controlled the trade routes in the region, erecting a network of commerce within the great walls that surrounded Hausa cities within her dominion. According to the Kano Chronicles, Queen Amina conquered cities as far as Nupe, and also ruled Kano and Katsina for thirty-four years. There were also female teachers, spiritual leaders, political activists and agents of change. In the former Bornu and Hausa states, for example, women had important political and religious functions, with female functionaries ruling the female population. The queen had a pivotal position, and in the pre-Islamic

Hausa rituals the 'bon cults', women played a major role and served as intermediaries. Female scholars also initiated members of the same sex and organised pilgrimages to Mecca.

Another significant figure was Asma'u bint 'Uthman b. Fodio, or Nana Asma'u. The daughter of Usmān dan Fodīo, she was a religious scholar, poet, educator, community leader and political commentator. A nineteenth-century Muslim West African women of great repute, she played a major role in political, cultural and intellectual developments in West Africa. Nana Asma'u was heavily involved in the machinery of the Sokoto caliphate, acting as an adviser to her brother, the Sultan of Sokoto Amīr al-Mu'minīn Muḥammad Bello, and writing over seventy works in subjects such as history, theology, law, the *Sunna* and women's roles in the Qadiriyya community. Dedicating herself to the education of Muslim women, she used her poetry as a teaching tool in the classes she held as part of the Yan Taru movement and eventually established the first major system of schools and other institutions of learning throughout the Sokoto caliphate. A more recent female Islamic sufi scholar Malama A'ishatu Dancandu from Niger, fought for women's and girl's education through the Islamic notion of the right to knowledge for all, defiantly positioning herself in between patriarchal indigenous traditions and French colonialism.

Whilst the experiences of Nana Asma'u and Malama A'ishatu Dancandu as leading figures in the spread of Islam in West Africa contrast sharply from the repertoire of 'docile', 'veiled' and 'oppressed' Muslim women, misunderstandings around women's place in Islam and the position of women in Muslim culture persists. Muslim women in West Africa should not be approached as monolithic objects of curiosity, as the experiences of women in Islamic cultures is extremely varied. Similarly, identifying Muslim women is not a simple task, due to an array of ethnic and class diversities. Yet, assumptions abound on what a Muslim, particularly a Muslim woman looks like, how she acts and what she thinks.

October 2018. It is a cold Wednesday evening in Lesotho, and the end of months of planning, culminating in – what was deemed – a successful two-day event. The team behind it were all celebrating surviving an intense prolonged period of work, the twelve of us from different parts of the world – Zambia, Lesotho, Zimbabwe, Cameroon, Canada, Pakistan, South Africa, Mauritius, and of course, Nigeria – gathering around the table to kick back and relax. We had all met for the first time in person for this event, and living in different parts of the world, prior conversations had been via email or video conferencing. Face-to-face and finally able to loosen up a bit, our discussions that evening ranged from Nollywood and how the films are usually split into part 1, 2 and sometimes 3, South African protests, and even petrol prices across our different countries. And of course politics within our various regions was very definitely not left out of the conversation.

In the midst of it all, it was slowly revealed that amongst our group, a man from South Africa, a woman from Mauritius, and myself were all Muslim. My colleagues on the table all looked at me, 'I thought so with your name'. One of them stated, 'but I wasn't sure'. The slow realisation and surprise among others on that table that I was Muslim was as I had become accustomed to. I shrugged it off as I usually do. As explained, it is something I have come to expect.

What happened the next morning over breakfast was a little more fascinating. The three of us are from different parts of the continent but we bonded, laughed and shared our experiences of growing up as Muslim. One memory that stood out the most for all of us was how our Imams, religious scholars, in our respective Madrasa classes were all so terrifying and strict. I was reminded of something that growing up in my household gave me that I forever cherish – the privilege to be able to make my own decisions about my faith and belief. On the flipside, it further revealed how often people put me in categories that do not quite explain who I am. As on the table, I was the only one out of the three of us who people were most surprised by the revelation of my religion.

On my first work trip to India five years ago, the hotel organised an airport pick-up for me. The driver for the longest time would not let me get into the hotel shuttle. Zahrah Ahmed was a South Asian Muslim woman's name. To him, I was neither South Asian or Muslim – it was as if he could not fathom the idea that I, a Black Muslim, could exist. Yet, once he had accepted what, and who, I was, his reaction turned into one of endless questioning – around my family, my heritage, the nature of Islam in Nigeria and the like.

And there was the time in April of 2018, I Skyped with a South Asian woman based in Zambia prior to flying out there for work. We met in person a couple of weeks after that call. Once we got to know each other a bit better, the woman told me she was expecting me to be *a brown, Muslim woman*. Similar to the airport pick-up in India years ago, there was definitely an element of shock in knowing that I was Black, and not Brown. I have had similar experiences in England. Trips to clinics, dentists and opticians, for example, have led to double takes from everyone, including other patients, when my name is called out in waiting rooms.

These separate experiences that have occurred in three different parts of the world, at different stages in my life, could be linked to the reality that a large number of people from different walks of life do not automatically associate Islam with Blackness. Racism within the Muslim community has certainly played a large role in the erasure of Blackness over the centuries in Islam. Black Women have a further layer of invisibility and vulnerability, owing to our status as being Black and Female.

As such, by design of my name – and this erosion of Blackness in Islam – to others, I should be a Brown, South Asian, Muslim Woman. Yet, I am only one of those things – a Muslim Woman. I do find it weird that people often put me in categories that I do not see myself in, and – in some cases – insulting the assumption of what a Muslim woman is supposed to look like.

Muslim women are not solely Arab or South Asian or Middle Eastern. We are not solely hijabi. With the rise of modest fashion, we are not all stylish, fashionista, bloggers. And we are also certainly not submissive. Yet, these are some of the images that instantly pop into people's minds when they think of Muslim women. These are categories that someone such as myself does not neatly fit into. Similarly, Black Women, and particularly Black African Women, are not all Christian. And while I cannot claim to have experienced discrimination on the basis of my religion, what I have come to realise over time is that the fact others categorise me reveals their own perceptions and reactions towards me. It is also often something they are more bothered by than myself.

Endings are something I struggle with. This case is no different, especially as the questions around my name and my religious identity will not end with a neat conclusion. Confession time. Sometimes I want to say no, whenever I am asked the question 'Are you Muslim?' I want to know how people will react. It would probably be simpler if I said no. Follow-up questions might not proceed. Unfortunately, I am yet to say no. Despite knowing the real intention behind asking me the question 'Are you Muslim?' is really to ascertain how I – a Black, West African woman – can also be Muslim.

Living with divergent religious and cultural identities in my daily life initially came with its own complexities and contradictions. It certainly had an impact on how I perceived myself and made my way through the world. Growing up I was never quite sure where I fit in, and never spoke about this inner conflict. I also never mentioned what I was unless I was directly asked. Even then, I responded by choosing one side of me. It is now less difficult to live with the various parts that make me, but it required that I embrace my many identities simultaneously and create a space to exist and thrive with them. Moreover, it involved me seeing the privilege that came with being able to fit in to multiple social, cultural and religious situations.

While I do not believe my positioning is unique, I often wonder where the voice and discussions of a Black woman from a mixed religious, cultural and nationality background fits in current discussions on identity. There was certainly a nervousness, hesitation even, in me as I write – that my Muslimness would not be accepted, even within this critical space. This is because while in many parts of the world we may have made progress and strides in how we view and accept differences, elements of uncertainty and distrust still exists towards people who are seen as different. Moreover, in many parts of society, we are still learning how to talk about identities, especially those that fall outside of traditional understandings of (in my case) religion and culture.

Perhaps I should end by answering the question, What Am I? rather than 'Am I Muslim?' The truth? I still do not know how to answer that question with confidence. On the surface, I am probably more Nigerian than anything – owing to the fact that I spent the first seventeen years of my life there. I am also certainly more Muslim – not only because I was born into Islam, but it is also what I am. Yet, as my relationship with my different sides has developed and strengthened over the years, my identities seem to have created a symbiotic relationship with each other.

So, what am *I?* I am a Muslim woman, a Hausa woman, a Nigerian woman, a West African woman, an African woman, a Caribbean woman, with a Christian British-Caribbean mother and a Muslim Nigerian father.

ARTS AND LETTERS

JIHADIS

Tam Hussein

I once met a woman on the Syrian border who had spent several decades in Tadmor prison in Palmyra only emerging when ISIS had taken the town. I cannot verify her claim but she said she gave birth to her child in its dark dungeons underground, that child did not see the sunshine for seven years, and whilst she hated the Islamic State, she hated the Assad regime more. Nevertheless, for the region and the international community, Assad, is the better partner. He is a known quantity, better the devil you know as opposed to rebels with Jihadists in their midst. He can be dealt with using tried and tested policies of the past. In many ways, the Jihadis present themselves to be a greater conundrum in the region and indeed in the Muslim world as a whole. Assad is slowly but surely corralling the rebels and Jihadis into that province to finish them off. I doubt however, that he will, if the example of the Nigerian President Muhammad Buhari's is anything to go by.

In 2015, Mr Buhari claimed that *Boko Haram* or the Islamic State in West Africa was 'technically defeated' but after three years, its fighters are still hiding in the borderlands of Niger, Chad and Cameroon, 27, 000 dead and 2 million civilians displaced. The lesson being that fighters are far more adept at surviving than civilians and they will most likely escape. These Jihadis will present themselves to be a greater problem not only for the international community but also for the Muslim world as a whole. Estimates of foreign fighters vary from four thousand to forty thousand foreign fighters in Syria. There will be security experts scratching their heads asking what comes next and what should one do? And I don't mean to be pessimistic here, but I am not so sure there is a clear answer to solving the problem because the phenomenon of Salafi-Jihadism is part of a historical process that will have to be played out to its fullest extent. In many ways Salafi-Jihadis share similarities with the Jewish Zealots and Sicarii from fourth century BC; these Jewish extremists ignored established religious leaders, they were aggressive militarists unwilling to follow the Rabbis who were trying to come to a political solution with Rome. That sort of behaviour seems uncannily similar to Salafi-Jihadis. They seem to represent that strain of militancy within the Muslim world which is torn between coming to an accord with the West and resisting Western interference in its countries.

Admittedly, meeting Salafi-Jihadis fighting in Syria do have their peculiarities. In theory, they are meant to be absolutely devoted to their word, if they give you *Amān*, that is a promise of safety, then you are safe. In reality, they might just change their minds mid-way and then you're screwed. Even if you convert to Islam your fate may just be the same. The conversion of Peter or Abdul Rahman Kassig didn't prevent him from being killed. According to Jejoen Bontink, a former Belgian ISIS fighter, James Foley and John Cantlie, too had converted to Islam. How sincere their conversion was is irrelevant in the circumstances. In the Islamic faith as soon as one has uttered one's profession of faith one is as sinless as a new born babe, and has full rights as a fully-fledged member of the Muslim community, the *Ummah*. One thing you cannot do is to test *how much* someone, especially new converts, believe. But clearly these hostages who had ostensibly pronounced the Muslim testimony of faith hadn't been believed and were not granted those privileges that was incumbent on the Salafi-Jihadis. Instead they were tortured and executed brutally. From a Salafi-Jihadi perspective their lives should have been spared but this is when modern pragmatism intrude; they were white Westerners, fetched top dollar and would most certainly make the front pages; in such circumstances religious considerations could be fudged and put aside.

Now, of course, visiting these zealots I had a lot of things going for me. I was brown and Muslim, two qualities which in the circumstances worked in my favour. Perhaps, if I was taken as a hostage, I might not be as marketable as say a white journalist in an orange suit. I might not fetch as much in terms of a ransom, and there might even be a risk that no one would believe me to be a hostage. I can just see the Jihadis debating my fate saying: 'what they think he is one of us?! But he is *nothing* like us.' All that was needed was for the Press to lump me in with your bog standard Jihadi and I'd face the Mesut Özil ordeal: the dreaded multiple identity predicament where I had to *prove* that I wasn't like 'them', that I loved the Queen and her damn corgis. I can just see that tweed screwing up his face and inspecting my dirty straggly beard going 'hmm, is he really a journalist, dear? He certainly doesn't look like one to me'. How am I meant to look?

I have languished in prison, the beard has grown beyond hipster length, my hair is flea ridden; at best I could pass for a Salafi-Jihadi Count of Monte Christo; at worst Abu Bakr al-Baghdadi's cousin. Even if I declared my love for Queen and country I would still confirm every single prejudice of the Tweed, 'well you never know, does he drink wine? No Chardonnay? Oh dear.. oh dear...' This might just be a feeling, I don't know why, but I just feel that the money wouldn't be as forthcoming. I'm not saying the media is racist, I have a load of journalist friends but those who know, *know!* But then again the creative amongst the Salafi-Jihadis might just think that all of us are scum and might propose that I appear as an extra in their latest release: 'The Spy who got blown up in the Cold'. They will find a macabre yet creative way to send me away to my Maker. So you have to be careful and take your precautions when you go to meet Salafi-Jihadis.

So I made sure I catered for their peculiarities, as I scrambled across the border, I stopped smoking. I had stopped smoking from the age of fifteen and had given up frequently. Sometimes I stopped for years and then when the feeling betook me, usually when I was in the Middle East, when cigarettes were dirt cheap, the food was good, coffee was bitter and the sun was out I would just grab one from a friend and soon enough I'd be finishing off a pack of ten by late afternoon. But whilst I usually agonised about giving the cigs up which I inevitably did, filming this group of fighting Jihadis gave me just that added incentive to stop immediately in case some of them didn't like my terrible habit. I just didn't want their 'sincere' advice to turn into something else where they saw me as a brazen sinner contravening the laws of God and I found myself walking round London without the ability to stick two fingers up at a white man van. Salafi-Jihadis are an unpredictable lot. Thankfully, apart from the odd cigar, I have remained a non-smoker. Curiously, thanks to my experience with Salafi-Jihadis my belief in the existence of God has also been strengthened.

Prior to my visit I was messaging one of these Jihadis and he condemned me for not fulfilling my individual obligation to fight jihad. I tried to explain that I was a journalist, journalists don't fight. But this particular fighter who had a world vision directly proportional to his educational career which ended at the age of fourteen, threatened to kill me for offering such an excuse. His reasoning ran thus: By not fighting I had become an apostate and thus my blood was legitimate to slay. Or perhaps he was just angry suffering from Post-Traumatic Stress Disorder like many fighting men do. Men shouldn't spend too long a time fighting, it makes them unbearably hard.

But Providence had contrived that I should bump into that self-same Salafi-Jihadi who had threatened me on that very trip into Idlib province. And as I got off the motorcycle in the market thinking that my worst nightmare was coming true, there he was standing smiling at me warmly, his large frame hugged me and asked me for forgiveness for threatening to kill me. I hugged him so hard as if I was hanging on to dear life and I forgave him totally. Only God could have contrived such a thing and so my faith in God was strengthened. Now, of course I should add a caveat, the men I covered were by no means mere Jihadi zealots, there were all sorts of fighting men. The good, the bad and the ugly. And it struck me that they represented various aspects of the future of Jihadism especially relevant to countries that are faced with the Jihadi conundrum whether in Syria, Tunisia or Nigeria.

Ostensibly, there are three types of fighting Jihadi and I will cover each in turn. The pop-Jihadi who can easily be dealt with by the current security apparatuses. Then there are the Committed Jihadi and the Master Jihadi, those two are going to be far harder to deal with.

Some of these fighting men, the foreign ones at least, struck me as following the standard pop-Jihadi trope. They espoused the language of the Jihadism born from Afghanistan, their English accents had become tinged with Arabic. They, to my amazement, even used 'thus' and 'narrated' and so forth in daily life thinking that this made them more intellectual. But I want to be fair, these pop-Jihadis were not devoid of sincerity but they struck me as vacuous souls, predictable, unaware of who they were, and caricatures of who they wanted to be. They thought themselves to be lions when in actual fact they were just about everything in between; some were serious, some were comic, some were thugs, some were absolute gents and some were indeed as courageous as lions when the fight kicked off. I suspect they were the same sort of men you might find in the British Army and could be made to do anything providing they had the right military officer. If they had a good officer all was well, a bad one could spell a Mai Lai massacre. They were the sort of men who had killed and then nonchalantly said that the men they had killed were *murtadd* (apostates) so it was fine to shed their blood, and they didn't lose any sleep over it. Whenever an organised military force push, it is these types that disappear into the ether, they will hide in the nooks and crannies of Turkey or Chad whiling away their time. And then when the coast is clear they return to their home countries grizzled and weary telling the intelligence officers at the border that they had been on holiday in Dubai and think nothing of their experience. Except perhaps years later, when they comprehend the enormity of what they have done and they have to live with the consequences of their actions. You hope then, that Dostoyevsky's idea will ring true: that living with the crime is bigger than the punishment, for many pop-Jihadis will get away with murder.

There were other fighting men of course, the committed Jihadis, they were slightly older; Brits and Europeans who loathed social media, they wanted to protect the sincerity of their actions by not announcing them to the world. They appeared moved by the religious impulse and knew that their religious devotion should not be corrupted by bombast and showing off. They maintained that they fought only for God, not a political ideology, and it was paramount that these ideals be kept secret to protect their pristineness. These men intrigued me. They wanted to fulfil an obligation that they believed was incumbent on them. I met two Indians from Bangalore – an engineer and an accountant. Both men struck me as deeply pained by what was occurring in the Muslim community. But the question was how were they to express their wish to serve the Muslim community? They talked about how think tanks and the media, not wholly incorrect I should add, did not bat an eyelid as Jewish young men and women fulfilled their desire to serve their community in Israel but Muslim men were labelled otherwise.

But Jews had a state, they had an army with a semblance of military discipline, these Muslim men did not. They seemed trapped by modernity that invalidated their desire to 'serve' if you will, and also trapped by their traditions and stories, which espoused coming to the aid of their fellow Muslims. This theme was constant; the thread runs in Netflix and in Muslim salvation history. The hugely popular Turkish drama series Ertugrül is based on the historic founder of the Ottomans who came to the aid of the Seljuks against Byzantine incursions. Muslim Facebookers post the example of the Abbasid Caliph Mu'tasim Billah who, according to legend, went to the aid of a captured Muslim woman. Muslims swim in the history of this obligation and there is an immense guilt felt by the devout for their impotence and emasculation. Muslims have never seen themselves as a people who turn the other cheek after all, historically they were a fighting peoples, of empire, of power, culture and civilisation. Take the example of the polymath and West African scholar, Sheikh Uthman Dan Fodio who declared himself the leader of the faithful and established the Sokoto caliphate in the nineteenth century when the powers that be prevented Muslim religious devotions from being practised. The caliphate lasted till 1903 with the arrival of the British. These are powerful examples for Muslim youth.

But what about now? Exactly how should and can this impulse of Muslim young men be manifested in this day and age? In the past young men could go off to a Ribat, Sufi frontier fortress or if one lived in the Ottoman period join the Bekhtashi order with its close connection to the Ottoman army, to fight and worship at the same time. But the world is no longer a world of empires. There isn't a Muslim foreign legion, nor is there a caliphate. Nation states have been carved out of the Muslim world. Geopolitics and Western countries have already made it clear that the prospect of a resurgent Islamic State is a frightful prospect, and yet, there are still Muslims bleeding. And so the argument from current Muslim ideologues runs thus: this wouldn't happen if we had a Muslim state, if we had our own government, if we had our own army, if we applied our own laws, if we did all this God would give us victory and succour. And the young quite naturally reply: 'how do we achieve that?' And they reply: 'through blood, the rose isn't got except by putting one's hand on the thorns.' So how are young Muslim men to express this sentiment? The young see Western armies in the countries of their fathers. Facebook posts and rants are extremely unsatisfying; and so young Muslim men grapple with this conundrum. And as long as this question isn't resolved amongst Muslims they will not be at peace, and the language of Awlaki and Bin Laden will pull in Muslims from all over the world now that Pandora's box has been finally prized apart. It seems that the only language available to the young is the Jihadi militancy of al-Qaeda since any other sort of protest isn't validated nor understood.

This sentiment of young Muslims or *geist* if you will, cannot be combated with platitudes, ill thought out deradicalisation programmes and naff websites set up to combat social media. What many of these well-intentioned leaders and Imams don't realise, and I have seen this with my own eyes, is that radical preachers like British Islamist, Anjem Choudhury, and Yamani militant, Abu Baraa, have a constituency. They hit a nerve and are watched by some of these Jihadis in the heart of Syria rather than those they deem to be 'scholars for dollars' despite the vast difference in learning. There is a dissonance between the young and the imams. Anjem Choudhury is not religiously trained, he's a solicitor. Abu Hamza al-Masri is self-taught but when the no doubt erudite

Azhari sheikhs such as Ali Gomaa seemingly support Sisi's killing of innocents followed up by Habib Ali Jifri's support for his teacher, one cannot help but understand their predicament and anger. Religion is being used to keep the young tame and docile. Same goes for the late Ramadan Buti, the 'Shaykh of the Lavant', and indeed Sheikh Bin Bayyah, the Mauritanian professor of Islamic Studies, and his American student Sheikh Hamza Yusuf Hanson, who have adopted a Burkean position of being against revolution preferring the stability of authoritarian monarchies but to seemingly support a kingdom such as the United Arab Emirates seen by many as actively subverting the aspirations of millions of Arabs and Muslims for their own political ends, one can see why these young men will continue to fight. The issue is not that scholars can't work with the state, one of the Hanafi legal school's major jurists Abu Yusuf is celebrated for it, but when scholars don't act as their flock's lightning rod, or do not convey their sentiments to power, or are not sufficiently independent enough, the matter becomes hopeless and young men being young men, look for other avenues. When Father Gapon was killed, young Russian men and women looked for other avenues. Currently, surveying the Muslim world, Muslims are bleeding all over the globe. My Facebook feed is filled with images of Hindus killing a Muslim for the sake of two cows, an eight year old Asifa Bano getting raped, horrific images of Rohingya, innocent Mali Fula villagers killed in cold blood by hunters on the premise of anti-terror operations, not to mention Syria and Palestine - these news feeds have a profound impact on the soul of anyone who calls himself human, it affects even a cynical grown man like myself, what then of the young ones? So you see these men are going to be the grist for the mill. These men will stay on and hide in the nooks and crannies too but they won't return to their home countries. They will weather the storm and wait for that man who can organise them effectively.

And amongst these men is the Master Jihadi, for he holds the key to organising them. I have not met many like that but the one I found, quite by chance, in the guesthouse where I was staying in Idlib province. Abu Muslim was altogether a different sort of Jihadi: an everyman. In contrast, pop-Jihadis took pictures of themselves, sported all the paraphernalia of war, posted it on Instagram and fooled themselves into thinking that this was proselytising Islam. When in all reality, their hearts skipped a beat every time some follower 'liked' something they posted, Abu Muslim was nothing like that. I only met two people like him, one was a senior al-Qaeda figure, who

I didn't even want to shake hands with in case some drone decided to release its weaponry and obliterate me and the other was Abu Muslim. Abu Muslim, that is what he called himself, was different precisely because he was so ordinary. The Levantine Arab you saw standing next to you when you caught a *servis* or greeted you in the cafe. You'd pay him little regard unless he asked you for directions. The only distinguishing feature was his generous beard and hair that gave clues to his religious affiliation, otherwise he wore a T-shirt, track suit bottoms, sandals, a sun-bleached cap and a pair of glasses perched on his nose. Your paths would probably never cross. He could have been an agricultural worker from Homs or a tailor in Cairo, but it was the glasses I suppose, that gave him that engineering mien. I saw him riding pillion criss-crossing the town going from one place to another always on the move meeting important men. That's all he did all day.

And though he was never the Emir of the guesthouse I stayed in, there seemed to be an unspoken consensus that he was indeed its undisputed Emir. His suggestions seemed to be carried out. His men too didn't have that typical characteristic Jihadi look, none of those things were displayed on his closest followers. Two of them were beardless with open faces, they wore jeans, t-shirts, had their hand guns stashed discretely in the back or just slung lazily on the coat hooks when they weren't outside. They played with the cats, talked about such and such but generally they were as obscure as you could possibly think. If they sat in a minivan going through a checkpoint, the guard would probably let them pass thinking they were local barbers or worked in the market. I don't know if that was the reason they sported that look but they certainly embodied it. They were curious men, friendly and often asked me what the world outside looked like.

Whenever Abu Muslim came in to the guesthouse I saw how they got up, not because he was an Emir, but because he was their older brother and they just made sure that he was okay. And he did the same. When he saw signs of tiredness in me and in the men, Abu Muslim reached for the lemons growing in the garden, grabbed some ice from the fridge, squeezed the lemons, crushed them, added sugar and made us a drink reminiscent of a virgin mojito. Whilst I knew something of the other men, he seemed very illusive. I only caught his story from snatched snippets of conversations at the end of the day when I was putting my equipment away. He had kids tucked away somewhere safe. He moved unhindered or seamlessly through the Levant as if borders weren't even an issue. He had a technical background. When the guest house had a visitor or two, these brothers sat in a circle exchanging stories that only fighting men shared, but ultimately it was him they had come to visit. I got an idea of his importance when a visitor, a young fellow with a short beard, came in, shook hands and joined his two companions in the verandah waiting for him. He was like all of Abu Muslim's men, Palestinian. The three men were soon joined by a Maldivian fighter, the visitor asked about one of his countrymen he had fought alongside a long time back. The Maldivian Jihadi informed him that he had had been martyred. The visitor smiled, sighed and said he was brave in a short statement that served as a eulogy. Silence. Death had intangibly brought them closer. The other two men recalled some other events and it became apparent that each man was a seasoned fighter. I was told much later that the visitor had been close to Abu Muhammed al-Jolani, commander of the Syrian militant group Tahrir al-Sham, perceived as some sort of legendary figure by the men, and I guessed that perhaps the Palestinian had some business with Abu Muslim, and he did.

On one of the days I was working I realised that my GoPro was missing. There was a suspicious voice within that convinced me that maybe one of the men I was sharing the room with had stolen it. GoPros are expensive and moreover, very useful for filming combat footage for propaganda films. Of course I didn't express those sentiments openly but I did ask if anyone had seen the camera. Abu Muslim just said it was impossible that it could be taken. It was as if he guaranteed it. He insisted that I take my backpack apart, that it would be there, somewhere in my bag. He was absolutely certain that the GoPro was there, he believed in the integrity of his men. He was right, late in the evening when I did unpack everything I found the camera exactly where it was. I felt ashamed of thinking so badly of my hosts.

In the evening Abu Muslim served us some *Kebse* a Levantine rice biryani type dish. He brought it out from the dark kitchen and put the large round dish on the verandah where all of us sat down together to eat. I could only liken him to a doting mother, *not* a father. I heard the creaking sound of the iron gate open and one of the Palestinians brought over two cooked chickens that had been steam cooked so that their flesh were succulent and fell off the bones. Abu Muslim invited us to eat but felt that I was too shy with the food, he chucked in bits of chicken to my side of the large steel dish as all the men sat round eating the food chatting. It was crude but exactly how I would have expected him to behave. After the meal they prepared some tea and I saw Abu Muslim relaxing and that's when I asked him what his story was.

Surprisingly Abu Muslim was not shy in telling me that he was a master bomber. Of course I couldn't confirm his story, but according to Reuters, in March 2012, Damascus experienced two car bombs that killed twenty seven and injured a hundred. The cars had targeted the headquarters of the Syrian Airforce intelligence services and the Criminal Police Headquarters. Syria had fifteen such spy agencies competing with each other to make them supremely effective and brutal. They had been responsible for killings on an industrial scale. Abu Muslim had succeeded in destroying them both. The Syrian regime held al-Qaeda affiliated Jabhat al-Nusra responsible for the actions but it was Abu Muslim and his boys that did it.

'For three years I was the most wanted man in Syria', he told me satisfied as if it was a badge of honour. I didn't know how to feel about the bombings. On one hand revulsion twenty seven people had been killed and a hundred people had been injured. They could have been officers or they could have been innocent bystanders, all of them irrespective of their sectarian affiliations, would be leaving behind loved ones. On the other hand, I had spent a day inside the very intelligence headquarters that he had blown up. Syrians said that those who go in never came out and they considered my return a miracle. But I am Swedish and so the rules are very different for me. Nevertheless, they had hounded me for six months and changed me into a different person, due to their constant surveillance, harassment and spying in Damascus. I can live in a police state but I also know when a man hasn't lived in one when he belittles the freedoms we have in London. In Fara' Filistine they had presented me with a thick file asking me where I had been on such and such place, what my post-graduate research was all about and so on. I saw intelligence officers masquerading as Salafis complete in their *kufi* and *thobe*, and I heard the screams and shouts down the corridor whilst I was served tea and cigarettes having genteel conversations with my interrogator. Everyone knew that the Assad regime was a real police state worthy of an Arthur Koestler novel. Some of my friends had disappeared during my stay in Damascus. So I certainly understood why it was blown up.

Abu Muslim told me that the whole project had been a partial success. He had planned to launch various simulated attacks in the Golan and Lebanon to provoke an Israeli response and attempt to start a regional war.

When the Syrian state would fail to respond to Israeli aggression it would show the Muslim world what Syria really was: a sham and the people would rise up and overthrow it. I didn't know what to think of Abu Muslim, was he a demented megalomaniac or was there something of the 20th century revolutionary in him?

Abu Muslim was a son of history and geopolitics. He hadn't learnt his bomb-making skills from al-Qaeda but from his older brothers who were Salafi-Jihadis fighting the Israelis. He had been fighting Israelis in his mother's milk, he didn't know anything else. Had he been born earlier maybe he would be learning his trade with the leftists and the Abu Nidals of this world but it so happened that his older brothers were Salafi-Jihadists. The Abu Muslim would never go away.

When the Syrian uprisings broke out, Abu Muslim went to Syria like Castro's Cubans did to Angola, and offered his services. There seemed to be cross-pollination of sorts between his aims and al-Qaeda, and maybe he had become al-Qaeda or perhaps parts of al-Qaeda had become a little like him. I couldn't quite figure out where exactly that convergence had occurred, but at the same time what exactly was he and what did he represent?

Here was a man whose rage against the Israelis could be understood by all, but he was from the Western perspective at least, on the wrong side of the fight, acceptable only if he renounced political violence against the Israelis. But for Muslims, Abu Muslim is not a wholly unsympathetic character, he has some sort of constituency if you will, especially in the Middle East. And so he presents himself as a conundrum for Muslims, was he, Abu Muslim, an expression of modern Jihad? The future of asymmetric warfare? Or was he none of those things? An aberration? The Martial tradition within Islam would always exist but was Abu Muslim an expression of just that? Or was he doing something that many of us would do if we were put in those circumstances?

Had Abu Muslim been a classic pop-Jihadi, al-Qaeda type figure with all his zealotry, Abu Muslim would present himself as less of a question. But in the following days when Islamic State released their latest video, the whole town went crazy trying to buy enough data to be able to download it and watch it. It was like a movie release or some Fortnite update. One of the men in the guest- house obtained the gigabytes and now all the men sat around the laptop watching the film. It was a surreal experience. Whilst the pop-Jihadis sat round memorising its nasheeds (devotional songs) and played the film over and over again like some demented psychos watching it with an immature glee, Abu Muslim watched it like a political scientist. After the film, I asked him what he thought of the Islamic State. He said that they had an admirable project, that only they had a vision to build a state. That, to his mind, was a good thing. He believed that Muslims needed a state to take them out of their humiliated position. Muslims needed to determine their own destinies, all of that had echoes of anti-colonial rhetoric not jihad.

'What will you do if they start fighting other Muslims?' I asked, 'then I will put my guns down and stop fighting. I didn't come here to kill my fellow Muslims.' Yet again here was the Abu Muslim conundrum: he was a crypto-Islamic State supporter, not affiliated to them, not bent on global Jihad, not bent on fighting other fellow Muslims and yet the man justified the bombing of two intelligence headquarters knowing full well that there would be civilian casualties with Muslims amongst them.

Now that the Islamic State is on its last legs, one would expect that it is the end game for the likes of Abu Muslim. But the Islamic State might be a flash in the pan yet the Jihadis have shown the Muslim world that colonial borders are not fixed. I suspect that there will be many men like Abu Muslim dreaming of the Hummers breaking the Sykes-Picot border and laying low in nearby countries waiting and planning to give an expression to their political ambitions that cannot be expressed in the current geo-political climate or the Salafi-Jihadi project. It will be these men who will no doubt cause the future problems for the power-brokers of the region. I suspect the bombings in Suweida in July 2018 which led to the loss of 200 souls too had someone like Abu Muslim as its planner. Men like Abu Muslim have the expertise, the grievance and a degree of sympathy from a population who knows the dungeons of Middle Eastern dictators that will enable the likes of him to survive. The pop-Jihadi will disappear into the ether but men like Abu Muslim and his followers will remain in the Middle East, North Africa and indeed West Africa and will continue to plague the Muslim world and the West for many years to come.

FOLDS OF A GARMENT

Abubakar Adam Ibrahim

1. Inani

The sun kissed her lips as she lay in bed, infusing her with a translucent warmth. Squinting, Inani drew the curtains, speckled with yellow flowers, shutting out the sunbeams. Her feet recoiled at the touch of the tiles. Cold. The bedside clock said she had thirty minutes before her lecture so she braced herself, stiffening her muscles, and pressed her soles against the floor. The tiles were tanned, almost like her complexion. The warmth in her body prevailed.

In the mirror, a stranger looked back. Swarthy face and dishevelled hair, rebellious strands of which stood on end, the roots frayed. Regret, a slothful inky cloud, drifted like wind-borne shadows into her mind. If she hadn't gone out to watch the match the night before, Balaraba, her next-door neighbor, would have braided her hair for her. By the time she had got back, bearing the handed-down sweat of the men from the viewing centre, and glum over a Chelsea defeat, Balaraba had gone out to a study date with her boyfriend, condemning Inani's clump of hair to another night of wilderness.

Over the song of her shower, the shrill angry ring of her phone persisted. She knew it had to be her mother. Only she called like that, never taking a breather between rings, as if her finger hovered over the dial button, redialling with the same impatience with which she had lived most of her life, the same impatience that had caused an end to her marriage.

Inani learnt the story later, when she was fifteen, thirteen years after her father, who loved tossing her in the air, became a shadow that drifted in with the seasons for fleeting hours to see her. A father she sometimes spent the holidays with, when her mother, Ina, allowed. For most of her life, she did not understand why there was a new woman in their lives, why she could not live with her father and had to live with Ina who swung between depths of hysteria and despair with the consistency of a pendulum. Ina had thought her husband was sleeping with another woman and threw him out, no questions asked. By the time she gave him the chance to explain, three years had passed and his new wife was pregnant.

Inani almost slipped rushing out of the shower to take the call, irritated now by the ringtone and exasperated by Ina before she even spoke to her. The usual litany of questions followed. Inani mouthed them as her mother reeled them out: Have you eaten? Did you sleep well? How was your night?

The last one she hated the most. But she said *alhamdulillah*, as she had been taught to say.

She did not remember quite how the conversation segued into Ina's *akara* business – she had a class to prepare for – but when her mother mentioned an injury, a finger that took the knife while chopping onions, Inani's mind stilled.

'It's all bloated and it hurts like hell,' Ina said.

'Has it been attended to?'

'Yes, I went to the pharmacy. They cleaned and put some iodine on it. But it's really swollen, I can hardly work.'

Inani heard, beyond her mother's words, the habitual call for rescue Ina embedded in most conversations. By the time she put down the phone, Inani sat on the bed, breathing deeply, feeling the weight of her mother's expectations on her shoulders.

When her father left, or was made to leave, she became all her mother had. She did not know when distraction turned to hope but she knew when it became obvious, when she had got admission and Ina had started sending coded messages, of her hopes that Inani would graduate, build them a cosy flat with a porch and potted flowers hanging on the walls where they would live happily ever after. In every phone call since, this message had been emphasised – in every complaint of an aching back, a sliced finger or fatigue. Inani wanted to make her mother happy — would love to because she loved Ina. She just did not like how every call sounded like an SOS.

Fifteen minutes to lecture time, ten of which she would use to walk to the hall. She opened her wardrobe and sighed. Her figure-hugging gown stood alone on the rack. She would have laundered her clothes if she hadn't gone to watch that damned match. Grumbling, she slipped on the gown. It was the colour of happy skies, and accentuated her curves. With a touch of eyeliner, a dash of lipstick, she wrapped a white turban around her hair, as she had always done, and slipped on her backpack.

Now she had seven minutes for a ten minute walk.

Locking her door, she felt a furry softness wrapping itself around her feet.

'Tinkerbell,' she said.

The cat meowed in response, looking up at her.

'You sneaky thing.' She bent down and patted the grey fur. As she had done in the last three days, since the cat first turned up at her door, straggly and hungry, she went in to fetch some of her leftover food. It had inched closer and gulped it down. The second day, she saved it some food and gave it a name. By the third day, it was the farthest thing from her mind. She unlocked the door and fetched the food, leaned over and scraped the yam porridge onto a piece of serviette. If this went on, she would have to find it a plate to eat from. She felt the pressure first, tight gown straining against her body, then she heard the rip as the seams violently came undone.

'Ya Salam!' She looked around her and saw a gash, the length of her finger, running down her hip, revealing her nude-coloured chemise. Five minutes to eight. In her room, there was one piece of wrapper, the black blouse she had worn the day before, which smelled of sweat that wasn't hers, and a pair of jeans badly in need of laundering. On the door of the wardrobe, there was a long black hijab she used for prayers. Reaching for it, she threw it over her head. It unfurled over her body, falling down to her feet. She had never gone to school like that but it would have to do. At the door, she stopped and poured some water for the cat before hurrying off to school.

2. Balemi

Hara Balemi removed his glasses and rubbed his eyes. He knew they would be bleary, he could tell by the itch he felt in the corners. They told stories, his eyes, of the rare times he drank. Red was the colour stories of his night were always written in, the red in his eyes. His hangover eyes, his wife, Kubra, used to tease. But when she, standing behind him, touched his shoulders, it wasn't in the manner she had done to rouse him from a drunken slumber. It was in compassion. He reached out and squeezed hers.

'Do you want to cancel the lecture today?' she asked. 'I'm sure they will understand.'

He shook his head. 'What will be the use of it?' he asked. 'It won't change anything.'

She leaned in and kissed his balding head, pressing her bosom against his shoulders. He closed his eyes and savoured home, savoured her. In the fifteen years they had been married she had woven, with the diligence of a bird, a home for him in her heart. She had collected his dreams and hers and interlaced them into this nest.

The previous night, his mother in Gwoza had called.

'Pray for us,' she had said, her voice sounding like heartbreak. 'Pray for us.'

And the line had gone dead.

He called back but the phone rang out a few times. When he reached his brother, in the thirty seconds they spoke over sounds of gunshots, he learnt that Boko Haram was attacking Gwoza.

That was seventeen hours before.

Balemi hadn't been a firm believer in God but he kept a vigil that night, crossing himself, praying, as his mother had asked, and scouring for information. On social media he learnt details of the attacks on his village, and could picture the turbaned terrorists swarming down the hills he had played on as a child, shooting men whose names and stories he knew, taking women from whose pots he had eaten when he visited. With his village ripped to bits, the home Kubra had built for him in her heart felt ever more treasured. She too knew what it felt like to lose someone to Boko Haram. He too had held her, just as she was holding him now, when a woman with a vest strapped under her hijab had detonated it at the

Maiduguri market where her father had a spice shop. They didn't find all the pieces of him to bury.

'Cancel this lecture,' Kubra said again.

'I am losing my mind sitting here waiting for news.' Being so far from home made it worse, filled him with a sense of impotence. It would take him the whole day to travel to Gwoza, if it were even possible to access it, to rescue his family. 'Best if I go to class.'

'They will be safe, in Jesus' name,' she said. 'God will protect them.'

Amen rolled off his tongue and deposited itself in the middle of the room like deformed hope.

Standing before his students, sometimes he chased the train of his thought running around in his head. Sometimes he imagined images of his mother, taking refuge in a ditch, as he had been told by his brother. Or the images he had of Kubra's father when he had gone to identify the corpse. He shook his head, crossed himself and turned to write on the board just as a girl in a long, flowing hijab hurried into the class. He followed her with his eyes as she went up and down and aisle, looking for a seat. He had never seen her before, had he? The other students too turned to look at her, as if she were a stranger. She found a vacant seat in the middle row and sat down almost in the middle of the hall.

He breathed and resumed his lecture.

But she moved again, fiddling with something underneath her hijab. She stopped when she saw that he was looking at her.

By the time he started teaching, she had her head tucked under the desk so that only the gentle curve of her back was visible to him. He stopped, his heart racing. When her head came up, he half-expected her to jump up and shout something maniacal, for a flash of fire to rock the hall. But she slapped a notebook on the desk and bent down again, only to resurface with her pen.

Again Balemi continued.

Minutes later, his heart jumped when she started gathering her hijab around her. There had been suicide bombings in Maiduguri, on the campuses. Girls like her, in hijabs like hers.

'You, in black,' he said, deepening his voice, 'you there, stand up.'

She pointed at herself, eyebrows raised. Balemi nodded.

'Are you a student here?'

'Me, sir?'

'Yes.'

'Yes, sir.'

'What's your name?'

'Inani sir. Inani Lawal.'

'Imani?'

'Inani, sir.'

He seemed to contemplate the name. 'I have never seen you in my class before.'

'Me, sir? I have never missed your class.'

He considered her sceptically. 'Whatever, could you please just leave the class?'

'What?'

'Leave the class.'

'Why, sir?'

'I am not comfortable with you here.'

'I don't understand.'

'I am just not comfortable with you in my class. You are very . . . distracting.'

Inani gaped. 'Distracting, sir? Me?' She looked down at herself and then turned an incredulous eye to the class as if they could help explain it to her.

'Please leave the class,' he said again. 'Now.'

'May I know why, sir?'

'I don't have all day to explain the nature of the discomfort you cause me, and I am sure a good number of my students as well. So please, leave the class.'

Inani started gathering her books.

'And don't ever come back to my class . . . like that,' Balemi said turning back to the board.

Inani stopped gathering her books, the seconds in which she stood still resounded with silence. She wiped the tears from her face. 'Is this because of the way I am dressed, sir?'

Balemi started wiping what he had only just written on the board. He wasn't sure why. Behind him, there was a murmur. Students hurried to scribble what he had noted on the board.

He turned and saw Inani standing, arms folded across her chest.

'What are you still doing here?' he asked.

'Waiting for an explanation, sir?'

A trail of murmurs rose and fell.

'You will get none. Leave. Now.'

'Sir, with due respect, I have paid my tuition. I am a bona fide student of this school, this department. To the best of my knowledge I have not done anything to warrant being treated like this. I shall not leave without some explanation.'

Balemi leaned on the rostrum. Before him, there was an annoying, scary girl and the mystery beneath her hijab. In his eyes, there was the irritating itch. He did not know what to do with both.

3. Hajara

That morning, when Hajara saw Inani walking into the lecture hall, she did not recognise her at first. In the little over a year since she had known her, she could count the number of times, she had seen Inani in a hijab – the few times she had gone to the school mosque to pray and had borrowed one of the hijabs kept in the women section.

Two things had made her take notice of Inani when they were first ushered into the university gates as undergrads. Inani's blue turban, like a female version of a bottled genie, and her tired smile as she spoke to another girl in the queue. What Hajara read in her smile then was a fragility and that drew her to Inani. She was beautiful but someone needed to tell her that as a Muslim girl, she ought to at least wear a long dress over her jeans, not a t-shirt that read 'Eff It.' When they met at the department and Hajara had smiled at her, intent on passing on her message, Inani, leaning against the wall like a propped scarecrow, smiled and offered her space in the queue to Hajara.

But the ground for friendship wasn't that deep since Hajara was particular about the kind of friends she kept, especially since she hoped to be the Muslim Students' Amira. Inani wasn't keen on covering up, like a good Muslim girl, and outside their studies, their interests were as different as Lagos and Abuja.

'What kind of good Muslim girl goes to football viewing centres full of uproarious men, and debates Messi and Ronaldo instead of the caliphs?' Hajara had told her friends. 'But then again, one shouldn't expect too much from those tribal Muslims.'

She did not care that this was reported to Inani; she knew she had spoken her truth.

But still, they smiled at each other, and only talked when Hajara saw Inani at the mosque in borrowed hijab.

'Sister Inani, good to see you,' she had said. 'Come to the mosque more often.'

'I will,' Inani smiled.

The next time they met at the mosque, two weeks later, Inani had finished her prayers and was hurrying out just as Hajara had entered. There was only time for a smile and a *salam*. So when Hajara had seen a long flowing hijab with the face of a girl drifting into the lecture hall, her curiosity was piqued, until she realised it was only Inani.

And all this fuss Dr Balemi was making – his expression an illegitimate child of rage and fear – over Inani's hijab. He seemed uncertain what to do while Inani stood, arms folded underneath the generous folds of her hijab with her back to Hajara, who sat behind her.

'The way I see it,' Dr Balemi said, 'one of two things is going to happen. This person is going to leave this class or I will.'

Inani did not move.

Hajara brought up her camera, and with a few clicks photographed the scene before her.

Balemi nodded. 'If I leave this class, I assure you, I will not be coming back. Ever,' he said, addressing the class. 'You can ask her for your grades at the end of the semester.'

A groundswell of murmurs. A girl sitting next to Inani reached out and touched her hand, transferring compassion. Another, some distance away, said in a loud enough voice for the class to hear, 'Inani, please go nah. Please go, I did not come here to carryover this course.'

It was Rebecca, the belligerent girl Hajara had never liked.

'Because she wore a hijab to class?' Hajara countered.

Balemi stood still as the class erupted.

Hajara typed a message on her phone and sent it out. Then she typed a post on her social media profile, tagged the Muslim Students Society profile page and uploaded the photo she had taken. She pushed the post button and watched the upload line inch towards the other end of the screen.

4. Balemi

So much noise now, like the buzz of angry bees. Balemi's eyes were itching so badly he removed his glasses and rubbed them with the back of his wrist. The students were now banging on the table. In his heart, a pool of uncertainty collected, in the middle of which was an island of certainty — that he had made a mistake in the first place. He realised this as soon as the girl stood her ground, but that very act had condemned him to only one course of action. In the seventeen years he had been teaching in the university, he knew that defiance was only tackled by authority. Something about her restlessness unsettled him, stroking the beast of his fear. His students could sense it. Having asked her to leave the class, he had to see it through. The girl was still standing, calm amidst the uproar around her, arms folded. Something had to give her that confidence. Perhaps something concealed beneath the folds of her garment.

Kubra was right. He should have stayed home. He gathered his sheaf of papers, tapped the edges on the rostrum, closed his laptop and shoved it into his bag. He headed for the door, and walked out, a storm of appeals from the students falling at his feet like leaves of a wind-blown tree. The storm would die. The students would come and plead with him. He would give them conditions and the lessons would continue someday. All would be well with the world.

5. Inani

She started crying when Henry, one of the students, spat at her. He would have hit her if someone hadn't intervened when he charged at her. She knew Henry. She knew that he was the first person in his family to make it to university. She closed her eyes and imagined the six badges of hope pinned on his chest, one from each of his siblings. His frustrations she could relate to. In her mind, her mother's daily call for rescue echoed, her own dreams wilted. This was no country to mess with your lecturers.

As the noise swirled around her, and Henry's spit slid down her hijab, tears streamed from Inani's eyes. She took her bag and walked out, the heckling and cheers piercing her in equal measure as she went. She wanted to shut out the noise in her mind and her head.

At home she ripped the hijab off her head, derived some pleasure from the lock on the door turning and sat on the bed. Each teardrop ferried fragments of her hopes as they ran down her face.

Her phone rang. Tired of ignoring it, she got up and turned it off. Her face in the mirror, looked pale, a washed out dream. What would she tell her mother when she called? What would she tell the other students if Dr Balemi stuck to his words?

She opened her lowest drawer and stared at the white bottle of pesticide she had bought for the undesirables that had once plagued her kitchen. It spoke to her, this bottle, drawing her to it. Just a gulp, and everything, all of this, would be gone. She wouldn't have to explain anything to anyone. Gently, she pushed the drawer close. Curling up on the bed, her eyes travelled back in the direction of the drawer.

She was going to fail Balemi's course now, she knew. And Balemi would report her to their coven of lecturers. The years ahead would be tough, just because she ripped a dress in the morning. Thoughts and time flowed through her. She dissolved into them, a ghostly entity at their mercy.

Knocks on the door woke her from a light sleep. It was 5pm in the evening, her clock said. If she stayed really still, held her breath, whoever was at the door would get tired and leave. But the person thumped the panel with the persistence of her mother and soon Inani feared she would be left to find someone to fix it, if she didn't rescue it from the fist of whoever was out there.

'Salamu alaikum,' Hajara said as soon as Inani opened the door, breezing in. 'Why are you locked up in your room?'

'I just needed to be alone.'

'We have been trying to reach you on phone.'

'Who is we?'

'You have no idea what has been happening, do you?'

'No. What has?'

Hajara reached into her bag and handed Inani some papers. They were posters, with a photo of the class that morning. It took her a while to realise she was the person in black hijab standing in the middle of the class. The other posters had only texts.

For Our Security, We Need to be Open!
Stop Terrorism!
We Need to be Safe on Campus!
Security of Lives over Religious Sentiments!
Students' lives matter!

'What's this?' Inani asked.

'These were pasted on campus, a few hours ago,'Hajara said. 'They are also being sent out on WhatsApp and Insta. We are collecting them as evidence.'

'By whom?'

'Who else? Enemies of the hijab, of course.'

Inani sat down and held her head.

'We are not lying down and taking it like that. We are countering. We have lodged a formal complaint with the school authorities and as I speak, even the Sultan has heard about this case. We cannot allow sisters to be intimidated.'

'Who is we?'

'We. The Muslim students of course. You are trending, Inani. I can't believe you don't know what you have started by standing. I cannot tell you how proud we are. We have been trying to reach you. We need you to make an official complaint.'

'What? I don't want any trouble. I just want to attend lectures and . . .'

'Wake up, Inani. Lectures have been suspended. The school authorities need you to make a statement. Come on, dress up. A team of the MSS is waiting. There is a lawyer on ground. We are all waiting for you. You are not in this alone.'

Hajara crossed the room and fetched Inani's hijab which she threw at her.

'Here, wear your hijab. You can now not be seen without one.'

On reflex, Inani caught the garment. She had the weight of the world in her hand.

'No,' she said.

'What?'

'I said no. I am not going anywhere with you.'

'What are you saying?'

'I want you to leave. What does it matter if I am called a terrorist because I wore a hijab to class?'

'Don't be silly, Inani? This is about all of us?'

'Is it? What does a tribal Muslim girl know anyway?' Inani said, watching the horror crawl into Hajara's face. 'If you don't mind, I would like you to leave now.'

She closed the door behind Hajara, leaned on the panel and sighed. The next few days were going to be long. But deep down she knew it would be alright in the end.

FIGMENTS

Dzekashu MacViban

You struggle in vain to remember when it all started. But the more you think, the murkier it gets in your brain, to the point that you can't distinguish reality from daydream. You try harder, but all you can remember are the dog days in a dimly lit open office you shared in the Madagascar neighbourhood in Yaounde. Its white walls smelled of whitewash and mould.

That is when the migraines started, you think. But you are not sure.

Your head is pounding. The clickety-clack of keyboards is the only sound you hear all day. You are staring at an abysmal computer screen and the words on your word processor soon start to run into each other. Despite all this, you can't take a break because the company is always looking for excuses to take a slash at your meagre salary.

It is supposed to be an easy job. All you have to do is answer the phone, make appointments and reply emails, according to the job description. Maybe it's an over simplification of a job which can get really frenetic sometimes, like when you have to cover up for your supervisor – who happens to be your brother, and the reason why you have this job in the first place – when he is purportedly in a board meeting, but is actually banging his secretary in the elevator that is out of order. Or when your brother's boss, Madam M, asks you to spy on your brother, because she suspects him of embezzling company money.

The office is so small and so hot that you can swear the walls are gradually closing in on you. Ndoumbe, your brother, walks by, ignoring you. You don't mind. People have ignored you for most of your life, except when they needed something from you. In secondary school, you didn't have any friends, although people occasionally pretended to like you when they wanted to read your unlimited collection of comic books. It's not different here at work. Your coworkers talk to you only when they need a favour, like when their personal computers need fixing.

Once every year, Madam M organises end-of-year pool parties. You hate those parties because being around people makes you nervous.

The last party almost went well. Almost. It was at Mont Febe, a government-owned hotel that sits atop a hill surrounded by lush vegetation, overlooking the presidency and the conference centre. The former and the latter sit atop hills as well, surrounded by overzealous flora and fauna. These three hills shield the once-affluent neighbourhoods that sprawled beneath, as if sprinkled between them, from the outside world.

You couldn't take your eyes off the hotel's transparent sky-blue pool, surrounded by a terrace with hypnotic white circles, no matter how much you tried. Pools weren't accessible where you grew up, and those you knew were an eyesore: they contained sky-blue-turned-black-brown water, and when an initiative was taken to keep the water clean, it was not without consequence. Delinquency was birthed in the absence of neglect, and soon after, the once-clean pools contained floating chunks of excrement. This experience had marked you many years ago, so much so that you quit swimming classes without entering the pool.

At the end of the party, you had joined the others for a picture by the pool. Seconds before the picture was taken, your brother pushed you into the pool in what he pretended was an accident. An enlarged copy of the photograph now leans conspicuously in the office, and the morning sun's reflection on it seems to accentuate your discomfiture in that moment, captured by the camera as you were tumbling into the pool.

As far back as you can remember, Ndoumbe has always played mean tricks on you.

This year's pool party has been announced and your gut tells you that your brother is planning something behind your back. You wait for him in front of the office after work and confront him.

'Why do you keep doing this to me? I'm your brother!'

'If this is about Sabrina, it happened only once –'

'It's about the pool, last year!' you cut in quickly, trying to avoid bringing up Sabrina, your first love, who became your brother's baby mama before you could figure out what they were up to and why she wasn't returning your calls. Their picture currently drapes part of the wall of the old family house in Melen, a large framed photograph of Ndoumbe, Sabrina and Shey – their baby – hanging next to a large framed photograph of your parents standing by a Peugeot 504. Beside these two photographs, as if an afterthought, hangs a smaller picture of yourself, barely visible because it is partly masked by the artificial Christmas tree that has not been moved for the past twenty years.

'Bro, that thing be be na accident,' he replies, almost dismissively, in pidgin.

'But you know se i no fit swim nor? If i fo drown you fo do weti?' you reply.

He looks worried for a few seconds, and is about to reply when your coworkers walk out of the office building, and nod at you in acknowledgement as they pass by, ignoring your brother. You wonder why they nod at you. It's no secret that they think you are weird and they usually do everything to avoid you. Ndoumbe follows them down the street, leaving you by yourself.

You stand there awhile, speechless, and almost teary as the night slowly crawls up on you. At night you dream of an incident that happened a few years ago, when your brother wasn't yet a bully, and forget it almost instantly.

* * *

The next day you wake up with a headache and ignore it, hoping that it will disappear. At work, there's an envelope at your desk, with a note that says you have been laid off. The letter, signed by Madame M, says you are constantly distracted at work and are a liability to the company.

You head upstairs toward Madame M's office. The cool air from the AC numbs you almost immediately as you get to her office floor. You realize you haven't been upstairs ever since you were hired three years ago. You look around: there is a delivery man going from desk to desk sharing croissants, coffee is boiling in a brand new coffee machine, someone is drinking filtered water in a cup from the water dispenser in loud rhythmic gulps, and another person is taking a selfie with the immaculate white walls as background.

Her office door is open, so you enter without knocking, and show her the note from your desk, looking at her beseechingly.

'You had it coming. You are always daydreaming and hardly get any work done. Your performance reviews are disastrous,' she says.

'This is about Ndoumbe, right? He put you up to this, didn't he?' you ask. 'I too have dirt on him, he —'

'What are you talking about?' she blurts, almost annoyed. 'Who the hell is Ndoumbe?'

'Ndoumbe... Ndoumbe, my brother... who works at Human Resources,' you say, unsure why she is getting worked up.

'I don't know any Ndoumbe at HR,' she says. 'Stop wasting my time.'

'But... but...' You are taken aback and unsure why she is reacting this way and pretending not to know Ndoumbe. Then you say, almost whispering, 'You asked me to keep an eye on him because you suspected him of embezzlement.'

'What is this? Is this some sort of joke, because it isn't funny, and you are starting to get on my nerves,' she says.

Nothing makes sense anymore. You feel dizzy as you pack what is on your desk into a tiny box. You'd gone to Madame M's office to say 'You can't fire me, I quit,' but you'd instead walked out feeling something was terribly wrong with the world.

Ndoumbe is the only thing on your mind as you walk out of the building in Madagascar where the company you worked for rents office space. You are lost in a reverie and fail to acknowledge that you'd never return to this hell hole. You're struggling to find a comfortable way to carry the box containing all of your office belongings when you see your brother across the street. He is buying a cigarette. You jump into the road, waving at your brother, and the next thing is darkness and excruciating pain. You are not sure which came first as you pass out.

* * *

You wake up with bandages on a bed in a dimly lit room.

'Thank God, you're okay,' a woman says as you struggle to sit up. 'You've been unconscious for weeks.'

You try to say something but can barely open your mouth. She draws closer to you and says you'll be all right. Drowsiness takes over you and you fall asleep.

The next morning you are not awoken by rats scurrying their way across the room as they habitually chase and tease each other playfully in your apartment. You are awoken by the aroma of coffee that hangs all over the room, reminding you that you are in a stranger's house. You don't remember how you got here. Every part of your body hurts

The woman you saw the previous night sits by you. She says you were in an accident and she took you to the hospital. You were discharged weeks later despite your state because she ran out of money, and no family member had come to check on you. You are speechless. Grateful. Suddenly, you remember Ndoumbe and are overwhelmed by an avalanche of different feelings.

* * *

During the days that follow, you don't see much of her because she goes out in the morning and returns in the afternoon to change your bandages and feed you. She hardly talks and you are usually asleep or drowsy from the medication she gives you. At night she goes out late and returns in the small hours.

Weeks go by and you feel better, but you are still bed-ridden. You no longer have bandages. You've called your brother several times, but he hasn't returned any of your calls.

'I owe you my life,' you tell her one day. She is silent.

'How will I ever repay you? I will pay you back, even if it is in fifty years,' you say.

'You don't have to repay me,' she says. 'Besides, you have not completely recovered. You'll have to stay in bed for a while.'

You look at her and wonder if such people still really do exist.

You ask her about her medical knowledge. She tells you she's a medical student, then takes back her sentence and says she *was* a medical student. You're not entirely sure what the *was* in the sentence means. She says she does voluntary work now.

'Did you finish medical school?' you ask.

'No.'

'Why?'

'To cut a long story short, let's say I turned down a lecturer's advances. He said nobody had ever said no to him, adding that he always had his way. I never passed any of his courses or those of his friends after that.'

You feel sullen, outraged, powerless and bitter at the cruelty. You are reminded of lines from the beginning of Zadie Smith's *NW*: 'Shrivelled blossom and bitter little apples. Birds singing the wrong tunes in the wrong trees too early in the year.' You want to ask her if she reported the lecturer when you notice the look on her face: her eyes speak of the prelude of a broken dream long forgotten. You try to change the topic.

'Where do you go to every night?'

'You ask many questions,' she says

'One last question.'

'Yes.'

'What's your name?'

'Alice.'

* * *

Time goes by. It's hard to keep track because you sleep a lot. You can't tell for how long you've been in this apartment. You feel better and gradually become obsessed with where Alice goes every night. You know it is a bad idea to entertain these thoughts but curiosity is a stubborn lump in your throat.

You are alone. The sun makes its way through the partly open window and sits on your bed. You can hear the boisterous city bursting with activity and you realize you've never really looked around the apartment. The room smells like a pharmacy. You make for the window and open it completely. Looking down, your neck craned forward, you notice that you are on the fifth floor. You spend the rest of the day looking around the apartment.

You pretend to fall asleep after you've had dinner. You are gripped with guilt over your decision to follow Alice.

The door slams shut with a loud bang as she leaves the room. You jump out of the bed and go toward the window, look out and see Alice walking down the front stairs and onto the sidewalk. You hurry down the stairs as curiosity swallows guilt. Deep down, you know this is a mistake.

You are limping at length behind Alice on the street and she takes a bend. You hasten your irregular pace. When you take the turn, you realize that she has slowed down and do same. The street is peopled with loosely dressed damsels who flutter and flicker around street lights like moths, in a manner reminiscent of the cover of Donna Summer's 'Bad Girls' album. You can hear Donna Summer's voice in your head, singing 'she works hard for the money so you better treat her right'. One of the women greets you and asks if she's the one you are looking for. You ignore her, trying not to lose sight of Alice who has just entered a disco. 'Tant pis,' she says in French, and heads toward another stranger.

As you get closer, you notice that there is a long, endless queue meandering out of sight. You approach somebody in the queue and propose to give him your phone in exchange for some bank notes, which he heartily accepts. Once the exchange is done, you force yourself into the queue and those behind boo and curse.

After what seems like an endless amount of time, but is just about forty minutes, you finally make it to the door. The guy standing at the entrance is tall, with a '50s beat-up beatnik face that looks slightly funny because his tattoos look incomplete. You hand him the required amount and he lets you in. Once inside, you realize that you had not had the time to look at the name of the disco. The atmosphere inside is spirited and psychedelic. Your senses are taken aback by the sirens, glitter balls, strobe lights, spot lights, flash lights, light guns, battle lights, black light, and finally, red and blue Bengal lights flaring up.

You describe Alice to a waitress and ask if she knows her. She shakes her head from side to side. You ask another and she says that information is expensive, so you pull out a bank note and ask her if it is enough motivation. Her face lights up. You can barely hear each other over Eko Roosevelt's deafening voice reverberating as it ricochets on the sound-proof walls while he croons:

'Attends-moi, attends-moi, attends-moi... attends-moi, reste avec moi, je ne peux pas me passer de toi, je veux vivre avec toi...'

She snatches the bank note and says 'over there', pointing to the strip poles.

You head toward the adjoining strip section, which is less populated. You spot Alice... she is dancing alluringly around a pole, getting tips every time she undoes a button of her blouse.

You think about keeping a low profile but your eyes meet hers before you can do anything. She freezes immediately she sees you. You can't decipher the look on her face. Is it surprise, disappointment, shame or anger? She jumps off the mini stage without saying a word and, ignoring the spotlight that is on her, as well as the cacophonous catcalls, she retreats through the rear door.

You follow her, but a bimboy-ish bouncer stands in your way in front of the door. The other men who were watching her are confused, but get just as quickly over the incident, head to the next stripper, and start tipping her. You leave through the front and head straight to Alice's place, wondering why you'd followed her in the first place. You have a bad feeling about how she may react, so you hasten your pace. At length, one of your legs starts hurting. You'd ignored the pain initially when you left the comfort of the bed. You slow down. It is very late, but you have no idea what time it is. A chilly breeze sweeps past you and you start shivering. The night is silent, except for the ridiculous clip-clop sound the soles of your shoes make on the macadamized road as you limp.

After what seems like an endless walk in the silence of the night, you reach the building where Alice lives and look up to her window. There is no light. Maybe she's asleep or not back yet. You hastily open the main door which is unlocked and climb the steep, winding staircase leading to her apartment. You realize that when you left the apartment in a mad rush to tail Alice, you didn't pay attention to the surroundings. Finally, you reach her apartment on the fifth floor and open the door. As you turn on the light, you feel that something is not right. The light blinks a couple of times, then illuminates the apartment. It is empty. You blink out of surprise and head over to the rooms. They too are empty. The apartment reeks of misuse and abandon. The whole place is cold and smells of mold. You helplessly pace from one end to another, trying to make sense of what is going on. You decide to knock on the door of the adjacent room. A short, bald man wearing horned-rimmed glasses comes out and asks why you are disturbing his sleep. You ask him if he knows Alice. He says he is not a tenant and is crashing at a friend's here. You ask if his friend who rents the apartment is home. By now you are begging him. He goes inside and his friend comes out.

'Do you know where Alice, the girl who lives in this room, has gone to?' you ask.

'Are you her friend?' he asks.

'Yes,' you say.

'It's a pity. Alice died in her room two years ago and the room has been unoccupied ever since.

You swallow to hold back discomfiture. Your heart is beating fast and loud. You must be dreaming. You bite your lip to make sure that you are not, and it hurts.

'Nobody wants to live in the room because there are rumours that the room is jinxed, so it has been unoccupied for two years. Why are you asking me this in the middle of the night? Where did you know her?'

You are speechless. You muster almost all the strength you have left and apologise for interrupting his sleep. You throw one last glance at the apartment where you'd spent what seemed like more than a month, and you head down the stairs with a sullen face, confused.

Outside, you sit on the small stairs which lead to the main entrance of the building and try to make sense of what is happening. Nothing makes sense. It is often said that artists are creatures of infinite melancholy. You wonder if you have the soul of an artist. Your head starts aching. It is pounding, as if something from within wants to burst free.

Your mind drifts back to the day you were laid off. Had Madame M been right all along? After your mention of Ndoumbe, she'd pulled up the employee records, turned to the page listing HR employees, and then tossed the document to you. You'd picked it up, almost as confused as she was. In fact, she was no longer confused at that point, she was angry. You'd looked through the names twice, trying to find Ndoumbe Ngwananjam. Nothing!

She'd pulled out your psych evaluation and you'd stared at it with a preoccupied look, after she'd handed it over to you. Your family records with the company said you were an only child! How could that be real? And if it was, what exactly wasn't?

Nothing makes sense anymore.

You reflect on how meaningless your life has been and wish you were an insouciant, inanimate object with no worries. Or if you are to remain a living thing, you wish you were a tree. Without warning, a mango tree starts shooting out of your head, and you feel its roots digging deeper into you as it grows so fast and tall that its branches and green leaves scrape the old corrugated iron roof.

POEMS

Victoria Adukwei Bulley

Cristo Redentor

know / finally / that it is not the statue / that overwhelms. the soapstone
exterior / is not so noteworthy / the iron core is not noteworthy / nor
the head / downcast & leftwards just-so / with L'Oreal hair. it is not / the
roman nose or the hands / hole-punched / so clean / & bloodless / sans
cross. realise / it is not the statue that overwhelms / if you have to / say it
whelms at best. & yet it is not / the statue / the metal / or the stone / but
the mountain / the mountain / or rather / the statue the statue stands on.
& now / with your feet placed for the first time / below saviour's toes /
know / at last / that if there is a holy spirit / an *espirito santo* / to find here
/ on this mountain / redeeming you / turning some wrongness in you
right / know anyway / that it is not holier / than the thousands of older
holies / only taller / in a soapstone rendition. it is not / his figure that
astounds / it is not the soapstone / that asks to be fathomed / but the view
from here / which came first / & makes the jaw to slack / & falls the
mouth open / & moves the tongue to remark / in a tongue indigenous to
you / up here where there is no birdsong / but wind. it was never the
statue / that was large but *the land* / but *the land* / but *the land* that is / &
the sea / & *the sea* / & *the sea* that is / so endless & nothingness in sight /
until the next mass of land / past the soft horizon that *is* / & *is* / & *is* until
Africa. on the mountain / at his feet / your only questions: / in whose
world do you hold / this stubborn wilfulness to awe / at what you cannot
claim / to have made? what does it mean to sing / not of the world's
wonders but / what was built upon them? how / do you speak / of those
who came as guests / but christened this place / a *new world* ? / with which
words do you tell / of such blindness to wonder / wherein the mountain
was seen / but not *the gods* / *the gods* / *the gods* / there already.

Junk DNA Haiku

They would have thought the
      first sea-crossing would have been
their only & last.
      What odd seasickness
lives in me today beneath
      this unbeaten skin?
What memory of
      ghosts, what fear of abduction
do I carry now
      awaiting trigger,
asleep in my liberty?
      There is no answer
just a mute prayer
      that no part of me still hears
water against wood
      & begins to drown.
There is no knowing for sure
      what *junk DNA*
walks me through my days
      waiting to come into use,
maybe save my life.
      What happened back then
happens still; differently.
      What persists in me
knows this. Keeps a gun
      under the mattress, keeps watch,
too, differently.

THE FACES OF ABISSA

Ngadi Smart

Abissa is a tradition of the N'zema people of south-eastern Côte d'Ivoire and south-western Ghana. It comprises an annual fourteen-day festival and is a time of forgiveness and rebirth – a time to let go of all grudges and celebrate the past year through creative traditional wear, dance, music and spirituality.

During the festival, an accusation-repentance ritual is performed during which attendees are expected to 'come clean' as they take stock of the past year. Other unique highlights of this celebration are the attendees' faces decorated with Kaolin, a special type of white clay, and the cross-dressing: men will dress as women, while women will dress as men, as a form of performance to mimic those who have wronged them during the year.

These unlikely, fascinating sights – especially for a West African festival – make this my favourite place to photograph. I photographed this festival in 2016, and again in 2017, and in the future, wish to further explore the stories behind the different people that come to Abissa every year.

Culture, and the preservation of it, is very important for me as a West African visual artist with a focus on illustration and photography. I feel it is vital for African creatives, whether they are living on the African continent or part of the African diaspora, to have a hand in how they wish their country or continent to be represented. I have lived and studied art and design in the UK, Canada and the Ivory Coast, where I live and feel that we are the ones experiencing the various aspects of what it means to be African in the present age. We must show these various facets of what that entails.

Abissa is also an opportunity for some families to demonstrate their belonging to a symbol of power or wealth (water, fire, yams, aubergines). In this case, a regal pair bedecked in handwoven cloth wear matching palm nut garlands as their symbol of wealth.

A man poses with corn as his symbol of power and wealth. Agriculture was the foundation of the economy in Ivory Coast and its main source of growth, so it is no surprise that crops play such a huge part in the display of well-being, wealth and power.

A woman that is part of a group of attendees dressed in matching 'couple' outfits displays her well-crafted palm nut outfit as a sign of belonging to this symbol of power.

An attendee displays money as a symbolism for wealth and power, with Ghana Cedis and Guinean francs attached to her hat.

Children in matching outfits take a break in a section away from the drum circle. In a joyful atmosphere, children, young people, and the old all strive to offer their best steps at Abissa. Everyone is expected to .participate in the celebration

A group of young festival attendees proudly display their Kaolin
decorations.

REVIEWS

}

DECOLONISING
THE BOOK OF KINGS

Shanon Shah

There was once a young and handsome man named Zahhak, son of the king of a faraway land called Merdas. One day, the brave and ambitious Zahhak was approached by Ahriman (Satan) in the form of a counsellor, who advised him to kill his father and become king. Zahhak followed the advice of Satan, possibly with the complicity of his own mother, and became the king of his father's realm. Iblis (another name for Satan) then took the form of a cook and, every day, prepared Zahhak a feast of delicious meat, eventually turning the king carnivorous. Curious and grateful for this wonderful cook, Zahhak allowed him to ask for any favour he desired. Iblis said that all he wanted to do was kiss Zahhak's shoulders. Zahhak consented.

As soon as Iblis got his way, he disappeared into thin air and two monstrous serpents emerged from Zahhak's shoulders – exactly where Iblis had kissed them. Iblis then appeared to Zahhak as a physician and told him that the only way to prevent the monsters from devouring him was to kill two young men every day and feed their brains to the serpents.

While this was unfolding, a just king named Jamshid was ruling the world from Iran, but his reign was becoming undermined by arrogance and hubris. It was at this point that Zahhak accepted the invitation of the Iranian nobility to come to their capital, which he did and from where he proceeded to rule the world with terror and tyranny.

This is one of numerous stories told in the world's longest epic poem by a single author, the *Shahnameh* by Hakim Abolqasem Ferdowsi Tusi. Completed in the year 1010, the *Shahnameh*, the Book of Kings, is an epic of many empires but stories like those of Zahhak's make us ask whether it is a work that celebrates kings or if it is more cautionary and subversive. Or perhaps is it meant to do something else – something grander or more profound? And what do we make of the recurring murders of sons by fathers (and less often fathers by sons), and the role that mothers play? Where do we even begin with all the homo- and hetero-eroticism? These are some of the questions that Hamid Dabashi, Professor of Iranian Studies and Comparative Literature at Columbia University, puts forward in *The Shahnameh:The Persian Epic as World Literature.* As he phrases it, 'how are we to read the *Shahnameh* beyond its past and lost glories', especially today, when it is encountered mostly in English, not in the original Persian? If, like me, you are new to the *Shahnameh*, then some background is needed before the question's significance becomes clear.

Hamid Dabashi, *The* Shahnameh: *The Persian Epic as World Literature*, Columbia University Press: New York, 2019.

The *Shahnameh* consists of some fifty thousand couplets usually divided into three sections – the mythical, heroic, and historical. It narrates the global story of a people – referred to by its author Ferdowsi as Iranians – from the creation of the world to the Arab conquest of the Sassanian Empire in the 650s. But the land that Ferdowsi referred to as Iran is not the same as the modern nation-state – his was a term that encompassed an empire that interacted with other empires. None other than Alexander the Great has an entire story in the *Shahnameh*.

Ferdowsi (c. 940–1020) was born in the village of Paj near the city of Tus in the north-eastern province of Khorasan, a historical region that included parts of modern Iran, Afghanistan and Tajikistan. We know little about Ferdowsi – we do know that he was a young husband and loving father who was grief-stricken by the death of his young son. He makes a note of this in the *Shahnameh*, and such personal remarks are characteristic of the epic. Ferdowsi's patron was Sultan Mahmoud of Ghazna (r. 998–1002), a powerful warlord and the most prominent ruler of the Ghaznavid Empire (977–1186), which stretched from Iran's eastern front into the northern Indian subcontinent. The Ghaznavids inherited the already impressive achievements of their predecessors, the Samanids, and consolidated the Persian language and culture.

Historically, poem, poet and patron became intertwined, giving rise to folkloric traditions, including those that satirised the relationship between

Ferdowsi and Sultan Mahmoud. In one story, Ferdowsi offers his finished *Shahnameh* to the sultan, who had initially promised him a gold coin for every line. Regretting this promise upon seeing the completed fifty thousand couplets, the sultan offers him as many coins of silver instead. A disappointed Ferdowsi replies, 'Your Majesty, I just remembered a few additional lines, and I'd like to take my manuscript back and add them to the end of the book.' After giving away the silver coins to the sultan's retinue on his way out, Ferdowsi heads to a mosque where the sultan used to pray and scribbles graffiti on the wall intended for Mahmoud and other worshippers to see:

Oh you Sultan Mahmoud the world conqueror:

If you are not afraid of me be afraid of God!

For thirty years I suffered to write the *Shahnameh*

So that the King would appropriately reward me –

For sure the King was born to a lowly baker,

For he has given me the rewards enough to buy a loaf of bread!

If the King's mother were of a noble descent,

I would have been richly rewarded with gold and silver.

When Sultan Mahmoud heard of this, he sent his soldiers to punish Ferdowsi, but the poet fled to Baghdad and sought refuge under the ruling caliph there. Ferdowsi eventually returned to his homeland upon receiving news of his son's death. Sultan Mahmoud sent for Ferdowsi with the award that had initially been promised, but his delegation arrived as Ferdowsi's coffin was being carried to his grave.

Dabashi includes all of these tantalising vignettes to demonstrate the seductive and profound power of the *Shahnameh*. He also takes up the cudgels against Eurocentric notions of comparative or 'World Literature' which have yet to shake off their imperial hangover. He challenges, for example, David Quint's binary distinction of two trajectories in epic European poetry – the triumphant epic of the winners and the defeatist epic of the losers. Triumphalist epics include Virgil's *Aeneid*, Luís de Camões's *Lusíadas*, and Torquato Tasso's *Gerusalemme liberata*, while examples of defeatist epics are Lucan's *Pharsalia*, Ercilla's *Araucana*, and d'Aubigné's *Les tragiques*. Where would the *Shahnameh* fit within this framework? Is it an epic of conquest or an epic of defeat? According to Dabashi, it is neither. 'It is simply astonishing,' he writes, 'how radically different the *Shahnameh* is from both sides of this Manichaean binary Quint detects in European epics.'

Dabashi has no quarrel with European literary scholars analysing European epics. He does not even have a problem with European scholars engaging with literary works from outside the regions they are familiar with. What he criticises incandescently is the imposition of Eurocentric analytical frameworks upon non-European works which then inform the criteria of whether something can 'rightfully' be admitted into the canon of 'World Literature'. How can this be truly representative of *world* literature if the 'World' is defined through Eurocentric and subconsciously (or not-so-subconsciously) imperialistic eyes? This, he argues, has prevented the *Shahnameh* from being appreciated widely and deeply in its own right.

Equally reductive, according to Dabashi, are the polemical, selective, and 'overpoliticised' readings of the poem by the different regimes that have tried to legitimise their version of the modern nation-state of Iran. Dabashi is scathing about the major millennial celebration of the *Shahnameh* staged by Reza Shah (r. 1925–1941), the first Pahlavi monarch, in 1934. Reza Shah Pahlavi's militant manipulation of the Persian epic to justify his rule was all the more cynical given the situation that modern Iran was finding itself in – it had to cope with the upheavals of the constitutional revolution (1906–11), the collapse of the Qajar dynasty (1789–1924), and the chaos of recent foreign occupation.

Neither is Dabashi very forgiving of the treatment of the *Shahnameh* by the post-1979 Islamic Republic, which has either ignored it or used it selectively to forge a sense of Shi'i nationalism in the aftermath of the disastrous Iran-Iraq War (1980–88). Both approaches inflict 'epistemic violence' on the *Shahnameh* by tying it to a chair and beating confessions of pre-Islamic, Zoroastrian imperialism or delusions of Shi'i grandeur out of it. The poem is more exciting and complex than that – it contains positive references to Zoroastrianism *and* allusions to Shi'ism, and both add to the richness of its moral universe. In fact, Dabashi persuasively argues that the *Shahnameh* instantiates a paradox that is uniquely Shi'i – it laments impending doom at the same time that it celebrates imperial victory, just as it finds nobility and grandeur in righteous defeat. The epic's 'traumatic unconscious', in Dabashi's words, locate the *Shahnameh* within the legacy of Shi'i martyrdom and its models of political and spiritual power and protest. Dabashi is therefore also disdainful of the appropriation of the *Shahnameh* by leftist Iranian dissidents. By converting its stories and characters into political slogans, these activists inadvertently contribute to the nationalist dismemberment of the poem. They are merely upholding the framework that Eurocentric literary critics cling to, one that divides epics between those that are 'Western' and those that are not. How does it even make sense to talk about the *Shahnameh*'s 'Western' or 'Iranian' readers, when so many of its admirers now include Iranians in exile in the West, and indeed, when it has long been discussed by European intellectuals, just never acknowledged as occupying the same literary pedestal as the accepted 'classics'?

This book is at its strongest when Dabashi shows us what the *Shahnameh* means to him, a US-based Iranian academic, and his children and his life. Especially moving are the passages, such as this one, where Dabashi recounts the impact and inspiration the *Shahnameh* has had on his students at Columbia:

> They began to read it, cover to cover, story after story, like explorers upon a distant shore. Their initial hesitation to pronounce the Persian names of heroes they had not even known before eventually yielded to a far more confident encounter with the substance of the stories. They soon began to analyze, synthesize, theorize the intricacies of the text. Before the term had ended the *Shahnameh* had become integral to their moral imagination, to their political consciousness, to their understanding of where in the world they were standing. They remained who they were — American, European, Asian, or African — but now Ferdowsi's *Shahnameh* had entered their poetic consciousness. I began writing this book on the *Shahnameh* with their sense of wonder in me.

This sense of wonder grabbed me, too. The story of the despotic Zahhak, for example, reminded me of a story in one of the Malay *hikayats*, or royal chronicles — the legend of the Raja Bersiong (the Fanged King) in the *Hikayat Merong Mahawangsa*, a founding epic of my native state of Kedah. Like Zahhak, Raja Bersiong was also transformed by something his cook did. In this case, however, the cook was not an embodiment of Satan, but a nervous servant who had accidentally cut herself while preparing a vegetable dish. Raja Bersiong, however, relished the taste of blood and wanted more. He ordered more and more innocent subjects to be killed to satisfy his bloodlust, which even made him grow fangs, like a vampire. The Raja's subjects eventually revolted and overthrew him. Filled with remorse, he fled and extracted his fangs and threw them away in a place that became known as *Baling* (Malay for 'throw').

Despite the common thread of cannibalism as a metaphor for despotism, there is little resemblance between Zahhak and Raja Bersiong. For one thing, Zahhak is eventually not overthrown by his subjects but is defeated by Fereydun, who chains him in a cave on a mountain. Still, it did make me wonder about the reception of ideas and other cultural artefacts around the world. Dabashi is right — it's not that non-Europeans or non-Westerners need to lobby the gatekeepers of what counts as 'World Literature'. Even if these gatekeepers did expand their definitions in some way, we would still be trying to appease them, pleading with them to let us in. Instead, the reception of different literatures needs to be utterly de-Europeanised. Would this not make better sense of the appearance of Alexander the Great in the Qur'an, the *Shahnameh*, and the *hikayats*, rather than the tired division of civilisations into the 'West' and 'East'? Incidentally, there is much evidence of Persian influences on Malay culture, either directly or via Gujarat, including in concepts such as *pahlawan* (the warrior) and the sultanate.

Sadly, where Dabashi falters is when he tries to summarise tales from the *Shahnameh* later in the book, compared to his more alluring vignettes in the beginning. These summaries can get a bit laboured — the reader can only handle so many names, so many plot twists, and so many treacheries and dalliances in a short space, in addition to high-level literary analysis.

Perhaps the solution might have been to retain Dabashi's rich analysis, but to be more selective about the excerpts shared and characters introduced to the reader. As Dabashi writes, 'the central traumas of the *Shahnameh* dwell in the three stories of Rostam and Sohrab, Rostam and Esfandiar, and Seyavash and Sudabeh. These three tales bring out the most potent, visceral, and emblematic power of the Persian epic.' This is exciting stuff, but it could have been shown by systematically focusing on the development of these three accounts, either through quotes from the poem (which were somewhat lacking), or from more character-building and back story. Perhaps with more showing rather than telling, the postcolonial criticisms raised by Dabashi need not have been so loud and so frequently stated either – I lost count of the number of times the phrase 'epistemic violence' was used.

These flaws are not fatal. Read this book, whether you are new to the *Shahnameh* or you know it already. Dabashi will delight, entertain, inform, and educate you with his erudition and passion. The last sentence of the book is rather touching:

> Every time I have taught the *Shahnameh* in my classes, and now in this book, the summation of my thoughts and feelings about this precious book, I have thought myself blessed with the accidental privilege of having been born into Ferdowsi's language, whispered into my ears with my mother's lullabies, to be able to occasion one of such countless gatherings around his immortal text.

GIANTS, KNOWN AND UNKNOWN

Samia Rahman

The request provoked a wry smile. Could I possibly chair a conversation with Chase F Robinson at the Bradford Literature Festival in the summer of 2017? His recently published book *Islamic Civilization in Thirty Lives: The First 1000 Years*, was to be the subject matter and I relished the thought of discussing Islamic civilisation in the city of my birth. The tome arrived a couple of days later and I warmed to the teal hardback cover. The front was adorned with a detail from an eighteenth century Indian miniature featuring Timur, founder of the fourteenth century Timurid Empire in Persia and Central Asia and also the great-great-great grandfather of the first of the Mughal Emperors, Babur. I was instantly reminded of the Mughal Water Garden in Bradford's Lister Park. In recognition of the heritage of members of the local community, the garden is centrally located, sitting harmoniously alongside the Victorian splendour of Cartwright Hall. Islamic civilisation in thirty lives I mused as my thumb rolled over the writing on the back. The words jumped out at me: 'a unique introduction to 1,000 years of Islamic history'.

A substantial and meticulously researched piece of scholarship, the book reveals itself to be the culmination of a long-held enthusiasm for Islamic history courtesy of Robinson, professor of history and president of The Graduate Center at the City University of New York. He tells me he became enamoured by early Islamic history before the subject took on any of the urgency that seems to be applicable to all things Islam-related these days. Describing the trajectory of his 'innocent' emergence onto the field, he simultaneously acknowledges that we live in contrastingly malignant times.

We met in the Green Room in Bradford City Hall, half an hour before the session. It was an unscheduled meeting but one I had intentionally orchestrated after googling his image and calculating he would be there. I reassured myself that this is perfectly normal. I found Robinson tucked away in a corner, poring over a newspaper with a mostly-devoured plate of lamb *karahi* and *pilau* rice pushed to the side. It amused us both that he had never visited Bradford before. This is despite his having previously lived in the UK for fourteen years, after joining the Faculty of Oriental Studies and Wolfson College at the University of Oxford in 1993. Of course, there is no compulsion in Islamic historiography that demands UK-based scholars must become intimately acquainted with this Northern mill town. Yet, the fact that Bradford is so intrinsic to British Islam seems, however tenuous, a missed opportunity. I ponder notions of fractured engagement and ivory towers but my cynicism is misguided. Omitting Bradford from an itinerary of must-visit places in the UK in the late 1990s and the noughties was, let's be honest, perfectly understandable. The book itself is testament to a passion for the eighth and ninth century that effervesces as you turn the pages. For Robinson, this period is unparalleled in its significance, bearing witness to the birth of a religion, an empire and a people.

It is through the lives of these people that we learn the story of the first 1,000 years of Islam. I tell Robinson that I have a fabulous idea to introduce the topic by ironically relating the stale but oft-repeated adage that the beauty of Islam can never be appreciated if knowledge of the religion is based on the example of Muslims themselves. Robinson looks at me a little incredulously and gently discourages this opening remark. I realise then that perhaps I should have allowed my mind to process my thoughts for just a little longer before uttering them out loud. Robinson was likely aghast because, apart from telling jokes that seem to fall flat at the punch-line, my comment represented the absolute opposite of his objective in writing this book.

Chase F Robinson, *Islamic Civilization in Thirty Lives: The First 1000 Years*, Thames & Hudson, London, 2016

What *Islamic Civilisation in Thirty Lives* does represent is a series of narratives that rely on much more than abstract analysis to celebrate the rich diversity of Islam during that period. Robinson recognises the intense interest in Islam and Islamic history that pervades. His response to the current appetite for information is a resolve not to write a turgid, inaccessible academic research paper. Instead he deliberately chooses the medium of biography, a genre well-established in early Islamic history, to reflect the 'wide and inadequately-acknowledged spectrum of ideas, social practises and personal styles... hyper-rationalism, scepticism, inventiveness, iconoclasm and eccentric individuality,' because, during this period in history, 'dynamism, experimentation and risk-taking were the rule'. Telling the stories of the lives of notable individuals was a cultivated craft within the Islamic world from the seventh century onwards and it is no coincidence that for the author, this was the most powerful way to introduce a mainstream readership to that world.

Raising awareness of Islam's dynamic beginnings is a challenge Robinson evidently takes seriously. He presents us with thirty eclectic profiles to establish the idea of the individualism of Islam and Muslims. It is his way of deconstructing generalisations about the mythical archetypal Muslim and throws shade on simplistic and lazy assumptions about what is, in fact, a multitudinous world comprising diverse communities, traditions, cultures and singular lives. The personalities that feature among the Thirty are magnificent, inspiring and pioneering in their own unique ways, representing the heterogeneity of Muslim experience. The lesson for our times is clear.

It seems apt that my conversation with the professor would take place in Bradford City Hall's Chamber. The seat of local government offers a fitting context in which to discuss such a lofty subject as early Islamic civilisation. The audience gathers expectantly, they comprise a pleasing mix of backgrounds, and Robinson regales us with the story of his path to academia, how in his youth he developed a love for what must have been a particularly obscure specialism. I am curious to know whether there was a reason why the book chose thirty personalities, and it becomes apparent that the number was arbitrary. It could well have been thirty-five or twenty-five or forty-five. I am also keen to understand why he decided to limit his exposition to the first 1,000 years. This is, I admit, a loaded question. There is a perception that Islam's 'Golden Age' of intellectual excellence and creativity is very much a thing of the far flung past. A relic of a bygone era utterly unrecognisable when compared with the state of the Muslim world today. Could this focus on characters from the first 1,000 years of Islamic civilisation serve to validate such a view? Robinson counters that this is not the case at all. His decision to restrict his scholarship to this period is because 'the underlying economic and political framework of the pre-industrial Middle East began to undergo major changes. As a result, the 'early modern' or 'modern' societies that emerged generated fundamentally different cultural forms'. I am satisfied by this explanation.

There are more questions, however. Luminaries of early Islamic civilisation are abundant so how does one go about hand-picking 30? Robinson intersperses well-known icons with rather more obscure characters but what unites them is that they are paragons. The book features a range of exemplars from different disciplines: scientists, warriors, philosophers, politicians and artists as well as eccentrics and non-conformists. Each has been chosen for their humanness and ability to capture the imagination of the reader and challenge the dominant narrative of civilisational clashes and cultural incompatibility. Many names are familiar, from the Prophet himself, without whom any discussion of early Islam would be wholly incomplete, to al-Ghazali and our very own Ibn Rushd.

It is the surprises within the book that I find particularly enchanting. I am intrigued to read about 'Arib, courtesan of the Caliphs during the ninth century, one of Robinson's chosen thirty. She was born into the powerful Barmakid family of viziers, albeit in unconventional circumstances and certainly not as a result of marriage. As a young child she suffered a dramatic change in fortune when the family's influence declined. By some turn of fate she is sold into slavery, facing an uncertain and difficult future. However, by employing a mix of tenacity and skill she grows up to become one of the most acclaimed singers, musicians and dancers of her time. Her fame and celebrity knew no bounds and to my absolute glee Robinson describes the notorious beauty as 'a mix of Elizabeth Taylor and Amy Winehouse'. He explains that she 'confounds the social and gender categories that we typically impose upon Islamic civilization. A slave who sold her musical and personal services to the most powerful men of her time.' The example of 'Arib offers a commentary on a plethora of issues with which the Muslim world wrangled with. Slavery, sex, power and, of course, women.

It is on the issue of women that I feel Robinson's effort could have perhaps laboured to greater effect. Of the thirty lives that he lionises, only four are women. Of these four, one sells sexual services to powerful men, a fact that, as I have just discussed, both problematises as well as reinforces the complicated manifestation of misogyny in the society that Islam was revealed to. It is true to say that 'Arib was not only an outstanding performer of great repute and talent but also highly shrewd. She bought her own freedom and accumulated great wealth by the time she died aged ninrty. She went on to be lauded as a role model for other women and became something akin to a feminist icon, yet the dearth of female protagonists in Robinson's collection is too glaring not to notice. He is quick to acknowledge and accept that the number of women in his parade of excellence could indeed be greater and cites the availability of sources as a hindrance in his attempts to adequately reflect the impact of women on early Islamic civilisation. The scarcity of evidence of female lives does not indicate invisibility, but rather a gradual 'writing out' of women and silencing of voices as centuries of patriarchy sought to remould the past in its own vision.

This lack of reliable sources proved a great obstacle in the work of scholarship that the author was determined to undertake. The lives of women were just not sufficiently recorded and of those that were, they were likely to be vulnerable to disregard, neglect or were not well-preserved over the ages. Difficulties of historiography were not confined to issues of gender balance. Robinson describes the great lengths he went to extrapolate information about fascinating personalities who left only the tiniest clues about their lives behind. His starting point in bringing to life the virtually unknown twelfth century merchant millionaire Abu al-Qasim Ramisht was an inscription on the Ka'aba's Farewell Gate in his memory. Like a history detective, the author researched every detail offered in the memorial and, after taking the opportunity to briefly explain the Hajj pilgrimage which I found to be an excellent educational touch, explains that because 'it is about poverty and charity, the inscription gives us a glimpse into the world of medieval Islamic wealth.' Further investigation traces Ramisht's origins to Siraf on the southwest coast of Iran where it can be ascertained that he amassed his fabulous wealth in merchant trade and went on to fund the building of a hospice for Sufi ascetics.

Other problems of historiography that Robinson had to overcome were on the entirely opposite end of the spectrum. An over-abundance of material relating to household names such as the Prophet Muhammad brought with it an entire set of other issues. Working through the sources required separating fact from myth. Saladin, the first Sultan of Egypt and Syria and the founder of the Ayyubid dynasty famously had scribes and propagandists recording everything he did and said, to present an idealised vision of himself as an anti-Crusader hero. He epitomised the way in which facts are appropriated by certain periods in history to suit the contemporary context. The life of an individual can be re-told numerous times and the challenge for the biographer is to reflect this process while at the same time ensuring a forensic approach and an ostensible search for 'truth'.

What makes *Islamic Civilization in Thirty Lives: The First 1000 Years* a unique and ultimately successful work is the commitment and tenacity shown by the author. He places emphasis on challenging ignorance and misconceptions about Islam and Muslims, setting out to inform a mainstream audience about the culture of this sensationalised and deeply misunderstood world. At the same time, he ensures that the quality of research is beyond reproach and the book serves up lessons from the past about creativity, diversity and the human story that will serve us well to heed today. He may not yet have taken the opportunity to marvel at the delights of Bradford's Mughal Garden but perhaps researching a book on Islamic civilisation beyond the first 1,000 years will finally afford him that experience.

AFRICA IN SOMERSET HOUSE

Natasha Koverola Commissiong

When I visit central London and pass through intersection upon intersection of regally kept buildings with intricately embellished fronts of antique stone and wrought iron gates, I always wonder what the city would have looked like two hundred years ago. The upkeep of the capital's history, from street names such as East India Dock Road to antique artefacts controversially secured in polished glass boxes, walks a fine line between heritage remembrance and a bow to London's colonial past.

Somerset House, one of London's many refurbished grand sites, is a Georgian palace tucked away on the edge of the River Thames. This is the grand venue that opened its doors in October 2018 to host 1–54, the leading international fair for contemporary African and diasporic art. Running for its sixth year, 1–54 was originally founded by Touria El Glaoui, curated by Ekow Eshunhas and has rotating exhibitions in the United Kingdom, the United States and North Africa showcasing all of Africa's fifty-four countries and its diaspora with one hundred and thirty pieces of contemporary art.

As I walked across Somerset House's entrance to attend the fair, I passed a courtyard exhibition of geometric, life-size meditation tree sculptures created by South Sudanese artist Ibrahim El-Salahi. Pausing to look at the trees, had me thinking about the artistic process of translating contemporary notions of 'Africanness' and/or 'blackness' through art as well as the bridged divide from housing the art in a space such as the cobble-stoned grounds of Somerset House. Upon entering the lobby, my eyes bounced across a crowd of African art consumers and I spotted bedazzled chunky Gucci trainers with matching bum bags, forest green covered lips and a head full of twisted jumbo Marley braids. I wondered how my mauve coloured Turkish style maxi dress, bronzy Fenty highlighted cheekbones and middle parted slick bun compared. As I wove in and out of a largely mixed, yet predominantly French group of art sellers, buyers and visitors of African art, it seemed as if everyone was familiar with everyone and part of a well-connected clique of African art lovers.

1–54: Contemporary African Art Fair, Somerset House, London, 2018

The art had a loud presence occupying all of the rooms in Somerset House yet did not make any tangible sound, aside from a couple of audio-visual displays exhibiting on screens. Rooms were either segregated by artist or by the art gallery that housed their work with a couple of well-dressed representatives quietly distinguishing gazers from those who could buy from those who couldn't afford to ask the price. To say the least, the combination of the crowd and the art at 1–54 was an overwhelming and impressive display that left me with many thoughts. In my free time I do art, blog fashion, and carry out research on projects that pique my interest particularly on identity, 'blackness' and gender. Two interrelated thoughts came to mind after reflecting on my experience at 1–54: the first is contemporary representations of women in West African art through the body, and the second is the tension between Western consumption and appreciation of art in a space such as Somerset House.

'African art is functional, it serves a purpose. It's not a dormant. It's not a means to collect the largest cheering section. It should be healing, a source a joy. Spreading positive vibrations.'

Mos Def

In the words of 1-54's curator Ekow Eshunhas, this years' exhibition conceptualised blackness as an aesthetic by exploring three key things: how archive and vintage image reflects African diaspora identity and history; how portraiture emerges as a political medium to assert black visibility; and what African photography reveals about notions of 'Africanness'. Despite the overwhelming amount of art on display, a trio of West African artists caught my eye. Thus, my interpretation of the pieces sits comfortably within my own interest in gender dynamics and representations of black women through their bodies. Specifically, I found that the work of photographers Sanlé Sory and J.D. Okhai Ojeikere and painter

Modupeopla Fadugba highlighted how the 'West African woman' can be understood and translated through powerful black and white portraiture. The first photograph, Malienne Coquettes, is one of a series taken in

black and white Voltaic style 1970's portrait by Burkina photographer Sanie Sory, of two women standing on a tiled mosaic floor in matching floor length striped dresses and tall turbans woven in elegant styles to cover their hair. The portrait is a beauty shot with depth that focuses on the two *coquettes* (or flirts translated from French) and their hidden, coy confidence as each of their hands rests on slanted hips outward. Taken in the historic time of political upheaval and reconfiguration during the independence period across Africa, the photo exudes a vintage flare of two women oozing a fashionably modest aesthetic – could they be models, freedom fighters...or both?

The second photograph by Nigerian photographer JD Okhai Ojeikere captures another simplistically set vintage scene, remaking common

images into artistic platforms of observation, exclusively focusing on black hair. The series presented at 1–54 was of black and white photographs of the backs of women's heads, cropped to highlight intricately designed, culturally embedded hairstyles including parted twists, knots and braids. Interestingly, the historical trajectory of hair for black women in Africa and its diaspora has great depth. For cases in West African communities, a well-kept head translates as a woman's ability to embody a 'life-force and multiplying power of profusion and prosperity' and for groups in Nigeria, undone hair may be seen as an outward demonstration of bereavement, depression or poor hygiene. For both Sory and Ojeikere's photographs, the vintage aesthetic utilised here, pinpoints these West African women to a historical trajectory, allowing their blackness and their bodies to transcend space and time.

The third piece of art that captured my imagination, displayed not just the artistic skill attached to the medium used, but the unpopularised placement of black women's bodies swimming, participating in sport. It is uncommon in Western pop culture for black women's bodies to be visualised in historically 'white' athletic spaces, unless the outlier and now household name Serena Williams comes to mind. This type of representation has been transformed by Togolese artist Modupeola Fadugba. As a woman of African descent and former competitive swimmer, I have often been the only black person in the pool swimming, on the deck or in the audience cheering. This is not surprising considering that a survey by the Center for Disease Control found that 'an 11-year-old black child is 10 times more likely to drown than a white child the same age' due to histories of segregation and cultures adopted around 'whites only' athletic spaces. Now, seeing this representation emerge through art in a space such as 1–54 brings a refreshing voice to what it means to be black *and* be able to not only swim for survival, but to swim for leisure. Interestingly, the prominence of hair in Fadugba's painting makes yet another appearance, well kept in twists, beads and cornrows placed in neat buns atop the young girl's hair. The style sure beat my attempt at retaining moisture to my curly hair with bleached ends due to constant exposure to chlorine. Nonetheless, Fadugba's work is a mix of whimsical and vintage and nods to the need to rethink the corporeal representations of black women in unlikely spaces.

> 'Most striking about the traditional societies of the Congo was their remark-
> able artwork: baskets, mats, pottery, copper and ironwork, and above all,
> woodcarving. It would be two decades before Europeans really noticed this art.
> Its discovery then had a strong influence on Braque, Matisse, and Picasso.'
>
> Adam Hochschild, King Leopold's Ghost

Does the fact that 1–54 occupies a space such as Somerset House mean that there has been a shift in a Western appreciation for African art? Does a Western appreciation of this art continue to force African artists to depict things the Western gaze would expect, such as poverty or decolonisation, in order to be relevant? As founder El Glaoui stated in an interview with *Art Africa,* 1-54 'functions as a bridge between Africa and the West' and works 'in dialogue with organisations and initiatives beyond 1–54 and outside of London and New York, in order to make a dialogue possible beyond the fair itself'. In light of El Glaoui's goal, my observance of the audience of art sellers and art buyers as well as the thematic focus on the black female body that I found interesting, answering these questions is not straightforward. It is not straightforward because although the audience at 1–54 London was very mixed, those selling, buying and who physically own the space are predominately from a largely white European background.

However, ownership over the space can be complicated when someone such as myself, a young woman of African descent can engage with and be observant of the representation of West African woman through different art mediums that translate relevant topics such as hair, fashion and sport. Translating the ramifications of the European colony in Africa into works of art will forever be a reality for the African artist. This is because history cannot be erased and does play a role (consciously and/or unconsciously) in shaping the narrative that the artist puts onto paper, the way they engage with their medium and select their subject. Nonetheless, as interpretations of history in West Africa develop and African art becomes more accessible, the production of and content driven into the art itself evolves as well. I think what makes a piece of contemporary West African art relevant or considered worthy of being showcased in a space like 1–54 is when the artist is simultaneously able to use art as a tool to rewrite narratives of black and/or 'African' representation and reflect their personal inspiration into their work. For the three different representations of black West African women described earlier and the noted tension between what the artist is portraying and who predominately consumes the art, I think it is impossible for African art to escape the problematic gaze of the West.

There is something to be said about Somerset House's availability to host an event like 1–54, allowing it to take shape in its corridors. By providing space for representations of a gendered blackness and notions of an 'Africaness' to be explored and consumed in a historically white colonial space, the work of three artists came to the forefront, depicting watercolour and vintage photographic representations of black, women. However, the highly racialised dynamics in the 'opened' space at Somerset House of who can buy, sell and visit the art left me feeling uncomfortable – particularly when keeping in mind historical narratives of how black women's bodies have been set by Europeans.

FISHING IN AKURE

Gemma Edom

In a 2016 interview for Fiction Writers Review, Chigozie Obioma revealed the place of inspiration from which his Man-Booker nominated debut novel, The Fishermen, was born. Living in Cyprus but homesick for Nigeria, Obioma spoke to his father on the phone one evening: 'He told me of the growing closeness between my two oldest brothers, who, while growing up had a very serious rivalry between them. I started to think about the closeness and what it means to love your brother'. With this in mind, it is unsurprising that the novel feels like a sweet homage to unfaltering brotherhood, the oblivion of youth, and day-to-day life in Akure, Nigeria.

Told from the perspective of the youngest brother, packed full of imagery and interwoven between milestones in Nigeria's own story, it is these three themes which resonate throughout. But, how can those strands be brought to life beyond the page, I wondered? It was not long before I would find out as the novel has been cleverly adapted for the stage by Gbolahan Obisesan and revived by New Perspectives, under the watchful director's eye of Jack McNamara. Fresh from a sell-out run at the Edinburgh Fringe Festival, its season at the Arcola Theatre ended in December 2018, bringing new meaning to concepts of brotherhood, youth, and home as they are transferred from page to stage. The play remains true to Obioma's story, telling the tale of four brothers growing up in 1990s Nigeria. After their father moves away to a new job, the boys start fishing at a forbidden river, trailing single file to its river beds day after day. When on one trip they encounter the local madman, Abulu, who predicts their tragic collective future, the boys' relationships unravel, only to be reeled in instead by fate and fatalities.

The play begins where the novel leaves us, as brothers Ben, played by Michael Ajao, and Obembe, played by Valentine Olukoga, reunite and reunite and trace back their memory of those years. We immediately see the world through the eyes of a ten-year old; with lines rushing into each other and time measured through birthdays and favourite meals, it feels just how your little brother would excitingly recount his day at school: *and then, and then and then…* Perhaps the salience of this is unsurprising considering Obisesan grew up in Nigeria until the age of ten, which is also the age of the book's protagonist, Ben.

By stripping a novel busy with characters, down to just two brothers, we enter a near-imaginary realm, where children can spend hours absorbed in their own story, and see others only through the lens of their world. The way this is captured by the actors is certainly one of the highlights of the play. The actors' physicality bursts with energy and laughter as they jump from character to character, transforming from hysterical chickens to Mama Iyabo, Abulu the madman, to their stern father.

Chigozie Obioma, *The Fishermen*, Little, Brown, London, 2015

'The Fishermen', New Perspectives Theatre Company, Arcola Theatre, London, 2018

This playful storytelling device is made all the more striking set against Amelia Jane Hankin's stage design; a simple curved, raised stage across which a line of large metal poles snake horizontally, reminiscent of a river. As the siblings transform the poles into fishing rods and weave in and out of them, we are again reminded of youth, when even the most mundane objects can acquire any new meaning. This is really where the chemistry between the two actors shines through. Both mock each other and squabble over the order of events, yet their joyful playfulness, and the way they bounce off each other captures Obioma's intention of closeness brilliantly. They flit from laughing, arguing, trying to impress each other and resenting each other's' actions. This makes it all the more painful to watch as the play grows darker, and their relationships are torn apart, leaving each one isolated from those he loves the most.

While these reminders of youth and brotherhood are moving, it is the way the play intimately memorialises home that gives it such poignancy. Nigeria is felt through the play's events, at the church service, and in their mother's Ogbono soup, yet it also resonates far deeper into the structure and language of the play. To look at this, it is worth returning to the book, and Obioma's intentions for it. In the 2016 interview, Obioma identifies 'West African realism' as a common feature of his fiction writing. For him this captures the 'nuances of the West African grappling with western civilisation which it has adopted, but moulding it into a hybridisation of his own traditional culture'. He goes on to say that 'in the Igbo thought, there is no difference between the world of the physical and the supernatural'. This is abundantly clear throughout the novel, which is populated with vivid imagery. Ben sees other people 'as', rather than 'like' animals; Ikenna is a python that becomes a sparrow, Boja is a fungus, Obembe a search dog.

Without the stability of the page, these images run the risk of becoming lost, yet the play captures the space between the physical and the supernatural in a clever way. As the actors jump from character to character, their impressions give an air of pseudo-reality; of characters that are simultaneously real and imagined. What's more, the exaggerated physicality of these impressions bring to life the imagery so potent in the novel; Ikenna transforms from python to sparrow, from a coiled hunched back with prowling eyes to a helpless panicker, darting around the stage before settling, limbs limp, head to one side.

West African realism also shines through in the way different languages are used, each carrying with them their own set of meanings. The boys' mother generally communicates in Igbo, while the brothers speak to each other in Yoruba, the language of Akure. Despite being the official language of Nigeria, English is considered to be very formal, used by strangers and non-relatives to address you and, when switched into by family or friends, has the power of 'digging craters' between you and them. Often throughout the play, speeches would dart between English and either the Yoruba or Igbo, without translation. This creates a sense of multiplicity, of being simultaneous within the realities of these three languages, and for those in the audience that understand Yoruba or Igbo, this made the play even more close to home. Laughs came harder and quicker, seemingly sharing an inside-joke, and creating a deeper level of closeness between actor and audience.

The moments when the Agwu family's story collided with Nigeria's daily politics was a highlight for me. As was when the brothers meet MKO Abiola, becoming the children of the 'Hope'93' campaign as he runs for the presidency in the 1993 elections. Just two months later they are swept up in a riot, escaping the 1993 election uprising, which became a seminal day in Nigerian history. These two stories are an important reminder that events on the nation stage infiltrate daily lives in a variety of, often unmeasurable, ways. Unfortunately, these scenes are omitted from the play and, despite my enthusiasm for them, I do see why. By keeping the action as family-centric as possible, we remain in the Agwu bubble, and continue to view the world as they do.

We do however meet Nigeria in other ways. The brothers take us to a Sunday church service via an impressive impersonation of Pastor Collins, while other events, like Abulu's car crash and the court case, are recalled between each other as memories, allowing us to remember what they remember. While not as rich as the election action, we are given an intimate insight into the busyness yet rudimentary pace of day-to-day in Akure.

The play closes with a scene that marks the brothers concluding their reminiscing. Heading home to greet their parents, they sing together in Igbo as they troop off the stage. Despite the story's ever-darkening plot, notions of brotherhood and youth unravel before us, and we cannot help but notice that this is clearly a love letter to the idea of 'home'. Nigeria is preparing to head to the polls for the 2019 elections and as attention is focused on the big men battling it out on the national stage, 'The Fishermen' is an important reminder of the gravity of the lives of the rest of us – how it feels to be a parent, to hope, to learn, to love, to grieve and to fish in Akure, Nigeria.

ET CETERA

ON EMERGING HORIZONS

Oluwagbemileke Joy Jegede

I graduated at eighteen years old with a First Class Law degree from Fourah Bay College at University of Sierra Leone. Two years later, barely twenty, I became the youngest lawyer in the history of Africa and second youngest in the world. If you google my name, you will find pages and pages outlining this accomplishment and my graduation pictures with my beaming parents. I wonder if you are surprised that I have achieved all this? I know many people are, and that is why I am proud to tell the world that I, a black female, born and brought up in West Africa, has made history. To be a role model, to inspire others to pursue their dreams and aspire to limitless goals, this is what makes me humble.

I am certain there are a few African parents showing these pictures to their children and advocating how a law degree is the way to go. The funny thing is, my parents never even pleaded or encouraged me to do law as they believed fervently that each individual has their own unique gift therefore their own original path. As much I did love law and I would encourage many to pursue a law degree, there is more to me than my degree and my educational attainment. By my late teens I was working in Sierra Leone's top law firm and consulting on a regular basis with the best private consulting firms, but there did not feel anything overtly extraordinary about that. So many people I have met over the course of my young life, simply cannot believe that I have already graduated, entered the labour force market and am now undertaking a Masters at the London School of Economics as well as a Programme for African Leadership. Yes I have done amazing things, but I say this not out of arrogance but out of pride as I am one of many young people on the

African continent breaking continental records and becoming pioneers in their respective fields.

How did we get here? Well it starts with joy. Not me but the actual feeling of joy. By that I mean that feeling of ecstasy that consumes one when learning. I was born in Nigeria, but soon moved to Sierra Leone and lived most of my life there. I became notorious for being hungry for that feeling through asking way too many questions. I wanted to know everything about anything. It was a persistent and deep desire for knowledge. Maybe it started with the fact that I was born a girl in a part of the world where many did not have high expectations for my gender. Or the fact that being female also elicited a tired narrative of being a helpless victim who requires white saviours and a truck load of foreign aid money, that would never actually be spent on my wellbeing. But also, it could have been my age; being young in any part of the world makes older generations roll their eyes.

You always face challenges with what people will say, what people will think, how people will act, they way they will treat you. We have a culture of silence, which does not necessarily foster an environment for enquiry. When you ask questions, you risk being considered stupid or incompetent or maybe even haughty for not just accepting the status quo. Some people may think you are wasting your time learning things that do not have a short term or tangible benefit to you. And if you are a student, who seeks to know things and not just get the grade or tick the box, expect 'compliments' like Nerd and Geek. These are indeed compliments because they mean you are not just going through the motions, you are actually understanding and appreciating knowledge, and learning how it plays out in real life.

You can't. You don't know. You will see. You wait. These are all subliminal messages a girl like me might hear from the limits of her family compound to the outside world, screaming on TV. But I persisted. I kept on pursuing knowledge, even when it was hard, when it was elusive. Whilst my peers were still learning to count, read and write, at the age of nine I took the National Primary School Examinations. At twelve, I took the Basic Education Certificate Examinations, a regional examination taken in many English-speaking West African countries that signifies reaching the limits of basic education and heralds the beginning of pre-university years. My parents, ever-proud, asked jokingly if I would like to also attempt the West Africa Senior School Certificate Examinations. As my parents jubilated, I was already thinking how could I indeed undertake this new challenge. I was twelve, but not even a bit afraid, I knew the more I was climbing the schooling system the more I would be learning. The words of Ghanaian president the late Kofi Anan would often come to my mind: 'Knowledge is power. Information is liberating. Education is the premise of progress, in every society, in every family.'

By fourteen, I was attending the prestigious Fourah Bay College, University of Sierra Leone, as the youngest pupil ever admitted to the Law Department according to their records. That's when I got another admission letter from Amity University in India to pursue a Bachelor of Business Administration, a three-year distance learning programme. I had applied to Amity as a back-up plan, as Fourah Bay College's admission policy had an age restriction of eighteen for anyone applying to its undergraduate programmes. With tempting offers from my two top choices of college, I decided to do both.

During my studies, I ran for secretary of the Law Society and found myself competing against a student more senior in years and with significant experience. He already had a degree under his belt and had been a student leader of the student union. I was even asked to reconsider because I was a woman and young, but I refused to listen to that negative discourse. Against all expectations, my self-belief carried me all the way to winning the elections.

I am always going to be persisting, because it is that persistence that has opened doors, has allowed me to meet people of all walks of life, to travel in places I never expected, to learn new things that were beyond my scope. But I want to make one thing clear, there were many before me and there will be many more to come after me. I was very inspired by Nigerian teenager and programmer Tomisin Ogunnubi. At twelve years old she created My Locator, a mobile app which helps children who are lost. Available on the Google Play Store, it has already been downloaded over 1,000 times since its debut in 2016. Bright young Africans like Tomisin are making inroads in the tech industry, enticing the likes of

Facebook and Google to Nigeria, astounded at the incredible potential so often glossed over in the Western media.

In West Africa not far from Nigeria, Cameroon has established its own Silicon Valley, dubbed Silicon Mountain, located in the anglophone part of the country. In a nation that lags far behind in innovation on the African continent and ruled by an autocrat, no one expected that a group of young techies could succeed in establishing one of Africa's seminal tech hubs. Despite discrimination at the hands of a francophone-led government, this tech hub has continued to flourish from strength to strength

There are many more stories of young excellence emerging from West Africa. Ghanaian, young entrepreneur Mabel Suglo founded the Eco-Shoes Project, which manufactures shoes and accessories from discarded tyres and recycled materials and employs people with disabilities. Inspired by her late grandmother, who suffered discrimination due to her leprosy condition, Suglo wanted to create employment opportunities for people experiencing similar hardship. Her business now employs five artisans, and has manufactured over 1,000 pairs of shoes since 2014.

Then there is Sierra Leonean and Harvard and MIT graduate David Moinina Sengeh who was appointed Chief Innovation Officer for the Directorate of Science, Technology and Innovation at the age of just thirty-one. His thesis was on improving prosthetic comfort for amputees, a key concern for a country like Sierra Leone, whose war left as many as 27,000 people disabled. Sengeh has worked with Nairobi's IBM Research Lab on healthcare technologies in Africa, as well as with Innovate Salone, a social action project to nurture creativity and an entrepreneurial spirit among Sierra Leonean youths.

But young West Africans are not only breaking barriers as entrepreneurs. Erica Tandoh is a ten-year-old DJ making history in Ghana. Known as DJ Switch, Tandoh started DJing at just age nine and became famous after winning a TV talent contest. She is now the youngest DJ ever to win at Ghana's annual DJ Awards. Her bold energy and infectious happiness has enchanted many people on the dancefloor as she says: 'I picked the name DJ Switch because I switch up people's happiness'.

In sports, they say Africans can't swim but the Pina siblings from Cape Verde are showing us that we belong in the water as much as anyone, leading their country's Olympic team to Tokyo 2020. Based in the US, the three siblings Latroya, Troy and Jayla have already competed in a few races such as the Confederation Africaine de Natation Championship in Algeria. Latroya emphasised why swimming is more than a sport. Togolese alpine skier Mathilde Amivi Petitjean made her African counterparts proud at the 2018 Winter Olympics when she was given the title of *Reine des Neiges* [Queen of Snow], proving we can and will conquer the snow. In the same Winter Olympics, three Nigerian-Americans Seun Adigun, Ngozi Onwumere and Akuoma Omeoga made history as the first ever African bobsled team to qualify for the Olympics. It was the first time any Nigerian athlete competed at a Winter Olympics, when they appeared at the PyeongChang games.

The West often talks fondly of the revolutions that unseated autocrats in North Africa and the Middle East, forgetting that the Arab Spring shook the coconut trees down south and led to an African summer of resistance. Young people in West Africa have also led the way as activists in the political arena. Rooting out corruption is at the top of their agendas and they are sending a clear message to all those ageing presidents clinging on to power that their time is up. When President Abdoulaye Wade announced his third run for presidential re-elections despite being over eighty years old, the Senegalese said '*Y'en a marre!*' [We are fed up]. Despite Western media consistently trying to paint African youth as only capable of violence and mob rule being the norm, the youngsters of Senegal took to the streets to protest peacefully despite state police descending upon them. Political machinations led to Abdoulaye Wade being given the green light to run for a third term, despite it being unconstitutional, prompting the same young to rally the people of Senegal to once again peacefully mobilise and choose their next president through the ballot. Using hip hop songs and sketches in Wolof to inform ordinary citizens of their duty to vote, Senegal's 2012 elections saw young and old people joining enthusiastically the voting lines. Democracy at its best.

Inspired by the change sweeping Senegal, Burkina Faso youth defied President Blaise Compaore's twenty-seven-year rule, stunning a man that had been propped up by Western powers for years and had been complicit in the death of Pan Africanist hero Thomas Sankara. Through the hashtag #wili, named after the traditional Burkinabè Lwili Peendé cloth being worn by protestors, the Burkinabé revolution was truly televised via twitter with opposition activist Emile Pargui Pare saying: 'October 30 is Burkina Faso's Black Spring, like the Arab Spring.' Without giving up, young Burkinabés protested day after day. Storming key buildings in the capital, images emerged of protesters taking over the state television station. Eventually, Blaise Compaore was forced to bow down to the power of African youth.

In recent times, we've seen Gambia's Yahya Jammeh also loosen his grip after twenty-three years. Defeated by a contender no one saw coming, Jameh was not about to leave without a fight. It was only when neighbouring countries issued a warning that they would militarily intervene to uphold the voting results, did he concede. Ghana and Liberia saw smooth transfers of power between political parties. There were fears that violence would break out if parties took to the streets contesting results. However Nana Addo Dankwa Akufo-Addo who ran twice before with the New Patriotic Party (NPP), won a resounding victory against the National Democratic Congress (NDCC), which had been undefeated for many years. In Liberia, not only did power change between parties but it marked Liberia's first democratic transition in seventy-four years. Former footballer George Weah was sworn in as the newly elected president, becoming the fourth youngest serving president in Africa.

There are many more other examples of excellence in West Africa, across the continent and throughout its diasporas. Brace yourselves because it won't be stopping anytime soon. Africa is the youngest continent and showing no signs of decline, even when other continents are struggling with aging populations. With all this talk on African youth, you might think I am quick to dismiss my elders. Well, this is where you are wrong. It is their strength and wisdom that gives wing to young African people of today and I keep close to my heart Kofi Annan's words: 'To live is to choose. But to choose well, you must know who you are and what you stand for, where you want to go and why you want to get there.'

I aspire to do great things like my counterparts and follow the footsteps of the giants that have paved the way for us. I feel my place is in the public sector and I dream of being of service to my continent. It might sound like young whimsical idealism but I believe the future of the continent is in developing better, efficient and transparent governments. There is much work to do in re-imagining what my African state for Africa will look like. How can an African country be held accountable to the diverse group of people living within its borders? How can we empower citizens to seize control of their lives and have the confidence to demand higher standards of their government? How can we reinvigorate African education so that it does not reflect imperialist legacies, but celebrates Africa's history going beyond colonialism, celebrating its contributions to the world and making its offspring proud to hold their head high. I don't want to simply use my talents to climb the social, economical and academic ladders, but to use the knowledge, experiences and privileges I have acquired for a greater good than just personal gains.

Perhaps this is why so many young Africans are risk-takers. We know the world has low expectations of us to begin with. We know that if we fail, the privilege afforded to others will not shield us from the harsh reality of this world and we certainly cannot remain silent. If we fail, it's also not just us who fail. It's our families, our communities, our country, and anyone African, because as people with rich melanin we are always held accountable for the actions of one individual. I believe in the fundamental equality of men and women of all ethnic groups, all economic classes, and all age groups. My parents taught me that each individual is uniquely positioned to fulfil their destiny with the gifts that are unique to them, and as such we young people of Africa have a message and duty to the world. We are here to let others know that the pursuit of knowledge is infinite, that the struggle for opportunities is achievable, that dreams can be broken but always reborn under many skies, that our limit has no bounds.

Too often, the media has painted our beloved continent with broad brush strokes full of stereotypes: poverty devastating communities, jungles of HIV ravages, backward pockets of people fighting for religion or ethnicity or tribe under the watch of big bellied politicians, all in a country called Africa. This does not mean Africa has not seen war that has destroyed not just infrastructures, but people of all walks of life. That does not mean that poverty does not still stifle many. That politicians do not ransack the money from the very people who elected them hoping for change. That Africa is not a homogenous country but it is made of people so different, so beautiful, so dignified, who together proudly call themselves African.

Tomorrow may not be promised. But one thing is for certain: the glorious future that we have all been waiting for is at the frontiers of the African continent. The next generations are readying themselves for shaping a new and innovative Africa that would become a model for the world.

TEN TIPS FOR VISITING WEST AFRICA

Yovanka Paquete Perdigao

You might be thinking it's time to visit 'Africa', the place of wonder. If it's your first trip to this continent, naturally you'll begin by researching where to go, what to do, and what to eat. But before you set out on your journey, here's a handy guide. You will find in the corners of the internet, many articles about the dangers of stereotyping and floundering into tropes, but sometimes all that brilliant satire might not drive the point home. After all, how to distinguish between satire and truth, news and false news, if you know nothing about this part of the African continent? So here are ten handy tips that will guarantee you a delightful experience when visiting this place I call home. Not only that, you will be able to look smug next to your other friends who might have visited and done exactly what I advise not to – what is better than looking woke?

1. Note the Diversity

Begin by not referring to that one African country, that one place you went to volunteer, went on your honeymoon, went on your gap year, went to follow your Safari dreams, went to find a cure to your midlife sexual crisis, went to take pictures with snotty poor Africans or some animal who didn't ask you, as AFRICA. Not only are there fifty-four recognised countries in AFRICA but guess what, many of the people living in those countries are radically different. They have different cultures, traditions, religions, values, languages and even skin tone! I can't tell you how many times, I have had random people run up to me to excitedly tell me they have just been to Africa like I give a crap. Only to find out they went to a tiny Pulaar village in Senegal. Or that they didn't visit Africa but really went to Papua New Guinea. Yes that country is in the Pacific, not Guinea Conakry in West Africa. You know what? Just name that African country.

2.White Guilt

Next time you are in said African country, do go and confront the history of the Atlantic slavery. That should be your number one must-see sight to visit. Too often the impact of slavery and colonialism is poorly acknowledged and discussed. It was only 400 years ago that the first ships arrived in Africa to capture, beat, rape and enslave Africans to the Americas and other places. It was only fifty, forty and even thirty years ago that some countries gained independence. To understand the monumental impact these two legacies had on the African continent, one needs to walk through the many slave castles scattered on the West African Coast. To enter the tiny dark spaces where thousands were kept, unable to stand with dignity, in their own faeces, without water or food for days. To feel in those walls, the desperate scratching, trying to count the days, to walk through the door of No Return, where slaves left never to return home, you realise the unspeakable. What you must not do, is make the visit about yourself. The constant twisting your hands as you move through the Elmina Castle tour, trying to muster a tear whilst looking to meet the eyes of Africans just to let them know you are sorry. We don't want your pity. Just wallow in your white guilt and leave African people alone to mourn. If you really feel that bad, don't bother buying flowers to leave in the slave dungeons, we are happy to take contributions for reparations.

3. Don't do anything you would not do at home

You might have saved all your money to take the trip of a lifetime to drink Amarula with giraffes on the Serengeti, but please, going to Africa does not mean a free-for-all. First off, stop hugging the locals because you think Africans are welcoming. They do not like it. Would you run up to people on Oxford Street? Second, stop taking pictures of yourself surrounded by kids covered in dust and snot. Why? It's so cute! No it's not, you have not sought their parents' consent and I am pretty sure back home you would be arrested for taking pictures of kids in parks. Once upon a time, a well-meaning German tourist tried to take a picture of me and my cousins whilst on a boat to Gorée Island in Senegal. What did my father do? Respectfully told him not to. The tourist sneaked up on us and still took a picture. My father grabbed his camera and threatened to smash it. The man promptly ran away as my father got the police involved. So what have we learned? Your tourist privilege won't shield you when you do nonsense that you wouldn't even think of doing at home. And if you must insist, just remember that those kids posing in your pictures are probably laughing at you as they collect your meagre dollars, waiting for another idiot tourist that desperately wants one for the gram. #LoveAfrica

4. Love makes us do crazy things

Africa might be a place of great mystery and exoticism for you. All those books of white saviours rushing through dusty red roads in their 4x4s, for meetings in clubs called Tropicana where cannibal-eating soldiers, African nouveau riche, and Russian or Chinese gangsters convene, musters a delightful action-packed fantasy. White saviours always have a tryst with their Herculean gardener who oozes coconut oil (true story) or are seduced by an African woman invariably described as slim with big buttocks (not always a true story) dressed in a skimpy tight red dress by the bar. Don't do it. Just don't be that guy who went to Africa to sleep around and woke up the next morning, his credit cards gone, his pockets empty and no telephone. Or that middle-aged woman who left her husband for a cab driver, only to find out she was one of many girlfriends paying for his other kids. I still think about this poor French girl who went to volunteer in Burkina Faso and met who she thought was a loving dreadlocked rasta man at a beach. Clearly she did not follow rule number three, do not do anything you wouldn't do at home including dating people you wouldn't at home. She came back and told me that they were planning to move to the UK together in the coming year. In the meantime they were long distance, with her doing most of the calling, spending on flights to see him in Burkina Faso, sending money when he had fallen on hard times. Thankfully it lasted only three months — it ended when she found out that the boyfriend was actually dating not just her, but all five other friends who had gone to volunteer with her. They were all calling, seeing him, and sending money whilst he promised fidelity and marriage. Yikes.

5. 'Do you speak African?'

Issa no. Read point number one. Speak English, French or Portuguese, after all that's the legacy of our ex-colonial powers so might as well use it. Don't flick through your apps or dictionaries, trying to comically speak Pidjin or Twi, we have things to do. I did not do this on my first visit to Ghana, and strolled in to greet my family with a proud 'Akwaaba!'. Turns out no one in Ghana says Akwaaba, only white people. They use 'Eti sen' to greet people. Or the other time when I said 'Jambo' in Kenya. Yes, Disney lied to us, not everything is Hakuna Matata, especially when it comes to African languages. Also, under no circumstances should you correct an African's pronunciation, just because you took Yoruba at SOAS. It won't end well for you.

6. Strictly (no) Dancing

I don't know where this obsession stems from. Why must foreigners always try to dance in Africa. Resist the urge to dance. Even when Africans invite you to the dance floor. You don't have it in you, the jingle, the sauce, the flavour, the sway. Maybe you took classes back home, a bit of dancehall, kizomba, zouk and afrobeats to spice it up. Your teacher has complimented you plenty, when you go out you are the first person to bust moves on the dance floor and people circle around you, you might even be part of an award winning crew, or your one African homie told you you got this. I believe you, but your teacher, friends and that one African friend you are proud to have, are being nice because they care about you. Maybe you are actually decent but let those that were born in the rhythm, do what they do best and you just stay seated. You saw Theresa May tried it in South Africa. If you look closer, you can see she really believed she could pull this dancing business off. Suffice to say it did not end well. Unless you want to be a meme, do not dance.

7. 'Is it dangerous?'

I mean at any point in time in the United States, there are twenty-five to fifity serial killers on the loose. This is the same country that averaged at least one deadly mass shooting a month in 2018. And where do I start with the UK —have you seen Brexit? A prime minister incapable of negotiating a deal, held hostage by other EU leaders, and her own parliament as well as a party always ready to attempt a coup? Meanwhile there are cuts to the NHS, more and more people living on the streets, unable to afford basic living necessities such as housing and education, and almost every day a knife crime victim. Of course with this Brexit mess, I can't even cross over to France, although they are not faring any better with *gilet jaune* protests. If it sounds like a hot mess, that's because it is. I mean I have survived civil war three times, once in Guinea-Bissau and two times in Ivory Coast, but at least that was simple, all you had to do is run, in the West you might just die a slow death in front of the TV.

8.Volunteering

You might be asking, how am I a dick by volunteering in Africa? Oh friend, if only you knew. Maybe you woke up one day, fed up with your placid void of a life, looking for a meaning in your existence, watched the news to see ads of starving children that brought you to tears at the injustice of the world, broke up with your boyfriend/girlfriend after they cheated on you, and decided you would take all of your emotional shit to Africa. No baby, what are you doing? Africa has enough problems, we don't need more lost foreigners trying to find themselves at the expense of poor people, just to make themselves feel better for doing absolutely nothing. Why don't you stay home and volunteer in your local communities? I know nothing feels better than being a white saviour, but you would not just do Africa a favour, but a huge service to your community. Your country needs you, not Africa.

9. Pack the essentials

I know you eat peri-peri chicken at Nando's but bruv, African food is another territory. If you have a bit of melanin you might survive it, but if you are the other kind that colonised half of the world for spices and doesn't use any in their kitchen, I am looking at you Sally with the unseasoned chicken, you better carry Imodium and probiotics. If you get caught out here in these African streets, you will be praying even if you are not religious. First of all there are not many public toilets and in any case I would not recommend using them. Maybe you will be lucky to find a restaurant around, but if you are picky like me, jumping in a taxi to go home will be your best bet. Just pray the maddening traffic of West African cities won't be at its peak. Take it from someone with experience, I am from Guinea-Bissau but I learnt my lesson in Ghana when I decided to be adventurous and eat bushmeat. I was staying at my future mother-in-law's, and boy oh boy it was brutal. It was so bad I was convinced I had worms but thankfully no, but I did spend months on probiotics.

10. So now you've been to AFRICA

You read through this list and managed not to be a dick there. Congratulations! You went to [name of African country] and you confronted your ignorance or white guilt. You sensibly did not do anything you wouldn't dream of doing back home, including dating for the sake of having an ill exotic fling. You did not dance or even attempt to speak the language or ask any stupid questions. No, you took your probiotics and Imodium and minded your own business instead of volunteering where you are not needed, now your skin is glowing honey! One last piece of advice, when you are back home please consider not being a dick about your trip. What I mean is, when you meet an African person, you don't need to show them you've been to the continent, or burst into random facts or quote Mandela (first of all he is not West African) or worst say: 'When I was in....' just carry these lessons back home but without the *dashiki* you bought at the market. It just makes you look too keen.

CITATIONS

Introduction: The Lion's Story
by Yovanka Paquete Perdigao and Henry Brefo

To read about the history of Islam in Ghana see O. Bari, *A Comprehensive History of Muslims & Religion in Ghana*, Dezine Focus, Accra, 2014; and J. C. Hanson, *The Ahmadiya in the Gold Coast: Muslims Cosmopolitans in the British Empire*, Indiana University Press, Bloomington, 2017.

For discussions on postmodernism and postcolonial theory see Homi Bhabha, *The Location of Culture*, Routledge, London, 2004; Toni Morrison, *Playing in the Dark: Whiteness and the Literary Imagination*, Harvard University Press, Cambridge, 1992; Franz Fanon, *White Skin, Black Masks*, Grove Press, New York, 1952.

Architecture, Culture, Identity by Shanka Mesa Siverio

For a popular definition of a Starchitect consult: Wikipedia https://en.wikipedia.org/wiki/Starchitect and age of the 'starchitect' by Edwin Heathcote 26 January, 2017 https://www.ft.com/content/d064d57c-df01-11e6-86ac-f253db7791c6.

To understand diversity among architects see 'Race Diversity Survey: is architecture in denial?', 10 May, 2018, Richard Waite, Bruce Tether in partnership with the Stephen Lawrence Charitable Trust: https://www.architectsjournal.co.uk/news/race-diversity-survey-is-architecture-in-denial/10030896.article

Further reading on architecture and Africa includes: 'Being an African Architect in Africa', Mariam Kamara, February 2017: http://www.ateliermasomi.com/blog/post_id-4; Zaha Hadid in an interview with Lynn Barber for *The Guardian*, March 2008, https://www.theguardian.

com/lifeandstyle/2008/mar/09/women.architecture; David Adjaye RIBA + VitrA Talk: Sir David Adjaye with Lesley Lokko 19 September 2018; Antoni Folkers, 'Modern Architecture in Africa critical reflections on architectural practice in Burkina Faso, Tanzania and Ethiopia (1984-2009)'; David Adjaye unveils plans for National Cathedral of Ghana in Accra by Natasha Levy, 7 March 2018, Dezeen: https://www.dezeen.com/2018/03/07/david-adjaye-architecture-national-cathedral-ghana-accra/.

Also see Ziauddin Sardar, *How Do We Know: Ilm and the Revival of Knowledge*, Grey Seal Books, London, 1991; Structure your wardrobe: how to dress like an architect, Hanna Marriott, *The Guardian*, August 2018, https://www.theguardian.com/fashion/2018/aug/29/structure-your-wardrobe-dress-like-an-architect-this-autumn-pair-of-heels; and William Gibson, *The Economist*, December 4, 2003.

We Were Once Friends by Henry Brefo

For further information about Islam and the history of West Africa see I Wilks, 'Al-haji, Salim Suwari and the Suwarians: A search for sources', *Transactions of the Historical Society of Ghana*, No. 13, pp. 1–79, 2011; D Owusu, *Islamic Talismanic Tradition in Nineteenth-Century Asante*, Edwin Mellen Press, New York, 1991; W Tordoff, 'The Ashanti Confederacy', *The Journal of African History*, Vol. 3, No. 3, pp. 399–417, Cambridge University Press, Cambridge, 1962; T C McCaskie, *State and Society in pre-colonial Asante*, Cambridge University Press, Cambridge, 1995; I Wilks, *Asante in the Nineteenth Century: The Structure and Evolution of Political Order*. Cambridge University Press, Cambridge, 1975.

Griots by Jean-Ann Ndow

For more on Griots, see Patricia Tang, *Masters of the Sabar: Wolof Griot Percussionists of Senegal*, Temple University Press, Philadephia, 2007; and https://worldmusiccentral.org/2003/04/18/youssou-n%E2%80%99dour-%E2%80%93-griot-for-the-21st-century/ On oral traditions of West Africa, download the file from:

http://www.goethe.de/ins/za/prj/wom/osm/en9606618.htm
https://static1.squarespace.com/static/53cfd0e5e4b057663ea1bc61/t/57b1e0b746c3c406dd172afd/1471275383444/Oral+Traditions+of+West+Africa.pdf

Information on other references made in the article can be accessed from these sites:

https://www.cambridge.org/core/journals/history-in-africa/article/beyond-migration-and-conquest-oral-traditions-and-mandinka-ethnicity-in-senegambia/EE3BA9D9E35F5FEEF05A85A042FFE283

http://www.goethe.de/ins/za/prj/wom/osm/en9606618.htm

https://worldmusiccentral.org/2003/04/18/youssou-n%E2%80%99dour-%E2%80%93-griot-for-the-21st-century/

https://www.forbesafrica.com/extreme-execs/2015/02/01/person-year-1324/

www.jallykebbasusso.com

www.seckoukeita.com

Seeing African Cities by Peter Griffiths

The works cited in the article, along with other sources on which the research is based, include:

Y Admassie, 'Gated Addis' in R. Burdett, P. Rode, & P. Griffiths, *Developing Urban Futures* pp. 60-61, LSE Cities, London, 2018; AfDB, *Jobs for Youth in Africa: Strategy for Creating 25 Million Jobs and Equipping 50 Million Youth*, African Development Bank, Abidjan, 2016; AfDB, OECD & UNDP. *African Economic Outlook 2016: Sustainable Cities and Structural Transformation*, OECD Publishing, Paris, 2016; African Export-Import Bank, *African Trade Report 2018*, African Export-Import Bank, Cairo, 2018; E Y Alemayehu, 'Informal

Logics' in R. Burdett, P. Rode, & P. Griffiths, *Developing Urban Futures*, p. 62, LSE Cities, London, 2018; D Anderson & R Rathbone, *Africa's Urban Past*, James Currey, Oxford, 2000; S Angel, A M Blei, J Parent, P Lamson-Hall & N G Sánchez, *Atlas of Urban Expansion—2016 Edition*, NYU, UN-Habitat, and the Lincoln Institute of Land Policy, New York, 2016; Arcadis, *Citizen Centric Cities: The Sustainable Cities Index 2018*, Arcadis, London, 2018; J J Bish, 'Population growth in Africa: grasping the scale of the challenge', 11 January, 2016, *The Guardian*, retrieved 19 December 2018: https://www.theguardian.com/global-development-professionals-network/2016/jan/11/population-growth-in-africa-grasping-the-scale-of-the-challenge; M Bloomberg, 'How to Foster Innovation at Your Company: Follow the Data', 11 March, 2014, LinkedIn, retrieved 10 November , 2018: https://www.linkedin.com/pulse/20140311161751-32503052-how-to-foster-innovation-at-your-company-follow-the-data/ ; R Burdett, P Rode, & P Griffiths, *Developing Urban Futures*, LSE Cities, London, 2018; R Burdett, M Taylor, & A Kaasa, *Cities, Health and Well-Being*. LSE Cities, London, 2011; J Crabtree, 'Africa is on the verge of forming the largest free trade area since the World Trade Organization', 20 March, 2018, CNBC, retrieved 10 October 2018: https://www.cnbc.com/2018/03 /20/africa-leaders-to-form-largest-free-trade-area-since-the-wto.html; A L Dahir, 'This Ethiopian homegrown coffee brand is opening 100 cafés in China', 22 October 2018, Quartz retrieved 23 October, 2018: https://qz.com/africa/1432178/ethiopias-garden-of-coffee-to-open-100-cafes-in-china/; Eko Atlantic, 'Eko Atlantic City to accommodate 250,000 residents', 13 July, 2016, retrieved 19 December, 2018: https://www.ekoatlantic.com/latestnews/eko-atlantic-city-to-accommodate-250000-residents; Eko Atlantic, '*Why Eko Atlantic?*', 2018, retrieved 19 December, 2018: https://www.ekoatlantic.com/why-eko-atlantic/; *Encyclopaedia Britannica*, 'Lagos, Nigeria', 6 December 2018, retrieved 19 December, 2018: https://www.britannica.com/place/Lagos-Nigeria; F Fawehinmi, 'The story of how Nigeria's census figures became weaponized', Quartz, 6 March, 2018: https://qz.com/africa/1221472/the-story-of-how-nigerias-census-figures-became-weaponized/; D Fearon, 'Charles Booth, Mapping London's Poverty, 1885–1903' *CSISS Classics*, 2002; F Giorghis, 'A City in Flux' in R. Burdett, P. Rode, & P. Griffiths, *Developing Urban Futures*, pp. 59-60, LSE

Cities, London, 2018; E Glaeser, 'Paradoxes of African Urbanism', in R. Burdett, P. Rode, & P. Griffiths, *Developing Urban Futures*, p. 7, LSE Cities, London, 2018; P Griffiths, 'Africa's New Urban Agenda', in A. Sy, & C. Golubski, *Foresight Africa: Top Priorities for the Continent in 2017,* pp. 64-73, Brookings, Washington, DC, 2017; P Griffiths & A Gomes, 'Africa's invisible cities: a spatial data challenge?', working paper, LSE Cities, London, 2019; J V Henderson, 'Productivity and urban form', in R. Burdett, P. Rode, & P. Griffiths, *Developing Urban Futures*, pp. 8-9, LSE Cities, London, 2018; ILO, *World Employment and Social Outlook Trends 2016,* International Labour Office, Geneva, 2016; IMF, *Direction of Trade Statistics Yearbook,* International Monetary Fund, Washington, DC, 2017; S Kagana, A Hauerwaas, V Holz, & P Wedlera, 'City, Culture and Society', pp. 32-45, *ScienceDirect*, 2018; J M Klopp, 'Visualising popular transport' in *Developing Urban Futures*, 2018; Lagos State, 'About Lagos', 2018, retrieved from Lagos State Government: https://lagosstate.gov.ng/about-lagos/; L Lawanson, 'Transit Futures and Infrastructures – Lagos', *Urban Age Developing Urban Futures Conference,* LSE Cities, Addis Ababa 2018; L Møller-Jensen, R Y Kofie & A N Allotey, 'Measuring accessibility and congestion in Accra', *Norsk Geografisk Tidsskrift – Norwegian Journal of Geography*, pp 52-60, 2012; K Maclean, '*Social Urbanism and the Politics of Violence: The Medellín Miracle',* Palgrave Pivot, London, 2015; H M Meleckidzedeck Khayesi, 'Negotiating "Streets for All" in Urban Transport Planning: The Case for Pedestrians, Cyclists and Street Vendors in Nairobi, Kenya', pp103-126, *Antipode*, 2010; J-L Missika, 'Comparing Urban Development Models – Paris', *Urban Age Developing Urban Futures Conference,* LSE Cities, Addis Ababa, 2018; M D Nunzio, 'Requiem for Arat Kilo', in R. Burdett, P. Rode, & P. Griffiths, *Developing Urban Futures,* p. 62, LSE Cities, London, 2018; S Parnell, 'Planning Fundementals', *Urban Age Developing Urban Futures,* Urban Age/LSE Cities, Addis Ababa, 2018; E Pietersen, 'Place-making in Dissonant Times', in R. Burdett, P. Rode, & P. Griffiths, *Developing Urban Futures*, pp. 12-13, LSE Cities, London, 2018; D Satterthwaite, 'Agency of informality', in P. R. Ricky Burdett, *Developing Urban Futures,* pp. 21-22, LSE Cities, London, 2018; R Shawl, 'The New Flower', in R. Burdett, P. Rode, & P. Griffiths, *Developing Urban Futures,* p. 61, LSE Cities, London, 2018; P Spiker, 'Charles Booth: Housing and poverty in Victorian London', *Roof*, pp. 38-40, 1989; N Stern & D

Zenghelis, 'Locking-in Cities', in R. Burdett, P. Rode, & P. Griffiths, *Developing Urban Futures,* pp. 19-20, LSE Cities, London, 2018; D Sudjic, *The Language of Cities,* Penguin, London, 2016; R Thomas, *A new Italian scrapes the sky in Sandton',* Asset Magazine, Johannesburg, 2018; UN DESA, *2018 Revision of World Urbanization Prospects,* UN Department of Economic and Social Affairs, New York, 2018; UN-Habitat, *Streets as Public Spaces and Drivers of Urban Prosperity,* UN-Habitat, Nairobi, 2013; UN-Habitat, 13 April, 2016, *Nairobi County makes Public Spaces a priority*, retrieved from UN-Habitat: https://unhabitat.org/nairobi-county-makes-public-spaces-a-priority; UNICEF, *Generation 2030 / Africa,* UNICEF, New York, 2014.

Timbuktu by Hafeez Burhan Khan

To learn more about the dramatic smuggling of manuscripts out of Timbuktu in 2012 and 2013, see Joshua Hammer, *The Bad-Ass Librarians of Timbuktu*, (Simon & Schuster, New York, 2016) and Charlie English, *The Book Smugglers of Timbuktu* (William Collins, London, 2018). Also see online reports https://www.theguardian.com/world/2014/may/23/book-rustlers-timbuktu-mali-ancient-manuscripts-saved, https://www.theguardian.com/world/2014/may/23/book-rustlers-timbuktu-mali-ancient-manuscripts-saved and an overview of the geopolitical context can read by visiting https://www.theguardian.com/world/2013/jan/16/mali-guide-to-the-conflict and https://www.theguardian.com/world/2015/nov/25/the-struggle-for-mali

Further reading on the development of prehistoric urbanism in Timbuktu can be found in the PhD research undertaken by Douglas Park at Yale University and the myth of Timbuktu is explored by Peter Coutros at https://www.sapiens.org/column/off-the-map/timbuktu-archaeology/. Zulkifli Khair details the contribution of Timbuktu's University of Sankore to Islamic civilisation at http://muslimheritage.com/article/university-sankore-timbuktu, and a BBC4 documentary The Lost Libraries of Timbuktu can be watched at https://www.bbc.co.uk/programmes/b00hkb0z. Also, Henry Louis Gates Jr extols the intellectual riches of historic Timbuktu in his PBS series Wonders of the African World: http://www.pbs.org/wonders/

Photos are courtesy of The Block Museum of Art, Northwestern University's 'Caravans of Gold, Fragments in Time: Art, Culture, and Exchange Across Medieval Saharan Africa' exhibition.

Ousmane Sembène's Cinema
by Estrella Sendra

On Ousmane Sembène's films, see:

Films Domirev (Firm), Ousmane Sembène, Wongue Mbengue, Venus Seye, Mame Ndumbé Diop, Ndiagne Dia, Mariame Balde, Awa Sene Sarr, and Tabara Ndiaye. *Faat Kine*. San Francisco, CA: California Newsreel, 2001; Impact Partners (Firm), Gadjigo, Samba, Silverman, Jason, Sembène, Ousmane, Sembène, Alain, & Myhr, Ken (2016). *Sembène!* (Widescreen edition.). New York, NY: Kino Lorber; Les Films Domirev, Sembène, Ousmane. Niaye, 1964; Médiathèque des trois mondes. Sembène, Ousmane. *Ceddo*. [S.l.]: 2002; Médiathèque des trois mondes., and Ousmane Sembène. *Emitaï*; [S.l.]: Médiathèque des trois mondes, 2002; Newsreel (Firm), Sembène, Ousmane, & Ngũgĩ wa Thiong'o. (1994). *Sembene: The making of African cinema*. New York: Third World Newsreel; New Yorker Films, Sembène, Ousmane. *Guelwaar,* 1992; New Yorker Films Artwork, Sembène, Ousmane. *Xala*. [New York]: 2005; New Yorker Video (Firm), Ousmane Sembène, Abdoulaye Ly, and Abourah. *Borom Sarret: Black Girl*. [New York]: New Yorker Video, 2005; New Yorker Video. Sembène, Ousmane. *Mooladé* [New York]: 2004; Societe Nouvelle de Promotion Cinematographique, and Papa wongue Mbengue. *Camp De Thiaroye = Camp Thiaroye*. London: BBC, 1997.

See also:

Andrade-Watkings, Claire. 'Film Production in Francophone Africa.' In Gadjigo, Samba Gadjigo et al. (eds.). *Ousmane Sembène: Dialogues with Critics and Writers,* Amherst: University of Massachusetts Press, 1993; Apter, Andrew H. *The Pan-African Nation: Oil and the Spectacle of Culture in Nigeria*. Chicago, Ill.: University of Chicago Press, 2005; Barlet, Olivier. *African Cinemas: Decolonizing the Gaze*. London: Zed Books. 2000;

Bisschoff, Lizelle, and David Murphy. *Africa's Lost Classics: New Histories of African Cinema*. London: Legenda, Modern Humanities Research Association and Maney Publishing, 2014; Bekolo, Jean Pierre. 'Aristotle's Plost.' In Eke, Maureen N., Yewah, Emmanuel, and Harrow, Kenneth W., *African Images: Recent Studies and Text in Cinema*. Trenton, N.J.: Africa World Press, 2000: 19-30; Correa, Chérif A. 'Islam and the Question of Identity in Ousmane Sembéne's Film Ceddo.' In Vetinde, Lifongo J., & Fofana, Amadou T. *Ousmane Sembene and the politics of culture*. Lanham, Maryland: Lexington Books, 2014: 33-50; Counsel, Graeme. *Mande popular music and cultural policies in West Africa: Griots and government policy since independence*. Saabrucken: VDM Verlag, 2009; Dia, Thierno Ibrahima, & Barlet, Olivier. *Sembene Ousmane (1923-2007): Un dossier cordonne par Thierno Ibrahima Dia et Olivier Barlet en collaboration avec Boniface Mongo-Mboussa*. Paris: L'Harmattan, 2009; Diawara, Manthia. *African Cinema: Politics and Culture*. Bloomington (USA); Indianapolis (USA): Indiana U.P., 1992; 'The Iconography of West African Cinema.' In Givanni, June (ed.). *Symbolic Narratives/African Cinema*. London: BFI: 2000: 81-89; Dovey, Lindiwe. *Curating Africa in the Age of Film Festivals*. New York, NY: Palgrave Macmillan, 2015; 'Subjects of Exile: Alienation in Francophone West African Cinema.' In *International Journal of Francophone Studies*, 12 (1), 2009: 55-75; Fofana, Amadou T. *The films of Ousmane Sembène: Discourse, culture, and politics*. Amherst, N.Y.: Cambria Press, 2012; Gabriel, Teshome H. *Third Cinema in Third World: The Aesthetics of Liberation*. Michigan: University of Michigan Press, 1982; Gadjigo, Samba. *Ousmane Sembène: The making of a militant artist*. Bloomington: Indiana University Press, 2010; Givanni, June (ed.). *Symbolic narratives/African cinema*, London: British Film Institute, 2001;

Harney, Elizabeth. *In Senghor's Shadow: Art, Politics, and the Avant-garde in Senegal, 1960-1995*. Durham, N. C.; London: Duke University Press, 2004;

Harrow, Kenneth W., 'Kiné, la Nouvelle Femme africaine.' In *Sembene Ousmane (1923-2007): Un Dossier Cordonne Par Thierno Ibrahima Dia Et Olivier Barlet En Collaboration Avec Boniface Mongo-Mboussa*. Paris: L'Harmattan, 2009: 156-165;

Jaggi, Maya. Profile of Ousmane Sembène. The Guardian Review, 14 May 2005: 20-23;

Murphy, David. *Sembene: Imagining alternatives in film & fiction.* Oxford: Trenton, N.J.: James Currey; Africa World Press, 2000;

Murphy, David & Williams, Patrick. 'Djibril Diop Mambety.' In Murphy, David & Williams, Patrick. *Postcolonial African Cinema: Ten Directors.* Manchester: Manchester University Press, 2007, pp. 91-109;

Petty, Sheila. *A call to action: The films of Ousmane Sembene.* Trowbridge, Wilts: Flicks Books, 1996;

Pfaff, Françoise. *The cinema of Ousmane Sembène, a pioneer of African film,* Westport: Greenwood Press, 1984;

Pfaff, Françoise, 'Femme, je vous aime: Les femmes africaines dans les films de Sembène.' In *Sembene Ousmane (1923-2007): Un Dossier Cordonne Par Thierno Ibrahima Dia Et Olivier Barlet En Collaboration Avec Boniface Mongo-Mboussa.* Paris: L'Harmattan, 2009: 149-155;

Sendra, Estrella. 'Sembène!' In *African Studies Review.* Cambridge University Press, 59 (2), 2016: 317-319;

Tully-Sitchet, Christine. 'Une nouvelle AFrique est en train de naître. Avec les femmes. Elles sont épatantes.' In In *Sembene Ousmane (1923-2007): Un Dossier Cordonne Par Thierno Ibrahima Dia Et Olivier Barlet En Collaboration Avec Boniface Mongo-Mboussa.* Paris: L'Harmattan, 2009: 166-168;

Vetinde, Lifongo J., & Fofana, Amadou T. *Ousmane Sembene and the politics of culture.* Lanham, Maryland: Lexington Books, 2014;

Vieyra, Paulin Soumanou. *Ousmane Sembène, cinéaste: Première période, 1962-1971.* Paris: Présence Africaine, 1972.

African Yuang by Hang Zhou

On China's African Policy see Admas Bodomo editor, *Africans in China: Guangdong and Beyond* (Diasporic Africa Press, New York, 2016); Chris Alden, *China and Africa*, (Zed Books, London, 2007); Chris Alden, *China and Africa: Building peace and security cooperation on the continent*, (Palgrave Macmillan, London, 2017); Cabestan Jean Pierre, 'China's Involvement in Africa's Security: The Case of China's Participation in the UN Mission to Stabilize Mali', *The China Quarterly*, 235, 713-734, 2018; Hang Zhou, 'Dragon under the Blue Helmet: a quantitative analysis of China's motivation for participation in UN peacekeeping operations', African East-

Asian Affairs, 3, 31-61, 2013; International Crisis Group, 'China's Foreign Policy Experiment in South Sudan', Asia Report N.288, July, 2017; Jia Guo, 'China-Africa Health Cooperation in the Post-Ebola Era: Trends, Challenges, and Suggestions', *Global Review*, 47, 114-131, 2017; Y Lu, et. al, 'Chinese Military Medical Teams in the Ebola Outbreak of Sierra Leone', *Journal of the Royal Army Medical Corps*, 162(3), 198–202, 2016; Yanzhong Huang, 'China's Response to the 2014 Ebola Outbreak in West Africa', *Global Challenges*, 1(2), 1-7, 2017; On African literature see Bruce Humes website, http://bruce-humes.com/archives/category/african-literature-in-translation; see also Serge Michel and Michel Beuret, 'La Chinafrique : Pékin à la conquête du continent noir', (Pluriel, Paris, 2011).

Pan-Africanism by Nouria Bah

For more on the background to Pan-Africanism, see Hakim Adi, *Pan-Africanism: A History* (Bloomsbury, London, 2018); Godfrey Mwakikagile, *Africa After Independence: Realities of Nationhood with Photos* (New Africa Press, 2006); Richard M. Juang and Noelle Morrisette, *Africa and the Americas: Culture, Politics and History: A Multidisciplinary Encyclopaedia*, Volume 1 (Santa Barbara, 2008); Kwame Botwe-Asamoah, *Kwame Nkrumah's Politico-cultural Thought and Policies* (Psychology Press, Hove, 2005; and José Pedro *Castanheira, Qui a fait tuer Amílcar Cabral ?* (L'Harmattan, Cabo Verde, 2004).

The following websites also provide useful background history: Pan-African News Wire: http://panafricannews.blogspot.com/2010/04/50th-anniversary-of-of-africa-1960.html; African Union: https://au.int/en/history/oau-and-au
'What Was Jim Crow." Ferris State University: https://www.ferris.edu/jimcrow/what.html; 'Marcus Garvey', History.com.. https://www.history.com/topics/black-history/marcus-garvey

Everything I Am by Zahrah Nesbitt-Ahmed

On the history of Islam in West Africa, see: Benjamin Soares, 'The Historiography of Islam in West Africa: An Anthropologist's View' (*The Journal of African History*, 55, 2014); Nehemia Levtzion, *Muslims and Chiefs in West Africa: A Study of Islam in the Middle Volta Basin in the Pre-colonial Period* (Clarendon Press, Oxford, 1968); Margari Hill, *The Spread of Islam in West Africa: Containment, Mixing, and Reform from the Eighth to the Twentieth Century* (Stanford Press, Stanford, 2009); Nehemia Levtzion and Randall L. Pouwels (eds), *The History of Islam in Africa* (Ohio University Press, Athens OH, 2000) and Peter B. Clarke, *West Africa and Islam* (Edward Arnold Publishers, London, UK, 1982)

And on how Muslim women shaped the history of Islam in West Africa, see:

Beverly B. Mack and Jean Boyd, *One Woman's Jihad: Nana Asma'u, Scholar and Scribe* (Indiana University Press, Indiana, 2000); Beverly B. Mack and Jean Boyd, *Educating Muslim Women: The West African Legacy of Nana Asma'u, 1793-1864* (Interface Publications Limited, Oxford, 2013); Adeline Masquelier, *Women and Islamic Revival in a West African Town* (Indiana University Press, Bloomington, IN, 2009); Bovin Mette, "Muslim Women in the Periphery: The West African Sahel," in *Women in Islamic Societies: Social Attitudes and Historical Perspectives*, ed. Bo Utas (Curzon Press, London, 1983); J C M. van Seeten *Women and the Spread of Islam in West Africa: Their Changing Role in a North Cameroonian Town* (Leiden University, 1995); Jean Boyd, *The Caliph's Sister: Nana Asma'u, 1793-1865, Teacher, Poet and Islamic Leader* (Routledge, London, 1990); Jean Boyd and Beverly B. Mack eds. *Collected Works of Nana Asma'u: Daughter of Usman 'dan Fodiyo* (1793-1864) (Michigan State University Press, Michigan 1997); Ousseina D. Alidou, *Engaging Modernity: Muslim Women and the Politics of Agency in Postcolonial Niger* (University of Wisconsin Press, Wisconsin, 2005); and Margot Badran (ed.) *Gender and Islam in Africa* (Stanford University Press, Stanford, 2011).

CONTRIBUTORS

● **Nouria Bah** is a musician and writer ● **Henry Brefo** is pursuing a PhD in Ghanain chieftancy at the University of Birmingham and is a strategic advisor to Ugandan literary organisation: Writivism ● **Victoria Adukwei Bulley** is a poet and filmmaker ● **Natasha Koverola Commissiong** is a researcher, fashion blogger and artist ● **Gemma Edom** is a writer, currently based at the LSE Firoz Lalji Centre for Africa ● **Kalaf Epalanga**, founder of the record label, A Enchufada, is a musician with Buraka Som Sistema ● **Peter Griffiths** is a journalist and former managing editor of LSE Cities ● **Tam Hussein** is an investigative journalist and novelist ● **Abubakar Adam Ibrahim** is an award-winning Nigerian journalist, and author of the novel *Season of Crimson Blossoms* ● **Oluwagbemileke Joy Jegede**, the youngest person in Africa to qualify as a lawyer, is currently pursuing a Master's degree at the LSE ● **Hafeez Burhan Khan** worked as an archaeologist for English Heritage and Birmingham University before becoming a teacher ● **Dzekashu MacViban**, founder of the *Bakwa* magazine, is a writer, journalist and editor based in Yaoundé, Cameroon ● **Jean-Ann Ndow** is advocacy manager at the World Association of Girl Guides and Girl Scouts ● **Zahrah Nesbitt-Ahmed**, a senior technical advisor on women's rights, is a founder of the African literary blog, bookshy ● **Yovanka Paquete Perdigao**, a Bissau-Guinean writer, editor and translator, is assistant editor at Dedalus Books and 1/3 of the 'Not Another Book Podcast' as Postcolonial Child ● **Samia Rahman** is director of the Muslim Institute ● **Estrella Sendra** is a filmmaker, journalist, festival organiser and teaching fellow in Global Media Industries at Winchester School of Art, Southampton University ● **Shanon Shah** lectures in religion and social science at King's College London ● **Shanka Mesa Siverio** runs her own architecture practice in London ● **Ngadi Smart** is a Sierra Leonean photographer and illustrator who lives in Cote d'Ivoire ● **Hang Zhou** is a PhD candidate in the department of Politics and International Studies at SOAS.